C0-FYI-788

A LEGAL FRAMEWORK FOR BIOETHICS

NIJHOFF LAW SPECIALS

VOLUME 34

The titles published in this series are listed at the end of this volume.

A Legal Framework for Bioethics

Edited by

Cosimo Marco Mazzoni

KLUWER LAW INTERNATIONAL
THE HAGUE – LONDON – BOSTON

Published by Kluwer Law International
P.O. Box 85889
2508 CN The Hague, The Netherlands

Sold and distributed in the USA and Canada by
Kluwer Law International
675 Massachusetts Avenue
Cambridge, MA 02139, USA

Sold and distributed in all other countries by
Kluwer Law International
Distribution Centre
P.O. Box 322
3300 AH Dordrecht, The Netherlands

A C.I.P. Catalogue record for this book is available from the Library of Congress

Printed on acid-free paper
Cover design and illustration: The Bears Communications, Amsterdam

ISBN: 90 411 0523 9

© 1998 Kluwer Law International

Kluwer Law International incorporates the publishing programmes of Graham & Trotman Ltd, Kluwer Law and Taxation Publishers and Martinus Nijhoff Publishers

This publication is protected by international copyright law.
All rights reserved. No part of this publication may be reproduced, stored in a retrieval system, or transmitted in any form or by means, electronic, mechanical, photocopying, recording or otherwise, without the prior permission of the publisher.

Contents

6. The Right to Die

1. Introduction

Bioethics Needs Legal Regulation

Cosimo Marco Mazzoni*

In early 1994 I was in New York, contacting some colleagues who I hoped would participate in an international meeting I was organizing on the juridical aspects of bioethics, due to take place in Siena in July that same year. Most of the essays in this book are based on the papers presented at that meeting.

While I was in New York a colleague who teaches at Columbia University told me the following story, which had happened to a student of his not more than a year earlier. One morning the young man got a phone call from a former girlfriend who had moved to Germany. He hadn't seen her for some time, but she said she was in New York for a short visit and wanted to see him. They arranged to have dinner together. The student told her on the phone that he was about to get married and that he would bring his fiancée to dinner as well. As was only to be expected, the dinner *à trois* was not a huge success. In fact, as they left the restaurant, the former girlfriend asked the student to drive her back to her hotel. The current fiancée was so annoyed by this stage that she went off on her own and did not even try to get in touch with him for the next few days. But as the days went by, her annoyance gave way to anxiety, since he hadn't called her either. Eventually she decided to phone him but there was no reply. A few more days went by and the girl contacted the boy's parents: they had not heard from him either. By this stage they were all very worried and went to the police to report his disappearance. Several days later – at this point about three weeks had passed since the ill-fated evening – the girl got a phone call. It was him: 'I'm in a callbox, on X Street and Y Avenue: come and get me.' She rushed to the spot, found him and helped him into her car. He had obviously been drugged: he couldn't remember what had happened to him. She took him to a doctor who examined him thoroughly, finding him in a reasonably good state, except for a recent suture along his left side ... His left

* Professor of Law, University of Siena, Italy

Cosimo Marco Mazzoni (ed.), A Legal Framework for Bioethics, 3-7.
©1998 *Kluwer Law International. Printed in The Netherlands.*

kidney had been removed! He couldn't remember a thing. The girl from Germany was nowhere to be found. No sign of her anywhere.

This is just one of the stories, the many stories that are making the rounds, like fairy tales or horror stories of illegal markets, of human organs being bought and sold. These stories have been going around for years. True, we do not really believe these tales, or at least not the whole story, but they contribute to fuel a climate of alarmism and fear *vis à vis* one of the most dramatic issues of our times, a problem which was unknown – even unimaginable – just a few decades ago, but which is now so topical that it could even be considered a symbol of our modern times. Stories like this, especially the invented ones, can be exceedingly dangerous in that they make it difficult to elaborate a valid, serious transplant ethic, an accepted regulation for emergency therapeutical transplants. In fact, they undermine the legislative policies that attempt to introduce any form of legal regulation in the field. These stories also jeopardize the slow, difficult acquisition of a social ethos expressed through gestures of solidarity, without which no law can be effective. We can introduce excellent laws disciplining transplants and organ donation, but they will be totally meaningless and will have no hope of being properly implemented unless they are supported by a social conscience based on sentiments of solidarity.

Stories like this one, which supposedly occurred a couple of years ago in Manhattan, also tell us how flourishing – fiercely so – the illegal market is and how strong the demand is, compared to the level of the supply, still very low. The figure is well-known: on average, in Western countries, there are no more than 15 organ donors per million inhabitants.

Legislative history in the field of bioethics is no more than twenty years old. Some countries immediately adopted regulations disciplining specific sectors, others gave themselves legislation of a more general nature. Some countries have laws based on accepted principles, others have disciplines elaborated around concrete hypotheses. Some countries have given themselves legal codes that anticipate future developments, while others have laws clearly drawn up in fear of the future and of the evolution of new technologies, regulations consisting merely in a string of prohibitions. In some countries the legislator simply allowed the laws to develop out of the growing social acceptance of new technologies, whereas in other countries the role of the laws in this field is seen more as one of fostering a new social ethic. Some countries waited for the international community, i.e., supranational organizations, to intervene with general reference legislation, while others produced laws in an autonomous manner, reaffirming their legislative independence.

Lastly, there are also some countries – and Italy is one of them – which have produced no laws at all. There has certainly been a considerable debate on the issue, with highly significant contributions, in some cases based on the experience of other countries, in others on original proposals, but none of these contributions have succeeded in guiding the legislator. In recent years there have been a vast number of suggestions put forward, many proposals which have led to the formulation of several bills on individual subjects, or rather on key sectors in the field of bioethics. None of these law proposals has ever been adopted, since they were all invariably discarded during the parliamentary debate; neither did any of these proposals become generally accepted by public opinion, since the political scene in Italy shows little or no attention for topics related to bioethics. It is a fact that Italy has become in recent years a country noteworthy for its lack of regulation. The fact that Italy still has no law governing organ transplants or artificial insemination has meant that the philosophical, juridical, sociological and medical debate on these issues has become progressively harsher, with positions that are becoming increasingly radical and polarized. And at the same time the arguments put forth by the different parties have become shallower and poorer. The result is that today the positions of the opposing factions are even further apart than they were a few years ago. The scientific debate has become repetitive, it has fallen prey to sterile discussion for the sake of disagreeing, more intolerant than ever and firmly rooted in points of principle that each side now views as dogma.

The unique situation in Italy – which distinguishes it from other Western countries – is further aggravated by the fact that, like other countries (in some instances, even more so), the interdisciplinary debate, i.e. the discussion in non-specialized periodicals and in the mass media, has developed enormously, involving the social conscience of vast sectors of society. Although the general public has shown a considerable interest in issues related to bioethics, the attention dedicated to these issues by the political class has been negligible: it is almost as though Italian Members of Parliament and Government had no time for the problems connected to bioethics.

Thus, Italy finds itself in a unique position: a country which has suddenly opened up and become a free 'bioethical' marketplace, where there are no juridical regulations and no generally accepted moral rules either. This contrasts with the situation in the neighbouring countries, where the regulations exist and in some cases are very restrictive. Italy is now the country where daring new techniques of fertilization are experimented, where women over sixty can benefit from artificial insemination. In a word, Italy has become the country where the lack of laws has given rise to a personal and social ethic that bears no relation to objective behaviour parameters authorizing or condemning practices carried out by ruthless physicians who sell themselves on the marketplace as the sole dispensers of the revolutionary results achieved by scientific progress in recent years.

But it is necessary to add a further element, to complete the picture of the uniqueness of the Italian scenario, an element which can in part explain the origin of the divergence and the reasons why the positions have become so radicalized. In no other country like Italy has bioethics been divided into two families, two parties, two factions, which look at each other with mistrust, antagonism, suspicion, mutual accusations of falsity, with a constant conflictuality. The two factions are described (not without further criticism) as the 'lay' or secular faction, on the one hand, and the religious (i.e. Catholic, or confessional) on the other. And even the associations and institutions within which the two different viewpoints are represented are subjected to accusations of partiality, bias and one-sided behaviour. All appeals (some noble, others hypocritical) to return to conditions of mutual respect in the discussion and to remember that the ultimate ethical goal is the same for both parties, have gone unheeded. In recent years Italian politics has gained awareness of this unbridgeable gap; in fact, it exploits the division using it as an excuse for not legislating, for not reacting to the situation. Although the message the politicians are really conveying is of their total inability to intervene and express an acceptable judgment in a field where the intervention and judgment of politicians and legislators are absolutely indispensable. In practice, what is happening is that none of the innumerable law proposals put forth in recent years can manage to fight its way past the vetoes firmly laid out by the two opposing factions.

The relationship between bioethics and law is thus interrupted; it breaks down exactly at a time when the juridical importance of the issue is transformed or needs to be transformed into an actual law. The aspect I would like to examine more in depth here does not concern bioethics in relation to the law, or the juridical aspects of bioethics, or the contribution of jurists to bioethics. Rather it concerns the following stage: how such a relationship can be transformed into laws, into binding regulations. The adoption of recognized and accepted principles of individual and collective ethics must be confirmed by becoming included in a law, in the binding and compulsory rule which calls for a specific code of conduct.

The existing legislative void has also produced an important secondary effect. Surrogate laws, proposed and drawn up by private individuals or bodies, have come into being, and they now have all the pretensions of real laws. These are the ethical codes of conduct of the Order of Physicians, the declarations of principle contained in the documents elaborated by Ethics Committees. This is a specific characteristic of the principles set forward in the field of bioethics: the fact that codes of conduct originate from different and dishomogeneous sources. The statement of a principle or the enunciation of a behaviour code are frequently given the same absolute and peremptory connotation as a law, although they are proclaimed by committees and bodies that are not part of the nation's lawmaking institutions, by bodies that are often private but which have a marked vocation to use prescriptive language. In these cases the indication of a code of conduct formulated in a law-type language may sound like a law, but actually is no more than a recommendation which should be taken as a guideline, as a suggested protocol, emanating from a judgment of an ethical nature, which is very different from the meaning and importance of a juridical regulation, an encoded law.

In my opinion, not even the interpretation of a judge who identifies, collects and then formulates in terms of principles, guidelines and trends can take the place of the law in the formal sense. Naturally, I am referring here to written legal codes, where more and more frequently we can observe judges taking over the role of the legislative powers in the field of bioethics.

It is necessary to have a proper regulation from another point of view as well, in relation to what we might call the growing 'internationalization' of bioethics. From the very beginning, the discussion on issues related to bioethics was both interdisciplinary in scope and international in scale. The search for a common rule, capable of going beyond the considerable ethical and social differences, is still a difficult task, even if we were to concentrate only on European countries, each one starting from very different premises. One need only think of the role and of the lawmaking activity undertaken by the European Union in recent years. The general impression is that results in terms of the production of laws to foster a unified interpretation of the issues have been scarce and dominated by the need to reach a compromise between the opposite viewpoints, to the extent that the texts produced are almost ineffective as far as proclaiming general principles is concerned, and equally inefficient in making recommendations to the legislative bodies of the Member States.

My overall impression is that it is premature today to try and elaborate a series of uniform laws in the field of bioethics. The diversity of the current legislative context in the Member States of the European Union does not allow us to be optimistic as far as achieving a speedy legislative harmonization is concerned. The efforts of jurists today should address the social, ethical, political, religious, and even economic conditions of the individual Member States, where the search for an ethical principle and legal regulation appears very difficult: and the example of Italy can serve as a cautionary tale.

2. From Bioethics to Biolaw

An International Overview of Developments in Certain Areas, 1984–1994

Sev S. Fluss*

Entre les rêves parfois fous des savants, les désirs souvent illimités des individus et les angoisses volontiers millénaristes des laïques, c'est à la loi qu'échoit la rude tâche de délimiter le champ du permis – si possible en tenant compte de ce qui est ou n'est pas matériellement réalisable.

Sylvie Arsever, in an article entitled 'Bioéthique et Société', Journal de Genève et Gazette de Lausanne, 29-30 January 1994, p. 19.

1. Introduction

In a paper presented at the XXVIIIth CIOMS Conference (*see* footnote), a distinguished French jurist, Christian Byk, outlined national and international responses, both legislative or otherwise, to some of the key issues in bioethics and specifically the following: the extension of the right to autonomy in the reproductive health context, and in the context of refusal of treatment and 'right to die'; the new reproductive technologies: genetics; and the neurosciences. He also focused on developments during the period 1984–1994 affecting 'bioethics and its institutions' (i.e., academic and professional groups in the field; national ethics committees and the equivalent; and the

* Former Chief, Health Legislation, WHO, Geneva and currently Programme Manager for Human Rights, Office of Health Policy in Development. The views expressed are, except where clearly indicated, not necessarily those of the World Health Organization. The author alone is responsible for any errors, omissions, or misinterpretations. An earlier version of this paper was presented at the XXVIIIth CIOMS Conference on Poverty, Vulnerability, the Value of Human Life and the Emergence of Bioethics (Ixtapa, Mexico, 17-20 April 1994).

Cosimo Marco Mazzoni (ed.), A Legal Framework for Bioethics, 11-37.
©1998 *Kluwer Law International. Printed in The Netherlands.*

role of international organizations in bioethics). In this paper, initially presented at Ixtapa, I review developments in other areas, notably: human experimentation; organ transplantation; HIV/AIDS; professional ethics; and international cooperation and South-North perspectives. This review is, of course, not intended to be comprehensive and the materials cited may not necessarily reflect the latest developments in the countries, jurisdictions, or organizations concerned. Our thrust has been on endeavouring to identify the way in which discourse and debate have given rise, in some contexts, to legislation or other regulatory measures, whether internationally or nationally.[1] In other contexts, the debates continue and legislation is either pending or still on the distant horizon.

Two examples will be given to illustrate this point. In France, the substantive commencement of the national debate on the bioethics/law continuum occurred with the publication in the spring of 1988 of *De l'Ethique au Droit*, prepared by the *Section du Rapport et des Etudes*, presided over by Mr Guy Braibant, of the *Conseil d'Etat* (a report that the French Government had requested in December 1986). That report was followed by a series of other studies, notably those prepared by Mr Franck Sérusclat, a member of the Senate; Mr Bernard Bioulac, a member of the National Assembly; Mme Noëlle Lenoir, a distinguished jurist (and now a member of the Constitutional Council); and Professor Jean-François Matteï, a professor of genetics and member of the National Assembly.[2]

The draft legislation prepared in response to these reports and other developments has not yet been enacted; at the time of writing this paper, consideration is being given to the following three Bills: a Bill on the donation and use of elements and products of the human body, medically assisted procreation, and prenatal diagnosis (Bill No. 957); a Bill on respect for the human body (Bill No. 961); and a Bill relating to the treatment of personalized data for the purposes of research in the health field, and amending Law No. 78-17 relating to data processing, personal card-indexes, and freedoms (Bill No. 962).[3] What is particularly significant in France is the sheer extent of the debate; the respective roles of legal specialists and politicians were elegantly

1 In order to keep this paper within reasonable limits, the bibliographical references have been deliberately limited.

2 For detailed information concerning the origins and scope of these reports, *see* Rullier, B., *'Le Parlement français et la bioéthique'*. Unpublished paper presented in response to a questionnaire drawn up by the British Section of a Project, supported by the Commission of the European Communities, of the Association Descartes, Paris, within the framework of BIOMED 1. For the most recent of the reports mentioned here, *see* Professor Matteï's report entitled *Rapport à Monsieur le Premier Ministre sur l'Ethique Médicale* (dated 15 November 1993).

3 The versions of the Bills available to WHO are dated 21 January 1994. I am grateful to Dr Gérard Huber of the Association Descartes, Paris, for these Bills; they underwent a Second Reading in the National Assembly during April 1994 and are scheduled for a Second Reading in the Senate on 17-18 May 1994.

described by Mme Simone Veil, the then Minister of State and Minister of Social Affairs, Health and Urban Affairs, in the following terms:

> *En tant que magistrat, j'ai toujours considéré que le droit est un moyen, certainement pas une fin en soi. Il revient au politique, responsable de l'ordre public – ce qui a joué en 1975 pour la loi sur l'IVG – mais aussi de l'ordre social, de fixer les règles que la société reconnaît comme justes, pour assurer le respect de valeurs supérieures. Les juristes doivent se plier à ces impératifs, politiques au sens noble du terme.* [4]

Lord Kennet has referred to the concept of 'from ethics to law' as a 'French slogan'[5] (it does indeed appear to be Braibant who used the term for the first time). Kennet goes on to make some very interesting and astute observations concerning British and French perceptions of the continuum:

> There is in human nature a scale of different possible reactions to the slogan: from ethics to law. At one extreme is the temperament which feels, if it's wrong, we must legislate at once. Let us forbid it in the Penal Code, or at least write it into the Civil Code, and if we can't do either of those, then let us outlaw it in some other code or body of law, such as the Public Health Code. The British think that is the French way.
>
> At the other extreme is the temperament which feels: if it's wrong, let us educate everybody to know that it is wrong, and that will surely solve the problem. At the very most, let us hope the professionals will regulate it in their own codes of practice; medical, nursing and so on. Above all, no new law. The French think that is the British way.

In the case of the United Kingdom, the debate on some key issues in bioethics was launched by the presentation, in May 1984, of the Report of the Committee of Inquiry into Human Fertilisation and Embryology (the Warnock Report).[6] A whole series of stages occurred thereafter, culminating in two items of legislation, the Surrogacy Arrangements Act 1985 and the Human Fertilisation and Embryology Act 1990. Other bioethics issues have not generally been extensively considered in Parliament, one obvious exception being the debates that preceded the enactment of the Human Organ Transplants Act 1989. For example, as far as the author is aware, there has never been a debate in either the House of Commons or the House of Lords on the ethical issues

4 Interview in *Le Monde*, 15 January 1994, p. 15.

5 *See* Lord Kennet's unpublished paper entitled 'Legislation and Regulation in Europe', presented to the European Conference on the Social and Ethical Problems Arising from Testing and Screening for HIV and Genetic Diseases: The Role of Parliaments and the Media (London, 20-21 January 1994), p. 12.

6 *See* Warnock, M., *A Question of Life: The Warnock Report on Human Fertilisation and Embryology*, Basil Blackwell, Oxford, 1985. *See* also Baroness Warnock's article on the 1990 United Kingdom legislation on human fertilization and embryology, as published in the WHO quarterly journal, the *International Digest of Health Legislation*, 1991, Vol. 42, No. 2, pp. 350-353.

raised by human experimentation corresponding to that which took place in the House of Lords, in the Summer of 1876, prior to the enactment of the Cruelty to Animals Act. As the Earl of Caernarvon stated in introducing the debate on the Second Reading of the Bill:

> The subject [of animal experiments] is not only an extremely painful, but it is a difficult and delicate one to deal with. On the one hand there is the danger of going too far; on the other, the danger of not going far enough: on the one side there is the strong sentiment of humanity; on the other, there are the claims of modern science. It is a sea strewn with rocks, and it is not easy to steer safely through them. ... I am sustained in what I feel to be the difficulty of the task, first of all by the feeling that legislation is right and necessary, next by the unanimity of the Royal Commission appointed to inquire into the subject; lastly by the fact that the conclusion of that Commission is in harmony not only, as I hope, with the general opinion of the intelligent and humane people of this country, but with much of the highest professional opinion – surgical, medical, and even physiological.[7]

These points clearly illustrate the passage from informed discourse on ethical issues to consensus-building and thence to legislation.

A particularly thoughtful and comprehensive report on issues relating to 'medical treatment and the end of life' was recently issued by the Select Committee on Medical Ethics of the House of Lords. This particular topic falls outside the scope of this paper, having been dealt with by Byk, but it is likely that this report will be useful to the political community, as well as lawyers, physicians, philosophers, ethicists and others concerned with this particularly delicate topic.[8] It will be interesting to see to what extent, if at all, the recommendations of the Select Committee are translated into legislation in the United Kingdom.

Tables A and B provide a brief summary of some of the key developments in the bioethics/biolaw continuum in France and the United Kingdom, respectively; they focus particularly on developments covered by Byk rather than in this paper, but do in a sense reflect the very different approaches in the two countries.

2. Some Institutional Aspects of Bioethics and Policy-making in this Area

While Byk has described some of the key institutional mechanisms, both national and international, in the field of bioethics, it may be relevant to draw attention to the major differences in national approaches. In some countries, for example France, a governmental committee has been established by way of legislation. Thus, the French National

7 *See Hansard* (House of Lords) for 22 May 1876, at column 1002 *et seq.*

8 *Report of the Select Committee on Medical Ethics*, House of Lords, Session 1993-94. 3 vols. Her Majesty's Stationery Office, London, 1994.

Ethical Consultative Committee for the Life and Health Sciences, created in 1983, has issued a whole series of Opinions [*Avis*]. Because of their particular relevance to Section V of this paper, it may be appropriate to cite those Opinions that have dealt with different aspects of human experimentation:

- Opinion No. 1 of 22 May 1984 on removal of tissues from embryos and dead human foetuses for therapeutic, diagnostic, and scientific purposes;
- Opinion No. 2 of 9 October 1984 on trials of new treatments in man. Reflections and proposals;
- Opinion No. 7 of 24 February 1986 on experimentation on patients in a persistent vegetative state;
- Opinion No. 8 of 15 December 1986 on research and the use of human embryos *in vitro* for medical and scientific purposes;
- Opinion No. 12 of 7 November 1988 on medical and scientific experimentation on subjects in a state of brain death;
- Opinion No. 34 of 9 February 1993 on the use of placebos in therapeutic trials on anti-depressants;
- Opinion No. 36 of 22 June 1993 on the application of somatic gene therapy procedures;
- Opinion No. 38 of 14 October 1993 on research ethics in the behavioural sciences; and
- Opinion No. 41 of 18 December 1993 on cooperation in the field of biomedical research between French teams and teams in countries undergoing economic development.

Five years after France, a Committee with an identical name was established in *Luxembourg,* while in *Belgium* a Consultative Committee on Bioethics was set up by an Agreement adopted in Brussels in January 1993. In *Italy,* a whole series of important recommendations and reports have been issued by the National Committee for Bioethics, a body attached to the Office of the Prime Minister. It is not without interest to point out that a mechanism now exists whereby the presidents or equivalent of these committees meet regularly to discuss matters of mutual interest, and in fact the most recent Conference of European Ethics Committees was held in Stockholm on 8-9 April 1994, under the auspices of the Council of Europe. Other European countries known to have such committees or similar structures include: Denmark (the Danish Council on Ethics); Finland (the Finnish National Research Ethics Committee); Hungary (the Hungarian National Ethics Committee); Malta (the Bioethics Consultative Committee); the Netherlands (the National Committee on Ethical Aspects of Research); Norway (the National Committee for Medical Research Ethics); Portugal (the National Ethical Council for the Life Sciences); the Russian Federation (the Russian National Committee on Bioethics); and Sweden (the National Council of Medical Ethics). Another model, encountered elsewhere in Europe, is for a bioethics committee or the equivalent to be attached to the Chamber of Physicians or another medical body. This is, for example, the case in the Czech Republic, Estonia, Germany, Poland, Romania, Slovakia, Switzerland, and Turkey.

An entirely different model is encountered in the *United Kingdom,* where a major role has been played by a private body, the Nuffield Council on Bioethics.[9]

Readers of this paper will be aware of the highly important series of reports issued in the *United States* by (1) the National Commission for the Protection of Human Subjects of Biomedical and Behavioral Research, and (2) the President's Commission for the Study of Ethical Problems in Medicine and Biomedical and Behavioral Research. At the time of writing, however, there is no national entity in the United States that addresses bioethical issues. Congress is currently considering whether to establish a new body at the federal level to deal with bioethics. As the Director of the influential Office of Technology Assessment of the United States Congress has stated:

> ... as Congress considers whether to create a new federal bioethics body, it can be guided by considering the strengths and weaknesses of these efforts. We believe that lessons from the past will prove instructive for the future. As the frontiers of biomedical research and technology continue to advance, it will become increasingly important for policy makers and the public to understand the ethical implications of such innovation.[10]

Interestingly enough, a limited number of developing countries have now taken steps to establish committees to address bioethical issues, notably in the medical research context. These include: Myanmar; Nepal; India; and Indonesia.

Finally, reference should be made to the Australian Health Ethics Committee (attached to the National Health and Medical Research Council); the National Council on Bioethics in Human Research (Canada); and the National Advisory Committee on Health and Disability Services Ethics (New Zealand; this committee has not yet been formally established, although there is a statutory basis for its creation).

9 For information on the nature of this body and of other United Kingdom entities, including government committees on bioethical issues, *see* Shapiro, D., 'A single national voice for bioethics: reflections from Europe', *Politics and the Life Sciences*, February 1994, pp. 22-23.

10 *See* the 1993 OTA Report, *Biomedical Ethics in U.S. Public Policy*, published by the U.S. Government Printing Office. For a comment on this process, *see* Schapiro, R., 'Another Bioethics Commission?', *Kennedy Institute of Ethics Journal*, 1993, Vol. 3, No. 1, pp. 77-79. That paper examines, *inter alia*, the possibility of a bioethics entity being based at the Institute of Medicine of the National Academy of Sciences.

3. The Internationalization of Bioethics

Byk's paper at the Ixtapa Conference described some of the relevant work of the Council of Europe, the European Union, and UNESCO, and referred to the important activities of the World Medical Association. All that needs be added at this juncture is to mention the growing trend towards the recognition of human rights and bioethics as being intimately interlinked. Particular reference should be made to the fact that, on 10 March 1993, the United Nations Commission on Human Rights adopted a decision (1993/91), entitled 'Human rights and bioethics'. After a series of preambular paragraphs (in which the Commission, *inter alia*, expressed its awareness of the 'rapid development of the life sciences and the dangers that certain practices may pose to the integrity and dignity of the individual', its desire to ensure that 'scientific progress benefits individuals and develops in a manner respectful of fundamental human rights', and its conviction of the 'need to develop a life sciences ethic at the national and international levels'), the Commission invited governments, the specialized agencies and other organizations of the United Nations system, in particular UNESCO and WHO, as well as other inter-governmental, particularly regional, organizations and non-governmental organizations, to inform the Secretary-General of 'activities being carried out to ensure that the life sciences develop in a manner respectful of human rights'. The Commission further invited States to inform the Secretary-General of legislative or other measures taken to this effect, including the possible establishment of national consultative bodies, with a view to promoting exchanges of experience between such institutions.[11]

Reference should also be made to the following paragraph, which appears in the Vienna Declaration and Programme of Action adopted by the World Conference on Human Rights (Vienna, 14-25 June 1993) on 25 June 1993:

> Everyone has the right to enjoy the benefits of scientific progress and its applications. The World Conference on Human Rights notes that certain advances, notably in the biomedical and life sciences as well as in information technology, may have potentially adverse consequences for the integrity, dignity and human rights of the individual, and calls for international cooperation to ensure that human rights and dignity are fully respected in this area of universal concern.

It is clear that this paragraph provides a valuable template for future cooperation in the field of bioethics, cooperation in which WHO can and no doubt will play a major role, not least in the light of a statement made by Dr Hiroshi Nakajima, WHO's Director-

11 The importance of such exchanges is highlighted in a recent US report, viz.: Office of Technology Assessment, Congress of the United States, *Biomedical Ethics in U.S. Public Policy*, U.S. Government Printing Office, Washington, DC, 1993.

General, in a speech delivered to the ninety-third session of WHO's Executive Board on 17 January 1994:

> My intention is to push for WHO's intensive involvement in the field of both human rights and biomedical ethics. With its global membership, long-standing experience in standard-setting, and specific technical expertise, WHO is uniquely equipped to facilitate reflection, exchange of data and experiences and consultation at the international level. As one distinguished member of this Executive Board very aptly put it: 'WHO should be the health conscience of humankind'.

In his Statement to the Forty-seventh World Health Assembly on 3 May 1994, he indicated his intention to request the participation of all Member States in 'drawing up a catalogue of the ethical issues related to health and the priorities they would wish WHO to take up'.

The Council for International Organizations of Medical Sciences has itself made many distinguished contributions to bioethics, particularly in the course of the first decade of the Dialogue described in table 1. It is noteworthy that the participants at the Ixtapa Conference endorsed a text, the Declaration of Ixtapa, setting forth a 'Global Agenda for Bioethics'. It is hoped that this will be available for distribution in the course of June 1994.

4. The Literature of Bioethics

The last decade has shown an astonishing increase in the number and range of books, governmental reports, and publications in the field of bioethics. While it would be beyond the scope of this paper to provide even a partial listing of some of the major contributions to the literature, reference should be made to: the forthcoming second edition of the *Encyclopedia of Bioethics*, prepared by the Joseph and Rose Kennedy Institute of Ethics at Georgetown University, Washington, DC;[12] the French-language databases generated by the *Centre de Documentation et d'Information en Ethique des Sciences de la Vie et de la Santé*, located at the National Institute of Health and Medical Research in Paris; such journals as the *Hastings Center Report*, *Bioethics*, the *International Journal of Bioethics*, the *Journal of Medicine and Philosophy*, the *Cambridge Quarterly of Healthcare Ethics*, *Trends in Health Care, Law & Ethics*, and the *Journal*

12 Scholars and others in the field of bioethics have had the task of accessing literature greatly enhanced by the documentation published by the National Reference Center for Bioethics Literature located at that Institute, notably *New Titles in Bioethics*; the *Bibliography of Bioethics* (Vol. 19, for 1993, has just been published); and a computerized database, BIOETHICSLINE. The Center also produces regular Scope Notes – thus, one dealing with foetal tissue research was included in Vol. 3, No. 1 (March 1993) of the *Kennedy Institute of Ethics Journal*.

of Law, Medicine & Ethics;[13] and a number of newsletters such as that issued by the Eubios Ethics Institute (located in Tsukuba Science City, Japan) – an excellent source of information on the vigorous and varied activities in Japan in the field of bioethics. Reference should also be made to the useful series of yearbooks in the field of bioethics, and to a 1990 publication of the Pan American Health Organization/WHO Regional Office for the Americas, *Bioethics: Issues and Perspectives*.[14]

As far as books are concerned, it would be cavalier not to mention: the massive tome, *Principles of Health Care Ethics*;[15] the Institute of Medicine/National Academy of Sciences publication, *Biomedical Politics*;[16] *The Ethical Dimensions of the Biological Sciences*;[17] the UNESCO publication, *Biomedical Technology and Human Rights*;[18] and the massive two-volume, 1270-page Final Report of the Canadian Royal Commission on New Reproductive Technologies, under a title that is apposite for many of the topics dealt with in this paper, namely, 'Proceed With Care'.[19]

5. Human Experimentation

Within the confines of this paper, it is not possible to do justice to the enormous amount of activity over the last decade in this area. Suffice it to say that there is almost an unprecedented number of international instruments that address the ethical issues raised by human experimentation. These are enumerated in table 2.

13 While it may be invidious to single out any one of these particular journals, the last-mentioned, produced by the American Society of Law, Medicine & Ethics, provides important perspectives on many health ethics/bioethics issues in contemporary medicine and public health; an example is the Special Issue (1993, Vol. 21, Nos. 3-4) devoted to 'The dual epidemics of tuberculosis and AIDS'.

14 While it would be outside the scope of this paper to enter into the vast area of the teaching of and research in bioethics, reference should be made to the newly established AMRO/PAHO Regional Program in Bioethics, located in Santiago, Chile.

15 Edited by Raanan Gillon, this book was published by Wiley (Chichester, England) in 1994.

16 This is a unique book in that it describes the move from ethics towards, although not necessarily to, law in the United States in a number of key areas such as mifepristone (RU-486); unproven AIDS therapies; the Human Genome Project; foetal tissue transplantation; and recombinant DNA.

17 Edited by Ruth E. Bulger *et al.*, this book was published by Cambridge University Press, Cambridge and New York, in 1993; it contains an excellent compilation of previously published papers on many key areas in bioethics.

18 Edited by Eugene B. Brody, this book was published jointly by UNESCO and Dartmouth Publishing Company, Aldershot, England, and was one of UNESCO's contributions to the World Conference on Human Rights.

19 This Report, released by the Canadian Government on 30 November 1993, defines the ethical framework and guiding principles that were used in guiding the Commission's deliberations. These guiding principles include: Individual autonomy; Equality; Respect for human life and dignity; Protection of the vulnerable; Non-commercialization of reproduction; Appropriate use of resources; Accountability; and Balancing individual and collective interests.

It should be emphasized that over the last decade a significant number of developing countries have introduced legislation dealing with human experimentation. These include: Algeria; China; Honduras; the Libyan Arab Jamahiriya; Mexico; Tunisia; and Zimbabwe.

6. Organ Transplantation

Ever since it first published a comparative survey of legislation in this area in 1969, WHO has been carefully monitoring all significant international, national, and subnational developments, and table 3 identifies those countries and other jurisdictions known to have enacted legislation on organ transplantation as of 1 March 1994.[20]

It should also be mentioned that, as early as 1986, the World Health Assembly commenced a series of discussions and debates on certain aspects of organ transplantation that had clear ethical and human rights implications. A process was initiated, the principal elements of which are indicated in table 4.[21] The Guiding Principles themselves have been extensively used at the national level in the formulation and drafting of legislation or guidelines. Two examples will suffice. The December 1992 Law of the Russian Federation on the transplantation of human organs and/or tissues (which came into force on 1 May 1993) includes a preamble indicating that the Law is 'based on the contemporary achievements of science and medical practice and [takes] into account the recommendations of the World Health Organization'. Draft Medico-Ethical Guidelines for Organ Transplantation, developed by the Swiss Academy of Medical Sciences, state in the preamble that the Academy based the draft on the most recent work of, in particular, the Council of Europe and WHO.[22] At the same time, WHO has also been monitoring the legislation that has specifically addressed commerce, and table 5 enumerates those countries and jurisdictions known to have, or to be considering, legislation in this area. Finally, careful attention has been paid to relevant international developments, illustrated in table 6.

In the process of developing its Guiding Principles, care was taken by WHO to avoid any pronouncements on issues that remain controversial and are still the subject of ongoing debates in some countries, such as the relative merits of the contracting-in (opting-in) and contracting-out (opting-out) systems and the acceptability or otherwise of determinations of death based on brain death; the latter topic has been the subject of continuing discussions in, for example, India and Japan.

20 For a recent compilation of legislation on organ transplantation, *see Legislative Responses to Organ Transplantation,* Martinus Nijhoff, the Netherlands, 1993.

21 For the text of the Principles, *see* '*Human Organ Transplantation: A Report on Developments under the Auspices of WHO (1987-1991)*', published by WHO in 1991.

22 For the text of the draft guidelines, *see Bulletin des Médecins Suisses*, 1994, Vol. 75, No. 5, pp. 168-170.

7. AIDS: A Multilateral Challenge

The last decade has witnessed a continuing increase in the number of countries and other jurisdictions that have enacted laws, regulations, or other measures aimed at the prevention and control of the HIV/AIDS pandemic. The initial regulatory measures were taken in 1983, as indicated in table 7. Since then, there has been a steady increase in the number of countries having such legislation, as indicated in table 8. At least in the developing countries, the 'peak' period for legislative/regulatory activity occurred in 1987, as indicated by table 9.

Ethical issues are addressed in a significant proportion of this legislation, and, particularly in some of the developed countries, attention has been focused on a number of problem areas, some identified by Bayer as early as 1988 (*see* table 10).

WHO has played a major role in influencing the configuration of legislation on HIV/AIDS; some of the key declarations, statements, etc. that have influenced policies and legislation are listed in table 11.

Finally, the literature on ethical issues raised by HIV/AIDS has grown almost exponentially since the first known compendium of papers that addressed legal/ethical/human rights issues.[23]

8. Professional Ethics and the Role of the Health Professions

Much could be said about the important role of the medical and other health professions in the development of 'classical' ethical standards for the members of these professions. Two bodies that have been particularly active in this area are the World Medical Association, which has, at successive World Medical Assemblies, adopted a series of declarations, statements, recommendations, and resolutions on such issues as: biomedical research involving human subjects; determination of death; euthanasia; foetal tissue transplantation; genetic counselling and genetic engineering; access to health care; the Human Genome Project; organ transplantation; *in vitro* fertilization and embryo transplantation; persistent vegetative state; physician-assisted suicide; terminal illness; therapeutic abortion; and torture and other cruel, inhuman, or degrading treatment or punishment in relation to detention and imprisonment. Reference should also be made to the work of the Commonwealth Medical Association, which is currently engaged in a project designed to develop 'Model Guidelines on Ethics for Physicians Practising in Developing Countries', directed particularly to physicians in Commonwealth countries.

23 *See Hofstra Law Review*, 1985, Vol. 14, No. 1 (this issue is largely devoted to a Symposium on 'Law, Social Policy, and Contagious Disease', with particular reference to AIDS).

9. International Cooperation and South-North Perspectives

Few indeed are the forums where health policy-makers, physicians, lawyers, philosophers, and others interested in bioethics can meet and discuss, and possibly even reach consensus on, issues that are relevant to developed and developing countries alike. Few also are the academic contexts in which such exchanges can take place. It is here that CIOMS is playing a major role, although it is not the only entity favouring such debate. Thus, in October 1994, the International Association of Bioethics will be convening the second International Congress on Bioethics, in Buenos Aires; that meeting will provide an excellent forum for scholars and practitioners in the Western Hemisphere, and elsewhere, to present their academic and research work.

UNESCO's International Bioethics Committee, currently in the initial stages of developing an international instrument on the human genome, is also placing strong emphasis on input from and the participation of experts from the developing countries. And, it can be anticipated that as and when WHO develops its own lines of activity in bioethics, every effort will be made to ensure geographically balanced participation.

10. Future Prospects

A report of a Conference held on 23-24 September 1992 on 'The Birth of Bioethics', held at the University of Washington, Seattle, appears in a Special Supplement to the November-December 1993 issue of the *Hastings Center Report*. One of the contributions, by Warren Reich, reminds us that the term 'bioethics' was first used by a distinguished oncologist at the University of Wisconsin-Madison, Van Rensselaer Potter. Potter is quoted as having formulated the objectives of bioethics in the following terms:

> The goal of this discipline, as I see it, would be to help humankind toward a rational but cautious participation in the processes of biological and cultural evolution... I chose 'bio-' to represent biological knowledge, the science of living systems, and I chose 'ethics' to represent knowledge of human value systems.

It is clear that, in the intervening decades, there has been enormous progress in the discipline. It was in May 1980 that progress in the discipline, notably during the 1970s, was assessed by one of the most distinguished leaders in the field, Daniel Callahan.[24] Callahan noted at the time:

24 Callahan, D., 'Shattuck Lecture – contemporary biomedical ethics', *New England Journal of Medicine*, 1980, Vol. 302, pp. 1228-1233.

> If one can discern various schools and currents in ethics, all drawing on old and deep streams in Western philosophical and religious thought, one can also discern some general developments that have had a profound effect on recent biomedical ethics. Perhaps the most important is the increasingly strong interaction between ethics, law, and regulation. One of the most important trends of the past decade has been the rapidity with which ethical debate has been taken to court, has been the subject of legislation, and has stimulated regulatory activity. One need only mention the Karen Ann Quinlan case, the Saikewicz case, human-subject regulation, the regulation of recombinant-DNA research, and so on, to signal that development. It has had two important consequences: an excessive emphasis on the language of individual rights, and a blurring of the distinction between law and morality.

The Shattuck Lecture (to the Massachusetts Medical Society) makes interesting reading even today, after a lapse of nearly one-and-a-half decades. Callahan identifies some of the key continuing issues, and defines what he described as the 'future agenda of biomedical ethics'. He points to one particular problem that will undoubtedly be of interest to practising physicians attending this conference, as well as to the ethicists:

> Those in ethics have learned, mainly by hard experience, that they will make little sense to practising physicians if they are not fully aware of the experience and details of clinical practice. It is simply not enough for those in ethics to roll up to the bedside the ghost of Immanuel Kant, John Stuart Mill, or G. E. Moore and provide instant moral diagnoses. It is hardly better to do the same with the writings of John Rawls. If the ultimate strength of ethics lies in its capacity to develop coherent modes of ethical analysis and comprehensive moral systems, it needs at the moment far greater skill in penetrating the often confused dynamic of the clinical setting. Only after a detailed analysis of the actual experience of the clinician (or a patient trying to work out a moral choice) can it be in any position either to invoke traditional theories or develop new ones.

Callahan could not have predicted just how extensive and far-reaching the debate on ethics, and the dynamic nature of the ethics-law continuum, have evolved in the 1980s and early 1990s. The debate in fact has grown to such dimensions that Sir Patrick Nairne, the former Chairman of the Nuffield Council on Bioethics, has affirmed: *'[Bioethics] is on the agenda for all of us'*.[25]

As WHO prepares its Ninth General Programme of Work, covering the period 1996-2001, it is clear that there is a growing awareness of the importance of bioethics. Thus, the draft version of that Programme affirms that:

> ... technological advances in medicine in the industrialized countries, especially in the field of genetic research and applied technology, are raising new issues of an ethical nature which call for urgent consideration at the highest levels.[26]

25 Quoted in *New Scientist*, 1994, Vol. 141, No. 1912, p. 13.
26 *See* WHO document A47/3, 9 March 1994, para. 14.

The document affirms further that WHO's directing and coordinating functions include 'the advancement and application of knowledge and the sharing of information in the field of health, including the bioethical dimensions'.[27] In discussing the question of 'ensuring equitable access to health services', the document states that:

> The significant advances, for example, in neurosciences and immunology have not always been applied widely in health care and services, and ethical questions are being raised more frequently with regard to the impact of developments in technology as well as to the accessibility and use of health technology and care and improvements in the quality of life. More and more attention is being given, in countries at all stages of development, to bioethics.[28]

No conclusion to this paper would be more appropriate than an extract from the speech delivered by Dr Zbigniew Bankowski, the distinguished Secretary-General of CIOMS, at a Symposium held in Washington, DC, on 26-27 April 1990:

> When we consider the world in all its diversity, it is strongly apparent that we need to achieve a common basis for policy transcending the viewpoints of each particular group. Of course, we must respect all that is deeply important to people, and this certainly includes their religious convictions, whatever they are. We can agree that dogmatism, fanaticism, and ideology are the enemies of tolerance, of careful listening, of reason, and of understanding and compassion for those who are different. They foster divisiveness and conflict, and the health of the people of the world is far too important for us to accept that. Instead, we should turn our efforts to identifying that core of principles on which we can agree, and should strive to have them adopted as a basis of an international code of ethics for health policy. We must live with the reality of disagreement about some issues, but we should do all we can to translate our considerable agreement into better health for mankind.[29]

27 *Ibid.*, para. 55.
28 *Ibid.*, para. 76.
29 *See* Bankowski, Z., 'Health policy, ethics, and human values: an international dialogue', in: Pellegrino, E., Mazzarella, P., and Corsi, P., Eds., *Transcultural Dimensions in Medical Ethics*, University Publishing Group, Frederick, MD, 1992, pp. 213-221, at p. 220.

Table A: 'From Bioethics to Biolaw' – The Case of France

Date	Author	Subject	Source of mission/Forum
Oct. 1984	National Ethical Consultative Committee (CCNE)	Recommendation for legislation on human experimentation	
Feb. 1988	Guy Braibant *(Conseil d'Etat)*	Report on *The Life Sciences: From Ethics to Law*	Prime Minister (in Dec. 1986)
Dec. 1988	Parliament	Law on human experimentation	
June 1991	Noëlle Lenoir *(Conseil d'Etat – now Conseil Constitutionnel)*	Report on *At Life's Frontiers: For a French Approach to Biomedical Ethics*	Prime Minister (in Oct. 1990)
Feb. 1992	Bernard Bioulac *(Deputé)*	*Information Report on Bioethics*	National Assembly (in Oct. 1990)
Feb. 1992	Franck Sérusclat *(Senator)*	*Report on the Life Sciences and Human Rights: Towards an Uncontrolled Transformation or a French Approach to Legislation*	Parliamentary Office for Assessment of Scientific and Technological Choices (in Dec. 1990)
Nov. 1993	Jean-François Matteï *(Deputé)*	*Report on Medical Ethics*	Prime Minister (in June 1993)
April 1994	National Assembly	3 Bills on various aspects of bioethics	Second Reading
May 1994	Senate	3 Bills on various aspects of bioethics (as amended by National Assembly)	Second Reading

Table B: 'From Bioethics to Biolaw' – The Case of the United Kingdom

Date	Author/Entity	Subject matter	Requested by
July 1982		Establishment of Committee of Inquiry into Human Fertilisation and Embryology	UK Government
June 1984	Warnock Committee	Report on Human Fertilisation and Embryology	
July 1985	Parliament	The Surrogacy Arrangements Act 1985	
1986	Department of Health and Social Security	Legislation on Human Infertility Services and Embryo Research (Consultation Paper)	
Nov. 1987	Government	*Human Fertilisation and Embryology: A Framework for Legislation* (White Paper)	
Nov. 1990	Parliament	The Human Fertilisation and Embryology Act 1990	
July 1992	Parliament	The Human Fertilisation and Embryology (Disclosure of Information) Act 1992	
Jan. 1993	Human Fertilisation and Embryology Authority (HFEA)	Sex Selection (Public Consultation Document)	
Jan. 1994	HFEA	Donated Ovarian Tissue in Embryo Research and Assisted Conception (Public Consultation Document)	

Table 1: Major Milestones in the Programme on Health Policy, Ethics and Human Values – An International Dialogue of the Council for International Organisations of Medical Sciences

Event	Location	Date
XVIIIth Round Table Conference on *Health Policy, Ethics and Human Values – An International Dialogue*	Athens	29 October - 2 November 1984
Conference on *Health Policy, Ethics and Human Values*	New Delhi	March 1986
XXIst Round Table Conference on *Health Policy, Ethics and Human Values: European and North American Perspective*	Noordwijk, Netherlands	2-5 June 1987
XXIInd Round Table Conference on *Ethics and Human Values in Family Planning*	Bangkok	19-24 June 1988
Seminar on *Health Policy, Ethics and Human Values: An Islamic Perspective*	Cairo	24-25 November 1988
XXIVth Round Table Conference on *Genetics, Ethics and Human Values: Human Genome Mapping, Genetic Screening and Gene Therapy*	Tokyo/ Inuyama City	22-27 July 1990
XXVth Conference on *Ethics and Epidemiology: International Guidelines*	Geneva	7-9 November 1990
XXVIth Round Table Conference on *Ethics and Research on Human Subjects – International Guidelines*	Geneva	5-7 February 1992
XXVIIIth Conference on *Poverty,Vulnerability, the Value of Human Life and the Emergence of Bioethics*	Ixtapa, Mexico	17-20 April 1994

Table 2: Selected International Instruments (Current or in Preparation) Regulating Research on Human Subjects

Organisation	Title	Status
Military Tribunal (Doctors' Trial, Nuremburg, 1946-1947)	Nuremburg Code (1947)	Final
United Nations General Assembly	International Covenant on Civil and Political Rights (1966) Article 7)	Final
World Psychiatric Association	Declaration of Hawaii II (July 1983)	Final
Conférence Internationale des Ordres et des Organismes d'Attributions Similaires	Principles of Medical Ethics (January 1987) (Articles 18-2)	Final
Council of Europe	European Prison Rules (February 1987) (Rule 27)	Final
World Medical Association	Declaration of Helsinki IV (September 1989)	Final
Nordic Committee on Medicines (Nordic Council)	Good Clinical Trial Practice (December 1989)	Implemented in all Nordic countries
Council of Europe	Recommendation No. R (90) 3 to Member States concerning Medical Research on Human Beings (February 1990)	Final
European Community	Notes for Guidance on Good Clinical Practice for Trials in Medicinal Products in the European Community (July 1990)	Final (entry into force: July 1991)
CIOMS and WHO	International Guidelines for Ethical Review of Epidemiological Studies (1991)	Final
United Nations General Assembly	Principles for the Protection of Persons with Mental Illness and for the Improvement of Mental Health Care (December 1991) (Principle 11, paragraph 15)	Final
CIOMS and WHO	International Ethical Guidelines for Biomedical Research Involving Human Subjects (February 1993)	Final
WHO	WHO Guidelines for Good Clinical Practice (GCP) for Trials on Pharmaceutical Products	In preparation (likely to be finalized in 1994)
Council of Europe	Protocol (to proposed Bioethics Convention) on Medical Research	In preparation (date of finalization uncertain)

Table 3: List of Jurisdictions Known to WHO/HQ to have Legislation on Organ Transplantation (by WHO Region)

European Region		
Austria	Greece	Slovakia
Belgium	Hungary	Spain
Bulgaria	Italy	Sweden
Croatia	Liechtenstein	Switzerland (17 Cantons)
Czech Republic	Luxembourg	Turkey
Denmark	Norway	United Kingdom
Finland	Portugal	former-Yugoslavia (status of legislation unclear)
France	Romania	
Germany (new *Länder* only)	Russian Federation	
Region of the Americas		
Argentina	Cuba	Paraguay
Bolivia	Dominican Republic	Peru
Brazil	Ecuador	USA (Federal and all States and District of Columbia)
Canada (all Provinces and Territories)	El Salvador	Venezuela
Chile	Guatemala	
Colombia	Honduras	
Costa Rica	Mexico	
	Panama	
Western Pacific Region		
Australia	Philippines	Vietnam
Japan	Singapore	
Malaysia	Tonga	
Eastern Mediterranean Region		
Cyprus	Lebanon	Tunisia
Iraq	Libyan Arab Jamahiriya	
Kuwait	Syrian Arab Republic	
African Region		
Algeria	Niger	Zimbabwe
Malawi	South Africa	
South-East Asia Region		
India (Union and Bombay, Karnataka, Kerala, Maharashtra, Tamil Nadu, Union Territory of Delhi)		Indonesia
		Sri Lanka

Table 4: Principal Stages in the Development of WHO's Guiding Principles on Human Organ Transplantation

Date	Event	Participants
May 1986	39th World Health Assembly discusses organ transplantation	Member States
May 1987	40th World Health Assembly adopts resolution on 'Development of guiding principles for human organ transplants'	Member States
May 1989	42nd World Health Assembly adopts resolution on 'Preventing the purchase and sale of human organs'	Member States
May 1990	WHO convenes informal Consultation on Organ Transplantation (Geneva)	20 experts + WHO Secretariat
Oct. 1990	WHO convenes 2nd informal Consultation on Organ Transplantation (Geneva)	5 experts + WHO Secretariat
Jan. 1991	87th session of the WHO Executive Board recommends endorsement of Draft Guiding Principles on Human Organ Transplantation	Members of the Executive Board
May 1991	44th World Health Assembly endorses Guiding Principles on Human Organ Transplantation	Member States
Sep. 1991	WHO publishes *Human Organ Transplantation: A Report on Developments Under the Auspices of WHO (1987-1991)*	

Table 5: List of Jurisdictions Known to WHO/HQ to Have Legislation on Commerce in Human Organs (by WHO Region)

European Region		
Austria	Greece	Switzerland
Belgium	Hungary	Turkey
Croatia	Italy	United Kingdom
Denmark	Luxembourg	former-Yugoslavia (status of legislation unclear)
Finland	Romania	
France	Russian Federation	
Germany (new *Länder* only)	Spain	
Region of the Americas		
Argentina	Costa Rica	Panama
Bolivia	Cuba	USA (Federal and all States and District of Columbia)
Brazil	Dominican Republic	Venezuela
Canada (all Provinces and Territories)	Ecuador	
Chile	Guatemala	
Colombia	Honduras	
	Mexico	
Western Pacific Region		
Australia (all States and Territories)	Hong Kong (final approval pending)	Singapore
Eastern Mediterranean Region		
Cyprus	Kuwait	Syrian Arab Republic
Iraq	Lebanon	Tunisia
African Region		
Algeria	South Africa	
Malawi	Zimbabwe	
South-East Asia Region		
India (final approval pending)	Indonesia	
	Sri Lanka	

Table 6: Selected International Responses to Commerce in Human Organs, 1970-1994

Organization	Response
Transplantation Society	1970 Statement
Council of Europe	May 1978 Resolution
Council of the European Society for Organ Transplantation	Oct. -Nov. 1983 Policy position
Transplantation Society	Sep. 1985 Guidelines
37th World Medical Assembly	Oct. 1985 Statement
Annual General Meeting of the European Dialysis and the European Renal Association	July 1986 Statement
Council of Arab Ministers of Health	March 1987 Draft Law
39th World Medical Assembly	Oct. 1987 Declaration
Conference of European Health Ministers (Council of Europe)	Final Text of Nov. 1987
XIV International Congress on Penal Law	Oct. 1989 Resolution
First Joint Meeting of the European Society for Organ Transplantation and the European Renal Association	Dec. 1990 Resolution
World Health Assembly	May 1991 Resolution
European Parliament	Discussion on Schwartzenberg Report, and adoption of Resolution, September 1993
First International Conference of Medical Parliamentarians	February 1994 Declaration
Steering Committee on Bioethics of the Council of Europe	Discussion in June 1994 or subsequently on Draft Protocol on Organ Transplantation to the Draft Bioethics Convention

Table 7: Elements in the Regulatory History of AIDS

A chronology of some key events (January-December 1983)		
Jurisdiction/organisation	**Date**	**Subject**
British Columbia	31 January	Reporting
CDC (Atlanta)	4 March	Reporting
California	23 March	Reporting
Sweden	8 March	Reporting
Austria	16 March	Reporting; HCWs
Denmark	30 May	Reporting
Alberta	8 June	Reporting
France	20 June	Blood safety
Council of Europe (CM)	23 June	Blood safety
Greece	14 July	Reporting; blood safety; HCWs
New Jersey	14 July	Research funding
New York	30 July	AIDS Institute; information
Italy	3 August	Case detection; reporting
New Zealand	15 August	Reporting
Turkey	18 August	Prevention
Norway	23 August	Reporting
California	29 September	AIDS Advisory Committee; funding education
Germany	15 October	Research
Israel	18 October	Reporting
Council of Europe (PA)	23 November	Human rights
Ontario	22 December	Reporting

TABLE 8: The Growth of HIV/AIDS Legislation – 1983-1994

Countries, etc. known to have legislation as of December 1983			
Austria		Italy	
Canada (Alb.; BC; Ont.)		New Zealand	
Denmark		Norway	
France		Sweden	
Germany (the then Federal Republic of)		Turkey	
Greece		USA (CA; NJ; NY)	
Israel			
Additional Jurisdictions introducing legislation between 1984 and 1987			
Angola	(1987)	Kenya	(1987)
Australia	(1984)	Libyan Arab Jamahiriya	(1987)
Barbados	(1985)	Liechtenstein	(1987)
Belgium	(1985)	Luxembourg	(1984)
Belize	(1987)	Malaysia	(1985)
Benin	(1987)*	Malta	(1986)
Bermuda	(1984)	Mauritius	(1987)
Brazil	(1985)	Mexico	(1985)
Brunei Dar es Salaam	(1987)	Monaco	(1986)
Bulgaria	(1985)	Mozambique	(1986)
Burundi	(1987)	Netherlands	(1987)
Canada	(1985)	Niger	(1987)
Chile	(1984)	Panama	(1985)
China	(1987)	Paraguay	(1985)
China (Province of Taiwan)	(1986)	Peru	(1987)
Costa Rica	(1985)	Philippines	(1986)
Cuba	(1986)	Poland	(1986)
Cyprus (Sovereign Base Areas)	(1987)	Portugal	(1986)
(the former) Czechoslovakia	(1984)	Republic of Korea	(1987)
Dominican Republic	(1987)	Romania	(1985)*
Ecuador	(1985)	(the former) USSR	(1985)
Egypt	(1986)	Rwanda	(1987)
Finland	(1985)	Singapore	(1985)
(the former) German Democratic Republic	(1986)	South Africa	(1987)
Grenada	(1986)	Spain	(1985)
Guatemala	(1986)	Sri Lanka	(1987)
Haiti	(1987)	Switzerland	(1986)
Honduras	(1987)	Syrian Arab Republic	(1987)
Hungary	(1985)	Thailand	(1985)
Iceland	(1986)	Togo	(1987)
India (Goa)	(1987)	United Kingdom	(1984)
Indonesia	(1987)	Uruguay	(1984)
Iraq	(1987)	Venezuela	(1984)
Jordan	(1987)	(the former) Yugoslavia	(1986)

**Text unavailable to WHO*

Additional jurisdictions introducing legislation between 1988 and 1994			
Albania	(1992)	Italy (Umbria)	(1992)
Algeria	(1989)	Japan	(1988)
Argentina	(1988)	Kyrgyzstan	(1992)
Bahrain	(1990)	Lebanon	(1990)
Bolivia	(1988)	Madagascar	(1990)
Chad	(1991)	Mongolia	(1989)
Colombia	(1988)	Oman	(1990)
Comoros	(1988)	Saint Lucia	(1991)
Croatia	(1992)	São Tomé and Principe	(1989)
Djibouti	(1991)	Saudi Arabia	(1990)
El Salvador	(1988)	Senegal	(1990)
Equatorial Guinea	(1988)	Tunisia	(1989)
Estonia	(1992)	Uganda	(1992)
Gabon	(1989)	Ukraine	(1991)
Guinea-Bissau	(1989)	Uzbekistan	(1992)
Guyana	(1989)	Vietnam	(1989)
Hong Kong	(1988)		
Date of legislation Unknown			
Bahamas*			
Cyprus*			
United Republic of Tanzania*		** Text unavailable to WHO*	

Table 9: Year of Initial Introduction of HIV/AIDS Legislation in Developing Countries/Jurisdictions (according to information available to WHO's Health Legislation Unit)

1984	Chile - Uruguay - Venezuela
1985	Barbados - Bermuda - Brazil - Costa Rica - Ecuador - Malaysia - Mexico - Panama - Paraguay - Singapore - Thailand
1986	China (Province of Taiwan) - Cuba - Egypt - Grenada - Guatemala - Malta - Mozambique - Philippines
1987	Angola - Belize - Benin - Brunei Dar es Salaam - Burundi - China - Dominican Republic - Haiti -India (Goa) - Indonesia - Iraq - Jordan - Kenya - Libyan Arab Jamahiriya - Mauritius - Niger - Peru - Republic of Korea - Rwanda - Syrian Arab Republic - Togo
1988	Argentina - Bolivia - Colombia - Comoros - El Salvador - Equatorial Guinea
1989	Algeria - Gabon - Guinea - Bissau - Guyana - Mongolia - São Tomé and Principe - Tunisia - Vietnam
1990	Bahrain - Lebanon - Madagascar - Oman -Saudi Arabia - Senegal
1991	Chad - Djibouti - Saint Lucia
1992	Uganda
1993-1994	None

Table 10: Some Early Questions and Issues in AIDS Law and Policy (Bayer, 1988)

Should public settings, like gay bathhouses, that facilitate multiple sexual contacts be closed?
How should those most at risk from HIV infection be discouraged from donating blood?
How aggressively should antibody testing, under conditions of confidentiality, be encouraged?
Is anonymity in testing preferable to confidentiality? And, if so, under what circumstances?
Do unconsented blinded seroprevalence studies represent an unacceptable invasion of privacy? Do they entail an unacceptable limitation on the ability to warn the infected of their infectious status?
Should the results of antibody tests be reportable – with full identification – to public health officials?
Should contact notification programmes, so central to the history of venereal disease control, be applied to AIDS?
Are there circumstances when the duty to warn unsuspecting sexual partners should take priority over the duty to protect confidentiality? Under what epidemiological conditions?
Should prisoners or others in confined settings be subject to mandatory testing?
Should inmates infected with HIV be segregated?
Should intravenous drug users be provided with sterile needles even if such a move would be perceived as 'weakening' the public health concern about impact of drug abuse itself?
Should public health officials invoking the power of quarantine have the power to control those who are infected with HIV and who willfully and maliciously expose others to risk?
R. Bayer, AIDS, Vol. 2 (Supplement 1), pp. 5217-5221 (1988).

Table 11: Some WHO Declarations, Policy Statements, Etc. on HIV/AIDS (1987-1994)

Report of the Consultation on INTERNATIONAL TRAVEL and HIV Infection	Geneva, 2-3 March 1987
Report of the Meeting on Criteria for HIV SCREENING Programmes	Geneva, 20-21 May 1987
Statement from the Consultation on Prevention and Control of AIDS in PRISONS	Geneva, 16-18 November 1987
Report of the WHO Meeting on Criteria for the Evaluation and Standardization	Stockholm, 7-8 December 1987
Report of the Meeting on HIV Infection and DRUG INJECTING Intervention Strategies	Geneva, 18-20 January 1988
London Declaration on AIDS PREVENTION (adopted on 28 January 1988 by the World Summit of Ministers of Health on Programmes for AIDS Prevention	London, 20-28 January 1988

Report of the Consultation on NURSING and HIV Infection	Geneva, 7-9 March 1988
Report of the Consultation on the NEUROPSYCHIATRIC Aspects of HIV Infection	Geneva, 14-17 March 1988
Statement from the Consultation on AIDS and the WORKPLACE	Geneva, 27-29 June 1988 convened by WHO in association with the ILO
Statement from the Consultation on Criteria for International Testing of Candidate HIV VACCINES	Geneva, 27 February - 2 March 1989
Proposed International Guidelines on UNLINKED ANONYMOUS SCREENING for the Public Surveillance of HIV Infections	June 1989
Consensus Statement from the Consultation on HIV Epidemiology and PROSTITUTION	Geneva, 3-6 July 1989
Consensus Statement from the Consultation on AIDS and SEAFARERS	Geneva, 5-6 October 1989
Report of the Second Consultation on the NEUROPSYCHIATRIC Aspects of HIV-1 Infection	Geneva, 11-13 January 1990
Consensus Statement on How to Achieve a Safe and Adequate BLOOD SUPPLY by Recruitment and Retention of Voluntary, Non-Remunerated Blood Donors	Geneva, 8-11 April 1991
Report of a WHO Consultation on the Prevention of Human Immunodeficiency Virus and Hepatitis B Transmission in the HEALTH CARE SETTING	Geneva, 11-12 April 1991
Consensus Statement from the WHO/UNICEF Consultation on HIV TRANSMISSION AND BREAST-FEEDING	Geneva, 30 April - 1 May 1992
WHO Guidelines on HIV Infection and AIDS in Prisons (issued in March 1993 as an outcome of Consultation on HIV/AIDS in PRISONS	Geneva, 15-17 September 1992
Statement from Consultation on COUNSELLING AND TESTING FOR HIV INFECTION	Geneva, 16-18 November 1992

NOTE:

Reference should also be made to the following: resolution WHA41.24, adopted by the Forty-first World Health Assembly in May 1988 (this resolution specifically addressed the need to 'protect the human rights and dignity of HIV-infected people and people with AIDS … and to avoid discriminatory action against and stigmatisation of them in the provision of services, employment and travel'); and the Global AIDS Strategy (published by WHO in 1992 as No. 11 in the WHO AIDS Series).

From Bioethics to Biolaw

Linda Nielsen[*]

> *Piet Hein:*
> 'We shall have to evolve
> problem solvers galore
> since each problem they solve
> creates ten problems more'.

1. Introduction

Regulation in the area of biotechnology is being enacted in many countries all over the world. The extent, content and form differs quite a lot, and the interaction between bioethics and biolaw can be expected to be on the agenda nationally and internationally in the years to come. In this essay, emphasis is put on biotechnology in relation to human beings, i.e., especially assisted reproduction, prenatal diagnosis, genetic therapy, genetic testing and screening, etc.

Regulation in this area must take into account the characteristics of biotechnology and biomedicine.

First, the legislator traditionally has had scruples about interfering in these areas

(a) because they concern the special relationship between the doctor and his patient;
(b) because the area has a bearing on 'the freedom of research', and to a certain extent freedom of contract;
(c) because judicial intervention in pregnancy and birth is seen as intruding into an area which is normally seen as the sphere of the individual and the family, not a sphere of public intervention.

Second, when the collective choice for today and tomorrow is taken it is essential to try to find out if there is consensus on the ethical questions and their solutions. In this

* Professor Dr. juris, University of Copenhagen, Denmark

Cosimo Marco Mazzoni (ed.), A Legal Framework for Bioethics, 39-52.
©1998 Kluwer Law International. Printed in The Netherlands.

respect it may be sensible to have ethics committees with the purpose of creating debate amongst the public and hopefully reach consensus. This way ethical questions and the regulative responses are becoming part of the democratic process.

Third, it has to be taken into account that the biotechnology area is a very dynamic and fluctuant area. This means that it calls for flexibility regarding regulation.

Fourth, it has to be recalled that the area is both of national and international importance. Cultural differences have to be taken into account when the legislation is made. On the other hand a ban in one country may lead to people going to other less restrictive countries to obtain what they cannot have back home. This kind of forum shopping is seen among others in the area of assisted reproduction – sometimes called 'procreative tourism'. Thus both national and international measures are called for.

Last but not least, it must be remembered that legislation and regulation in the area is a means, not a goal. It is important to be very clear about what is supposed to be achieved by making regulations of some kind. Legislation does not necessarily make people ethical.

2. The Basic Dilemmas

The legal choice reflects the ethical choice, which includes the balancing of different interests and values. The challenge is to obtain all the advantages of the biotechnology revolution and to avoid the disadvantages: To avoid becoming prisoners of progress, but to control the development and to guide it in the directions wanted by the community in question. One of the problems is trying to *foresee* possible and realistic consequences. Another is to agree upon *which* consequences are *unwarranted*. Finally, they must be *balanced* against other values. The basic dilemmas may be put the following way:

THE BASIC DILEMMAS:

Protection of:	**Protection against:**
– Autonomy	– Coercion and compulsion
– Human dignity	– A reductionistic view of life
– A private space	– Social control
– Equity	– Discrimination
– Fairness	– Stigmatization

Balanced against fundamental societal interests:

- Freedom of research
- Freedom of contract
- Efficiency in medical care
- Efficiency in public administration

After the ethical choices have been made, the next step is trying to find out how the interests and values in question are best protected, and *how* unwanted consequences are best avoided or minimized. What remedies do we have at hand?

3. Different Forms of Protection

The key problem here is *how* unwanted consequences are best avoided or minimized. Very different methods may each play a part.

a. Information and education
   This may raise awareness and contribute to protect human dignity and protect against genetic discrimination and stigmatization. This education should inform the public, and especially health care professionals, social workers and journalists. Multidisciplinary *Councils of Ethics* may fulfil an extremely important task in this respect. It is sometimes said that change of law is good, but change of attitudes is better.

b. Quality of services and scientific measures
   - *Sufficient scientific foundation* is essential.
   - Openness as to the procedure. The status of a new technique urges openness as to the procedure.
   - Quality of services is of extreme importance, especially as private institutions and persons may perform activities in the biotechnology area.

c. *Codes of conduct* may provide guidelines for professionals securing that quality control and integrity concerns are adequately taken care of, and that non-biased counselling is secured. Moreover, standards of good medical practice may secure a high scientific standard.

d. *The courts.* The judicial route may settle disputes, but has its limits, among others the uncertainty as to the outcome of the case, the time it takes, and the fact that it does not offer a comprehensive solution to the problems associated with biotechnology.

4. The Role of Law

Regulation is another well-known protective measure. It must be remembered that legislative intervention, a last-resort means of control and sanction, is bound to create some stumbling blocks. We must take the time to weigh the pros and cons of legislative intervention, consider public opinion, define the ethical bases on which to act and take pains to avoid dogmatism. Regulation may happen through informal or formal law. Probably both instruments are needed.

Regulation may have different functions[1]:

- A *norm-setting function*, declaring certain values and interests as worthy of protection against any infringement. In the present context, protection of human dignity, protection against genetic discrimination and prohibitions of germ line therapy, cloning, cross species fertilization, the creation of chimeras and measures regarding the foetus are paradigm examples. They are part of the vocabulary of who we say we are and who we want to become. This function is based on the vision that law may be educational – a way of implementing ethics.
- A *protective function*, balancing the protected values against other interests, providing sanctions for abuses and minimizing risks to patients and others affected by biotechnology. An example may be protecting potential children who might be born following assisted conception and another example people in a vulnerable position, i.e. applicants for work, insurance, etc.
- A *regulative or declarative function*, securing clarity and certainty in handling controversial areas of bioethics. The legal status of many bioethical practices is unclear in the absence of parliamentary interventions. Law may secure that the persons involved know what is accepted/not accepted so they can act accordingly. This way law may also stabilize confidence between physician and patient by providing reliable rules for their relationship. Examples are regulation of the right to abortion or prenatal diagnosis, the doctor's right/duty to deny access to assisted reproduction; rules dealing with aspects of confidentiality in respect of genetic knowledge obtained during the course of prenatal screening; and the (non-)disclosure of the identity of gamete donors for children born as a result of assisted conception.

5. Legal Intervention in Biotechnology Area? Pros and Cons

The crucial question is that of determining the extent to which biotechnology should be the object of legal scrutiny and control.

a. The arguments in favour of introducing some kind of regulation or control are centred on the following topics:
   - Reserving to the medical profession, etc. the right to decide on issues of life and death is seen as an improper derogation from an area of legitimate public concern. According to the proponents of this opinion the law, even if it is

1 *Albein Eser*, 'Legal Aspects of Bioethics' in *Europe and Bioethics, Proceedings of the 1. Symposium of the Council of Europe on Bioethics*, Strasbourg, 1985, pp. 41-42.

imperfect, is at least one means of controlling the biotechnology area in the interest of the community as a whole.

- Moreover, it may be necessary to protect those who face the risk of being placed in a bad position. This may be the case for the unborn child being conceived by a seventy-year-old woman; it may be the case for an applicant who does not want to undergo genetic testing and may learn that s(he) suffers from an incurable disease; or it may be the case for future generations, who should have the right to a world where we have taken care of the environment and culture in a responsible manner. To say that these people in a number of situations are entitled to say yes or no may not be sufficient, when the person in question is in a dependent situation, for instance as an applicant to work or insurance. Informed consent does not necessarily present sufficient protection. The choice here is not real. Protection of integrity and unfair discrimination may necessitate formal regulation.
- The individual person, who is to give informed consent, may be so eager to obtain medical intervention, rights, etc., that the person in question is not sufficiently aware of the long-term consequences of biotechnology. Consequently the long-term consequences are best taken care of through formal control and regulation.
- Finally, parliamentary intervention may be appropriate with the aim of securing public acceptance of new biotechnology. The democratic process secures openness as to the use of new biotechnologies and a broad debate and consensus, which means that development in this sensitive area is part of the democratic process.

b. The arguments against making legislation in the area are centred on the following topics:
   - It is said that overreacting may do more harm than good, especially because biotechnology is a very sensitive area. Sometimes it is heard in international conferences that a new disease has emerged, namely HIL, 'Highly Inappropriate Legislation'. Such legislation may limit research possibilities in an unnecessary and unfortunate way. According to this view intervention by the law is too blunt a way of tackling the delicate ethical dilemmas which doctors have to face: The individual conscience guided by personal experience and the ethical codex of the profession must confront and resolve the day-to-day ethical issues of medical practice.
   - This way of thinking is strengthened by the fact that development is so fast in this area that it is very difficult to legislate in an adequate manner. Autonomy for the responsible researchers and persons involved in research, procreation, etc. may be seen – and is seen by certain groups – as the best way of securing research and development. Freedom of research may be seen as an advantage in itself and may also be seen as the most efficient way of improving health and health care.
   - Moreover, rejection of control and regulation may be seen as a belief in responsibility and self-control by the responsible persons of the area. This may

produce the background why researchers and doctors often seem to regard regulation with a certain reluctance. It may be seen as unnecessary to control the development until some kind of abuse has been documented. It is said that legislation does not make people ethical.

- There may also be problems controlling that the legislation is taken into account, which in these sensitive private areas, i.e., insemination, may give rise to difficulties.
- Finally a ban in this international area may have as a consequence that cloning, genetic testing, assisted procreation, etc. is moved to another country.

c. In my opinion the problem of introducing legal rules into human affairs stems from the comparative vagueness with which legal rules must inevitably be expressed.

- Once rules acquire a more specific meaning, usually through judicial pronouncements, they allow very much less room for manoeuvre, and can be more restrictive than was originally intended by the framer of the rule. The effect of this can be to distort people's behaviour through the fear of litigation or prosecution. One may then be concerned not with doing what one feels to be right, but with doing with one feels to be the legally safest thing to do.
- Informed consent in the area of biotechnology is of extreme importance, but can be seen as an individualization of ethics, which may be the superstructure of selfishness. Thus, more common solutions are necessary where informed consent does not provide adequate or sufficient protection. Autonomy does not protect the weak and future generations. This leads me to the conclusion that formal regulation is necessary in the areas where such interests are at stake. Legislation should be supplemented by information, education, scientific measures and professional guidelines in the form of codes of conduct. This may especially be of interest with the aim of securing quality services, scientific standards, genetic counselling, etc. If law, education, information, etc. interact ethics is likely to get the best possible protection.

6. How Should Legislation be Enacted?

Regulation may have different levels:

- *Object of protection* – Individual or society at large?

  This includes the choice between *pluralism versus universalism.* The trend in western culture has for a number of years been pluralism and individualization, which tends to embrace ethics, too. This has led to moral pluralism via individual autonomy administered by informed consent. When informed consent is used, information, transparency and openness are important ingredients in the protection. Also the necessity of balanced presentation and time to think things over, seems important. The wish to obtain national and international solidarity may speak in favour of universal solutions in some areas.

- *Timing – ex post facto*, current or anticipatory.
  This includes the dilemma of a *slippery slope versus exaggerated legislation*. Another of the basic choices is whether there is a belief in the possibility of control and sticking to the limits. If protection against long-term unwanted consequences is seen as essential, and there is little belief in the ability to keep within the limits set by law in the first place, the fundamental way of protection is regulating specific kinds of research, research methods, etc., or registration. Worries as to the factual possibilities of *control* – of use or of fulfilling the scientific demands – may lead to setting limits which are not linked to the use, but to an earlier stage, to secure that the use is controlled properly. The risk is making exaggerated legislation, which may give a false picture of reality and erode the belief in the purpose of legislation.
- *Location* – Clinic, professional group, administration or government?
  Professional control at *clinics* or by the *medical profession*[2] may secure the quality of medical treatment and include ethical considerations, but leaving health professionals alone to set the ground rules in so complex a field as biotechnology, puts a very heavy burden on them. Regulation in this area is a matter of social policy, too, and must in my view not be left to the professions that are directly involved. *Councils of ethics* may be clinical, local or national and may play an important role as an independent agency of reflection and recommendation that is respectful of the full range of sentiments on biotechnology.
- *Form* – Prohibition, procedural measure, permit, secrecy, criminalization.
  The urgent need for flexibility in this fluctuant, developing area makes formal legislation less adequate in some areas. Legislative intervention may be sweeping or compartmentalized. It is urgent that the regulation secures consequence, predictability and equity.

7. Different Models of Protection and Regulation

MODEL 1: INDIVIDUAL CONTROL - THE PRIVATE ORDERING APPROACH

A system of private ordering presents an approach to biotechnology which leaves the protection to the participants. Of course this approach will have different consequences in different cultures and different legal systems.

If no regulation is made the following consequences may be stressed:

The *advantage* of this approach is the belief in autonomy and responsibility for the individual – self-regulation by responsible persons and institutions. Also, no situation is treated as a problem until it occurs to be so – no premature and exaggerated

2 The number of clinical ethics committees around the world has grown astronomically over the past ten years. Their role is essentially an advisory one.

legislation is made. Finally no regulation is made which cannot be surveilled and controlled by the authorities, and thereby an undermining of the belief in legislation is avoided. A law that is enacted and subsequently proves to be unenforceable is likely to be ignored, thereby missing its target altogether. There are also fears that, despite appearances, legislation would not necessarily give everyone adequate protection. Moreover, there may be a risk of passing legislation hastily under pressure from the public opinion and the media, where there is still no consensus.

The *disadvantage* is that, generally speaking, the most powerful will be in the stronger position, and the vulnerable groups may be left unprotected against abuse. Moreover, this approach fails to answer any of the fundamental questions raised by the application of human genetics and it does not provide conscientious researchers, doctors etc. with the guidelines they are seeking. It also creates difficulties in terms of the administration of justice. Finally, it may often be difficult for the individual to see and understand the long-term and societal consequences of the choice. The individualization of ethics, represented by informed consent, may have the consequence that long-term considerations tend to recede into the background, overridden by actual needs. Examples are assisted reproduction and embryo diagnostics, where a couple's wish of *in vitro* fertilization, donation, sex-selection, investigation for a number of diseases, etc., may be easy to understand, but the consequences for perception of embryos as 'things to freeze, donate etc.', and thus dehumanization, risk of eugenics etc. are overridden.

This kind of control seems especially fit for health care questions, whereas it seems *insufficient* where societal interests are at stake, or where respect for other people necessitates regulation. Examples are: a) criminal offences; b) where the person involved is incapable of giving consent (children, incapacitated adults, etc.); c) situations where risks of discrimination or stigmatization are at stake.

EXAMPLES:

Italy can be said to be an example of the *laissez faire* attitude. In Italy artificial reproduction, the treatment of human gametes, the human embryo, etc., is not regulated by law. Private IVF centres remain in a legal void, unfettered by either law or morality. Owing to large differences of opinion concerning the nature of family and of reproductive liberty, all of the bills introduced to address these matters have failed to pass.[3]

MODEL 2: PROFESSIONAL CONTROL AND ETHICAL COUNCILS – THE LIBERAL APPROACH

This approach is not as regulatory as the two approaches described later, but it emphasizes the *procedure* and the *norm-setting function* of law. Codes of ethics may guide the health

3 Cf. among others Linda Nielsen and Stefano Nespor, *Genetic Test, Screening and Use of Genetic Data by Public Authorities*, The Danish Centre for Human Rights, 1993.

area, and ethical councils may encourage debate. In areas of sharply conflicting values a Council of Ethics may be the best mechanism for generating broadly acceptable solutions. Given a diverse, representative membership, resources for the gathering of information and sufficient time and commitment to conduct liberat, a council can achieve a moderate consensus that is sensitive and responsive to a wide range of interests of concerns.

This approach seems appropriate where health care is concerned and the doctor/patient relationship is essential (e.g. genetic counselling).

EXAMPLES:

England may produce an example of the liberal approach.

The United Kingdom enacted legislation in 1990: The Human Fertilisation and Embryology Act. The main vehicle for the legislation is the Human Fertilisation and Embryology Authority (HFEA), which is a statutory agency with a wide range of responsibility. HFEA is primarily a licensing body concerned with three main areas of activity: The storage of gametes and embryos; research on human embryos; and any infertility treatment which involves the use of either donated gametes or embryos created outside the human body. In addition, HFEA is charged with maintaining a register of information concerning donors, treatment services, and children born following licensed services; publicizing services which centres and HFEA itself provide; producing advice and information to centres and publishing a code of practice to which centres should adhere or aspire; and providing information to donors, to potential patients and to children born following regulated services.[4] It has been said that the Act provides the attempt in English law to provide a comprehensive framework for making medical science democratically accountable.

British legislation does not even extend its regulatory ambit to all treatments currently in use, let alone prohibits them. Certain infertility treatment services are permitted only under a treatment license which will be necessary for IVF, AID, egg donation etc.

MODEL 3: COMMUNITY CONTROL – THE CAUTIOUS REGULATORY SYSTEM

This approach includes a number of quite elaborated safeguards. The model emphasizes the protective function, while at the same time fulfilling the regulatory function. Between the polar extremes of the State as oppressor and the State as protector-liberator lies a spectrum of supportive roles the State may assume in fulfilling its democratic mandate, namely, as dispute arbiter, health service provider, public financier, lawmaker, researcher, protector of public health, safety and human life, and strong and benevolent defender and promoter of human rights. The precise roles are deter-

4 Cf. Derek Morgan and Robert G. Lee: *Human Fertilisation and Embryology Act 1990.*

mined partly by historical and still evolving State roles, partly by fundamental and evolving values that define and structure legal relations between the individual, the family and the State.

The *advantage* is that the legislation secures some safeguards, which are not easily overruled, while at the same time the possibility of permissions makes the system more flexible than the prohibitive. The *disadvantage* is, that the cautious regulatory system may turn out to be too permissive or too restrictive, as things develop further. A binding legislation, which is difficult to alter, may be inadequate in these fluctuating and fast developing areas.

This model may be seen as appropriate in all the areas.

EXAMPLES:

Scandinavia and France present examples of this attitude towards biotechnology. This legislation contains provisions about donation of gametes, cryopreservation of human eggs and embryos, to a certain extent about anonymity etc. Moreover, the legislation in Scandinavia includes provisions that fertilized eggs may only be kept outside the woman's womb for 14 days from conception, that research on embryos is prohibited to a certain extent, and that cloning, cross species fertilization, etc. are banned. [5] The legislation also introduces ethical committees. In Denmark, the Council of Ethics was established in 1987, with the mission of examining biomedical and ethical questions, producing proposals for legislation, and informing and encouraging debate amongst the population. The Danish scientific, ethical committees were established in 1992, and have the task among others to approve biomedical research projects which include research on living human individuals, human gametes or embryos, etc.

The background for this attitude in Scandinavia may be connected with the widespread public health service and the welfare communities, where public interaction is part of the everyday life. Also the strong position of women's movements, which have been opposed to the new reproductive technologies, etc. may have some impact.

The comprehensive legislation in France of 1994 may also be seen as a way of implementing a cautious regulatory system.

MODEL 4: COMMUNITY CONTROL – THE PROHIBITIVE SYSTEM

This system emphasizes comprehensive protection at an early stage, and provides regulation by law with few exemptions and often backed with penalty.

5 The content of the legislation in Denmark, Sweden, and Norway can be found in: Linda Nielsen and Derek Morgan, 'Prisoners of Progress or Hostages to Fortune', *The Journal of Law, Medicine and Ethics*, 1993, 21:1. However, legislation had to a certain extent been amended, among others the Danish legislation on assisted reproduction in 1997.

The *advantage* is that things never 'get out of hand' because of the principle that what is not forbidden is normally allowed. Also, a temporary ban gives time to consider the adequate kind of regulation properly, without facing the risk of people considering certain methods as their 'right'. This problem is well known from assisted reproduction, IVF, where it probably would be hopeless to cancel the IVF programme once it has been established. The *disadvantage* is that prohibitions are made before problems arise. Also, the early regulation may turn out to be too prohibitive when compared to the needs and advantages that arise in practice.

This model will probably have its strongest position where economic areas, e.g. insurance and maybe work, are concerned.

EXAMPLES:

A *temporary* ban – a moratorium – has been known in Danish legislation concerning embryo research, where a temporary ban has now been replaced by legislation allowing specific kinds of embryo research. It is also known from the area of gene technology and environment.

Germany presents an example of the prohibitive system. The legislation contains a number of provisions in relation both to assisted conception treatment services and research. The wide spectrum of prohibitions are backed with penalty (Embryonenschutzgesetz). A similar restricted attitude can be found Austria, where legislation was enacted in 1992.

There are probably historical reasons for this prohibitive attitude in Germany. Moreover, the structure of decision-making covering the activity all over Germany is of importance. This partly explains the emphasis on penal provisions.

8. The Bioethics Convention

The European Parliament approached the topic of Biomedicine in the Bioethics Convention of November 1996.[6] The Convention contains a number of articles stressing the norm-setting and protective role of law:

ARTICLE 1 (PURPOSE AND OBJECT)

Parties to this convention shall protect the dignity and identity of all human beings and guarantee everyone, without discrimination, respect for their integrity and other rights and fundamental freedoms with regard to the application of biology and medicine.

6 Council of Europe: 'Convention for the Protection of Human Rights and Dignity of the Human Being with Regard to the Application of Biology and Medicine: Convention on Human Rights and Biomedicine, Directorate of Legal Affairs, Strasbourg, November 1996.

ARTICLE 2 (PRIMACY OF THE HUMAN BEING)

The interest and welfare of the human being shall prevail over the sole interest of society or science.

ARTICLE 5 (GENERAL RULE)

An intervention in the health field may only be carried out after the person concerned has given free and informed consent to it.

ARTICLE 21 (PROHIBITION OF FINANCIAL GAIN)

The human body and its parts shall not, as such, give rise to financial gain.

ARTICLE 12 (PRIVATE LIFE AND RIGHT TO INFORMATION)

Everyone has the right to respect for private life in relation to information about his or her health. Everyone is entitled to know any information collected about his or her health. However, the wishes of individuals not to be so informed shall be observed. In exceptional cases, restrictions may be placed by law on the exercise of the rights contained in paragraph 2 in the interests of the patient.

ARTICLE 22 (DISPOSAL OF A REMOVED PART OF THE HUMAN BODY)

When in the course of an intervention any part of a human body is removed, it may be stored and used for a purpose other than that for which it was removed, only if this is done in conformity with appropriate information and consent procedures.

ARTICLE 15 (SCIENTIFIC RESEARCH)

Scientific research in the field of biology and medicine shall be carried out freely, subject to the provisions of this Convention and the other legal provisions ensuring the protection of the human being.

ARTICLE 18 (RESEARCH ON EMBRYOS IN VITRO)

1 Where the law allows research on embryos in vitro it shall ensure adequate protection of the embryo.
2 The creation of human embryos solely for research purposes is prohibited.

ARTICLE 13 (INTERVENTIONS ON THE HUMAN GENOME)

An intervention seeking to modify the human genome may only be undertaken for preventive, diagnostic or therapeutic purposes and only if its aim is not to introduce any modification in the genome of any descendants.

ARTICLE 12 (PREDICTIVE GENETIC TESTS)

Tests which are predictive of genetic diseases or which serve either to identify the subject as a carrier of a gene responsible for a disease or to detect a genetic predisposition or susceptibility to a disease may be performed only for health purposes or for scientific research linked to health purposes and subject to appropriate genetic counselling.

9. Conclusion

Although there are differences between the different countries which are not easily bridged, it is apparent that some core approaches regarding biotechnology are desirable. *International* regulation may enlarge the protection and provide further equality, whereas *national legislatio*n can take the local culture, religion, etc. into account, is easier to change and may be more precise. When considering the content of international regulation*, consensus* carries the risk of 'harmonization downwards', where the regulation is based on the lowest common denominator, whereas *moral pluralism* carries the risk of underestimating the danger of cloning, genetic testing and screening, etc. to human dignity and the social dimension – discrimination, etc.

POSSIBLE INTERNATIONAL CONSENSUS

- Protection against genetic discrimination.
- Securing autonomy in health care?
- Exchange of information, experiences, etc. might encourage comparative bioethics and ultimately lead to a wider extent of communal bioethics.

POSSIBLE EUROPEAN CONSENSUS

- Council of Europe: Bioethics Convention; dignity, integrity, autonomy, privacy, non-discrimination.
- EU: Data Directive (privacy). Patent, Biotechnological inventions.
- Restrictions on genetic tests in insurances and maybe employment (EU)?
- Securing the quality of services. Professional guidelines for doctors?

THE INDIVIDUAL COUNTRY

- Encouraging public debate and promoting public education on biotechnology and its ethical implications.
- Encouraging the setting down of national Councils of ethics.
- Securing equal access to clinical genetic services.
- Social security and health care provisions.
- Provisions regarding the status of the embryo, embryo research, access to IVF, donation, anonymity, etc.

CODES OF CONDUCT

- Genetic counselling.
- Prenatal diagnosis.

URGENT NEED FOR RESPONSIBLE CHOICES FROM EACH INDIVIDUAL

It is essential that we try to produce public education as well as legal safeguards to protect the dignity, integrity, privacy and non-discrimination. The area of genetic testing and screening seems easier to reach consensus about than the area of assisted procreation, as religion is not as paramount as regarding, e.g., the status of the embryo. International measures may serve as safeguards *per se* and may serve as a basis for national measures according to the models described above. The Council of Europe and in some areas the EU may have an extremely important role in serving as the foundation and catalyst for international consensus, standards and reforms. But the individual country also has to 'fill in' the framework made internationally. Finally, we also have each and every one of us to make our personal choice and take responsibility. The sensitive biotechnology necessitates responsible attitudes internationally, nationally and individually. This is extremely essential for our common future.

Towards a Law for Bioethics

Paolo Zatti*

If one were to attempt to collect in an archive under the heading 'bioethics' everything that occurs in the world under this name, one would soon realize the huge gap that exists between the content of the archive and the current definitions of bioethics, the definitions, that is, that can be found in the best dictionaries. Bioethics is usually referred to as that part of ethics concerned with human behaviour in relation to life: or as a branch of knowledge which studies the relationship between bio-sciences and moral values. But, actually, bioethics was a branch of ethics, or at any rate a 'discipline' concerned with ethical issues, only as long as it remained a discipline confined to essays and textbooks. As bioethical debate and research has gradually extended beyond academic environments and established its own institutions, its authorities, its decision-making processes and its regulations, a new and highly complex phenomenon has arisen. Today's scenario conveys a new image of bioethics: it is no longer simply a branch of knowledge, but rather a multiform experience of consensus-forming around specific issues, moral choices, political and juridical options, concerning the relationship between science and human values.

From this point of view the transition from bioethics to 'bio-law' is not merely the transition from a level of ethical issues and options to a level of legislative problems and decisions. Rather it is the transition from a magma of scientific, social, institutional, communication, and consensus-forming experiences and facts, to interventions of juridical regulation. And it is in these terms that the question implicitly asked in the title of this paper appears singularly complex. 'Towards a Law for Bioethics': what relationship is being formed, and what relationship would be desirable, between bioethics (as described above) and law? How much, of our lengthy search for consensus, should be laid down in legal regulations? And which forms of juridical experience can best satisfy the needs of bioethics?

The issue is vast and difficult. I do not propose to address it as such, but simply to observe it from a specific viewpoint: what is – or what could be – the contribution of a jurist to the formation of bioethics; at which point and with what chances of success

* Professor of Law, University of Padua, Padua, Italy.

Cosimo Marco Mazzoni (ed.), A Legal Framework for Bioethics, 53-64.
©1998 Kluwer Law International. Printed in The Netherlands.

and at what risk does the specific competence of the legal expert fit into the process. Only indirectly will some considerations arise as to the final issue: how much and what type of law for bioethics.

Bioethics is a cultural field characterized by an impressive dissemination and proliferation of materials; to address the topic one needs to resort to a wide variety of languages which are not always governed by specific disciplines; the juridical question is usually closely linked to the description of the problem; and conversely in the rule of law we frequently can identify the final gathering point, the practical result of options chosen beyond the juridical horizon.

In a similar context, different and contrasting distortions can occur in the relationship between bioethics and law.

On the one hand, we can observe the tendency to conceive of this relationship in terms of a relationship between politics and expertise: bioethics as the field of choice and the law as the field of implementation. To put it in such a way as to flatter the wounded vanity of jurists: *l'entendance suivra.*

On the other hand, the integration of the languages occasionally appears to blur the boundaries between the different disciplines and cover up the specific connotations of the juridical problem – or of the ethical one, or of the sociological one – within a linguistic and methodological hybrid.

I hope I am not misunderstood. It is not my intention to state that the 'juridical' sphere has any form of supremacy in bioethical issues. I agree with what has been called the British Way (Lord Kennet, quoted by Sev Fluss) of interpreting the relationship between bioethics and legislative interventions. I am fully convinced that bioethical issues require first and foremost a consensus-forming process – although a consensus formed by propagation and imitation frightens me. The jurist must know that the rules he works with professionally are the result of a vast collection of needs, assessments and intentions that were born before and outside the legal world; the pedagogical or therapeutical duty of the law towards society should ideally address marginal behaviour patterns, and certainly not the core of commonly accepted choices and preferences.

I would simply like to stress two points of method, in themselves very simple and which are interrelated:

(a) the juridical issue does not arise at the end, but during the process of search for consensus; it contributes to the examination and formulation of options, not only in view of legislative measures, but also in order to establish an ethical core which is a prerequisite for a pluralist society;
(b) the acceptance of moral options in the order of the law is effective only if filtered through considerations of necessity, feasibility, and systematic compatibility with the rule of law.

To use a metaphor: a jurist cannot wait, sitting under the tree of bioethics, for the fruits of consensus to ripen so he can gather them in his basket; he is one of the team of gardeners and must use his tools, as well, to guarantee that the tree's branches grow strong, healthy and well-balanced.

To justify these generic indications and place them in a more concrete context, I will try to suggest some aspects of bioethics in which the juridical input influences the overall debate.

What makes bioethics so difficult – but also so fascinating – is the fact that we are wandering through a territory as yet uncharted, in which we cannot even recount to ourselves our experience.

If we could say to ourselves what birth is, what death is, what it is that lives in a woman's womb, what it is that lives thanks to the support of a machine, what a mother is, and a father, what identity is, what dignity is – we would have a language we could use to evaluate and to prescribe. But we do not know, or rather we have only a partial knowledge, without any certainties. Or we do not agree on what we know.

Looking at documents produced by Ethics Committees we see that often the members of these Committees find it wise or necessary to avoid giving a definition of the issues they are discussing. In a more pragmatic manner, they prefer to (or perhaps, *have to*) decide on what needs to be done without being able to put into words the issue they are deciding on.

On other occasions, instead, they clearly feel the need to make a preliminary statement, an attempt to put together a sort of 'common truth', an agreed definition of the object of the discussion: what do we mean by death, what do we mean by embryo, what do we mean by person, what do we mean by health.

I feel that juridical expertise can markedly influence these options. Jurists have long been aware that their profession is to 'do things with words', before they 'do things with rules'. The jurist knows that the pronouncements of the law are like preformative pronouncements and that they exercise this power through words.

Herein lies the origin of the virtues and flaws of juridical reasoning. The jurist is tendentially a baptist: he tends to believe that by giving a name to things – like Adam in the garden of Eden – the entire created world will become his subordinate. He suffers from the age-old habit of mistaking concepts for reality and from the illusion that the world can be subjugated by juridical 'baptisms'.

These are dangerous attitudes, which contribute little or nothing to the common discussion.

When faced with the difficulty of doing things with words, the specific skills of the jurist should consist in the power of analogic reasoning, in coming to conclusions strictly related to the premises, in keeping his arguments to the correct context: if the jurist abides by these skills, he will be well equipped to avoid the risk of exceedingly 'heavy' definitions which leave no space for legal realism, or conversely, prescriptions not based on sufficiently clear conceptual premises. And this will be a precious contribution to the consensus-forming process in bioethical issues.

A few points to think about – from my own limited experience.

(a) Relativity of qualifications
Bioethical debate on the issue of the beginning of human life is more sensitive than other topics to the problem of definition and 'baptism'. To qualify what is conceived – the embryo, the foetus, the viable unborn – as an 'individual', a 'man', or even more so a 'person', is an object of heated debate: supported and opposed with equal intensity. But both parties have in common the tendency to transpose the positive or negative option – the definition or non-definition – from the ethical plane to the juridical plane, in the conviction that the rule of the law must offer a practical sanction, the definitive answer to the moral question, so that we can finally have a consistent system of prescriptions to state definitively that the embryo is a human being ... or is not ... or is something but we do not know what.

Well, I believe that an interdisciplinary reflection on the issues relating to the beginning of human life can benefit from a premise which lies within the competence of a jurist, and which revolves around the complex use that juridical language makes of words such as 'person', 'subject', 'human being'. It is useful to stress that, for specifically legal purposes, qualifications which can appear contradictory are both valid, at the same time: in other words, it is possible and – in terms of a given order – it is 'true' to say, at one and the same moment, that the child who is about to be born and the viable foetus that is about to be aborted are protected by the law that punishes the killing of a man, and that neither one nor the other has a juridical capacity or is – technically speaking – a 'person' as far as the order of the law is concerned. And furthermore, this lack of general capacity or 'personality' does not mean that from other points of view – for example, as far as prenatal therapy is concerned – the foetus should not be considered as a man, and more specifically a child, on which an advanced form of parental right is exercised antithetically and synthetically to the women's right over her own body. And again, this in no way means that everything we are saying here, in the language of the law, when we speak of 'person', refers to that unborn being.

Naturally this perspective may appear totally schizophrenic to a moral philosopher, who – even if he supports the notion of considering the unborn a person – will have to agree on the point that the death of an embryo or of a foetus cannot be treated in all aspects exactly like the death of a man: and from this consideration he may agree on the need to qualify the embryo not in a 'totalitarian' manner, but defining and qualifying each case according to the situation.

(b) Approach based on contexts.
This brings me to the conviction that, in more general terms, jurists can give a significant contribution to the debate in bioethics by suggesting an approach based on contextual reasoning: to configure some sets of prescriptions, of rights and duties, which are suitable for a specific context and are not automatically reproduced in other contexts. Thus, for example, the distinction, in the case of the embryo, between the context of pregnancy and the context of in vitro fertilization will allow us to build up different consensus bases in the two contexts.

(c) Modes and 'weight' of the definition.
The jurist can give a useful contribution when he states his specific requirements in terms of legal definitions.

From the field of bioethics we have frequently received the message that it is inadvisable to define, that today it is necessary to regulate without defining.

And this is the solution that was suggested some time ago for the embryo: it was proposed to consider the embryo merely as a non-thing, something about which we can say what it is not, but not what it is.

The choice of non-definition or of negative definition derives from the difficulty or impossibility of reaching a consensus: we are nowhere near reaching a consensus on a premise of value. To postpone the definition means to avoid the risks we mentioned above, that is of providing definitions that are too 'intensive' and which, alongside the meaning, also proclaim the significance or the value of what is being defined.

In the juridical field we still have the problem of neatly circumscribing the *de facto* premise of the rule or legal conclusion. And, conversely, to qualify juridically does not always imply to establish, for a concept, an intensive meaning. The law often proceeds by more pragmatic 'extensive' definitions, which merely outline the area of reference of a juridical concept.

But not even this type of definition is ethically sterile. It does, however, allow for a less binding stipulation. For example, although it is not yet possible to reach consensus on a definition of the embryo that includes a full ethical qualification, it would be advisable, and is actually probably necessary from a legal point of view, to provide a purely extensive definition which could allow for a cautious approach to issues related to the formation, conservation, utilization, destruction of artificially conceived human embryos.

The stalemate in the ethical debate, in other words, does not necessarily have to have repercussions on the order of juridical language; and the partial stipulation suggested, or imposed, from the legal standpoint can offer a moment of truce in the battle between ethical positions difficult to reconcile.

The awareness of the specific requirements of each field of knowledge, and in particular of the legal field, seems to me an essential element in the bioethical debate from other points of view as well.

Bioethics is currently undergoing a vast process of internationalization, with a number of different factors playing a role. One of these, the most obvious but also perhaps the most powerful, is the circulation of 'materials'.

Circulation often means imitation and propagation. In the field of artificial fertilization and embryo status, for example, anyone wanting to examine the cultural heritage from the Warnock Report onwards could easily draw up a family tree of 'specimens' from document to document.

This is useful, but also dangerous. Hasty imitation, or servile imitation as one usually says when referring to products, means that sometimes we can underestimate the vast diversity of not only the social contexts in which the prescriptions and recommendations are to be applied, but also of the national juridical contexts.

It is obvious, for example, how the 'recommendation' of an Ethics Committee on the advisability of a particular regulation can exert a totally different effect in a written law context as compared to a setting of case law.

But, to give you a less obvious example, a recommended type of behaviour in the field of the neonatal treatment of severe malformations, of damage to respiratory centres, of anencephalic birth, cannot but interact with the way in which birth is defined, traditionally or legislatively, in the juridical environment the physicians work in.

Furthermore, the very juridical and social structure of the health care system means that certain indications made by Ethics Committees cannot simply be transferred from one country to another. For example, it may be that in Holland it is reasonable to ask a person's family doctor or his lawyer about his/her wishes as far as resuscitation are concerned, as is suggested in the document drawn up by the Nijmegen Ethics Committee. But anyone suggesting the same procedure in Italy clearly knows very little about our society and our health care legislation.

On other occasions the process of internationalization puts us in touch with different cultural premises which can immediately influence our juridical sphere.

One of the keys to the internationalization of bioethics is its reference to human rights (cf. 'Human Rights and Bioethics', decision 1993/1991 approved by the U.N. Commission on Human Rights). Human rights culture is certainly neither national nor continental: even in the juridical field it is characterized by a considerable degree of 'planet-wide' (to use a popular term) uniformity. But here, too, we must bear in mind the risk of generalization.

The rights of personality fall within the ambit of human rights, but it is up to the jurist to stress how, for example, the impact that a reference to privacy can have in North American bioethics sources as compared to European ones. And in fact, when building consensus on bioethics issues, it is a different matter to conceive of privacy as the source of all the person's rights, of the very relationship among individuals and between individuals and the State, in other words as the key element in the social compact, as opposed to considering it merely as one of the rights of personality, although a fundamental one.

I mean, there is a spontaneous harmony between the bioethical principles suggested by T. Engelhardt Jr. and the Constitution of Texas, whereas they have much less in common with the Italian Constitution.

And again, a characteristic feature of the elaboration of bioethics, which is reflected in the circulating 'materials', is that it integrates different languages, and especially prescriptive languages. And, similarly, those to whom these documents are addressed are equally varied and variously equipped to understand one or more of the languages used.

The result of this integration, in some documents, is a muddle of languages: the reader – and especially a person who reads the document without having an analytical understanding of the background – may not realize where the boundary lies between rules of professional conduct, jurisprudential and legislative rules, applicable here and now, and the proclamation of ethical evaluations which can be translated into behaviour codes, recommendations, or the proposed application of new deontological or legal regulations.

This impression is even stronger in the 'protocols' of behaviour drawn up by the Ethics Committees of public or private institutions, such as for example the Ethics Committee of a hospital. The intention is to provide a solution to the – often agonizing – dilemmas that the medical profession must face, allowing physicians and nurses to be guided by a series of pre-assessed cases or situations. But often the result is the production of documents in which the ethical perspective is not clearly distinguished from the deontological and the legal one; the solution offered consists of a sort of melting pot of indications on how to behave, a sort of guide '*dans tous azimuts*' which has the tone of a recommendation and the content of a legal case survey: a prescriptive Esperanto which may be valid as a general guideline, but which becomes disastrous when it is necessary to distinguish between the various orders of evaluations.

The person who will ultimately be using the protocol must be capable of separating the different perspectives and – more importantly – of understanding clearly what room for manoeuvre the legal regulation (critically interpreted) leaves to ethical options.

The role of the jurist in drawing up the protocol is difficult, although his contribution is precious. First of all, he must be willing to listen to and appreciate the ethical issues and options on which the Committee agrees, using all his professional expertise to integrate them, if possible, into the interpretation of the law with a sense of juridical realism. He must then accept the responsibility of outlining the limits of lawful behaviour, from the point of view of juridical regulations, but not simply by a pedestrian application of the major laws: he must explore all the possibilities and must foresee and contemplate not only the letter of the law and consolidated solutions, but also consider the evolution of the law, the probable, the possible – albeit very daring – decision of the judge.

Just to give you an example. In such a delicate issue as that of resuscitation, a superficial examination of the law which states that the obligation to provide medical treatment is unconditional (a position that is, generally speaking, also shared by the Nijmegen document) would give the physician or nurse a false notion, creating an excessive and unjustified gap between juridical evaluation and ethical evaluation, and make him think he is committing an act of conscientious objection of great consequence if he chooses to behave differently. A much more careful reading of the law would undoubtedly deprive doctors of some the false certainties they harbour on what is lawful and what is illegal, but would offer a much more articulated legal backing to their ethical options.

Lastly, the most complex question, on which I shall merely make a few considerations: What law for bioethics? What is the relationship between forming consensus on bioethical options and creating a new law, and in particular legislative sources?

It may be useful to recall here that the intention of the law is to 'do things with words'. The rule of law may certainly proclaim a value; but a good juridical system does not proclaim values that it cannot, within reason, also put into practice. And, above all, it does not proclaim values with prescriptions that induce clandestine behaviour, avoidance, *de facto* cancellation of the rule itself.

The possibility of achieving spontaneous application of the law; the possibility of exerting coercion so as to achieve application; the usefulness and compatibility in relation to the system: in other words, the effects of a rule on social conduct and on the overall order of law, these are the concerns of the jurist.

If consensus is the prerequisite for the juridical discipline, then we must also state that consensus can reduce the need for legislative innovation. I am not referring here so much to spontaneous 'virtuous' behaviour, since rules and laws, and especially prohibitions, act at the margins of social behaviour, where they can induce, and if necessary coerce, in order to reduce the number of 'deviations' from the most common ethical options. I am referring rather to the elasticity of the juridical systems, that is to the ability of applied law to adapt to new requirements. Case law and the study of precedents, assisted by doctrine, can perceive the need for a 'new' law and reduce the scope of regulatory void.

Thus, the Italian legal system has given itself a vast range of laws on personality without resorting hardly at all to the legislative source.

Of course, jurisprudence as a source can never be as articulated, as exhaustive, as free of doubt as a legislative intervention. Its role is more to identify guidelines, principles, assessments of what is lawful or illegal in more general terms, rather than to make up for the lack of a detailed discipline: there is no need for special legislation to state a principle of unlawfulness in a surrogation contract, whereas it can come in useful in defining the standards of efficiency of a health service. Conversely, the legislative statement of a principle can be both more difficult and more risky in a situation in evolution, where the jurisprudential 'trend' might perhaps offer a frame of reference capable of following the development of the issues and the changes in commonly held convictions.

And it is bearing these different characteristics in mind that we can establish a first criterion for disciplining legislative intervention in the field of bioethics, that is the criterion which advises us to restrict our innovations to necessary laws: to those rules, that is, which cannot be gleaned by interpretation or by reference to principles and which appear indispensable if we are to prevent irreversible trends in social conduct. In other words, we must discipline in order to guarantee the respect of interests that are at immediate risk, to safeguard principles that cannot defend themselves, and above all not to jeopardize the future.

From this point of view, an involuntarily cautious act has occurred in the 'Italian way' to bioethics as well (no discipline, so as not to legitimize). But it is equally obvious that a criterion of legislative economy and self-limitation can work only if the juridical setting – and especially the judiciary – is willing to identify and follow the majority consensus as it gradually evolves. We cannot follow the principle of necessary law if jurisprudence produces decisions such as the one passed by the Cremona Court, which pronounced a disownment of paternity in the case of a child conceived by a married woman with artificial fertilization, a procedure which had been agreed upon and decided by both husband and wife. Such decisions are in no way unavoidable if jurisprudence learns how to restrict the meaning of rules apparently of a general nature, such as the one that states that 'the mere declaration of the mother does not rule out paternity', thus allowing a married woman to declare the 'natural' origin of her child in order to draw up a birth certificate which does not attribute the paternity of the child to her husband (from the last Cassation, No.11073/92).

Necessary law must also be useful law (that is, effective and not counterproductive) and in this sense it is a possible law: a law which goes beyond a feasibility assessment from the point of view of the practical effectiveness of the rule and its enforcement. A possible juridical rule is one which offers good chances of spontaneous compliance and which can be applied in a compulsory manner in cases of disobedience.

There are many examples of inert, incoercible, useless laws. Rodotà has asked whether rules restricting access to artificial fertilization still make sense now that there is kit for home-fertilization available on the market.

A more complex and open to discussion example, and one which perhaps has a greater effect on the relationship between moral options and juridical regulations, is the case of the Italian law on abortion, which makes it illegal to perform an abortion even during the first 90 days of pregnancy unless there is a serious danger to the mother.

With no practical accessory, such as medical certification, this law has been considered platonic or hypocritical: Italian law is in other words making a pointless proclamation, a legal simulation concealing the substance, i.e. the mother's freedom of choice.

The ethical option that lies behind this law – not so much in the historic intention of the legislator, but rather in its objective motivation – is undoubtedly to prevent the life of the unborn child being sacrificed to values 'subjectively' deemed by the mother as worthy of this sacrifice.

The option has obviously been the object of a wide variety of opinions. As far as I am concerned, I agree on an ethical plane. The gravity of having to choose to abort, its intrinsic component of pain, does not eliminate the fact that there is an ethical problem in the level of importance of the motivations which make a woman choose to abort. As can be seen from the recommendation given to English women several years ago, to consider prenatal surgery as an alternative to abortion in cases of foetuses with hare-lips, small and easily remediable imperfections.

But on a juridical plane, the law requiring that there must be an actual danger for the mother's health runs the risk of becoming (and wanting to be) futile, in other words useless and in the long run counter-productive.

In my opinion, what we need to refer to is the criterion of usefulness of the law. An unenforceable law is not in itself useless, nor is it futile, if it possesses a significant systematic validity. In the case illustrated above, for example, this value would appear to survive. The rule, platonic in the specific context of legitimizing a decision to abort, is not platonic when it is used to establish the value attributed to the life of the foetus by the rule of law for conclusions relating to different matters, unrelated to abortion. It works, in other words, by giving a rank, a position to the 'good', that is, the life of the unborn child, obtained by comparison: this value is inferior only to the health of the mother, and only if the mother herself rates it as such.

And so we come to the third criterion. The 'new' law must be assessed not only from the standpoint of necessity and utility, but also according to the impact it will have on the system. What is needed is a consistent and compatible law.

First of all consistent within itself. Rodotà has stressed many times that if lesbian women are barred access to artificial fertilization, this is not compatible with granting legitimate access to artificial fertilization to single women.

Here, too, I would like to suggest another example, although I realize it is open to question.

Several people are proposing that we break the taboo on the organ market. In fact, though, there is a huge difference between the various positions, reflected also in a different use of language: the distinction between a market of organs – in other words, treating an organ as an available commodity, which can be bought and paid for, according to a fair trade model – and a market for organs, which involves the use of incentives to promote the propensity to allow the harvesting of organs, without direct payment, according to a donation model (Hansmann, Mazzoni).

I should just like to make a comment on the first of these two alternatives, the one that is furthest from the presumable direction the Italian legal system will take.

A new discipline introducing a relative contractual freedom into the domain of organ transplantation between living persons must not be examined exclusively within its specific context, that is as a serious erosion of the principle that physical integrity and health cannot be object of trade. The marketability of organs among living persons could, in my opinion, have a subtle fall-out, but one of fearful importance on the principles governing the physician-patient relationship.

Today the action of physicians is regulated in our law, as in legal systems similar to our own, by the principle of intangibility. Any tampering with physical integrity on the part of the physician is in itself a lesion, which can be justified either by patient consensus or by an actual state of necessity.

Consensus, in turn, is restricted by Art. 5 of the Civil Code, which prohibits one from disposing of one's body beyond the threshold of permanent lesion of physical integrity, except in those cases allowed by the law for transplantation. But beyond the actual law, the form of consensus that justifies the physician's intervention is not an unquestionable and arbitrary will to do of one's body what one wishes, but rather a consensus on an ultimate objective which is therapeutic, i.e. the preservation or the recovery, not just of life, but of physical and psychological well-being. A further issue arises from this, the frequently negative evaluation of consensus given for ultimate goals that are different from these: think of the distinction in cosmetic surgery between operations justified because they improve the patient's self-esteem and others whose purpose is to make the person more successful in the field of entertainment and show business. Here the idea of illegitimate consensus arises, since these are actions that go against commonly accepted mores.

I mention all these cases simply to stress how our legal system is characterized by a high threshold of consensus for tampering with one's own body, as long as the ultimate purpose of these actions is a high-ranking one (our right to good health). It is this high threshold that gives us the key of the relationship between physician and patient, obliging the physician not to attribute to his own assessments and decisions – albeit aiming at the 'objective' good of the patient – the power to justify his actions, since they alone cannot.

I think that, once we have introduced the principle that one's physical integrity can be decided upon, that one can dispose of one's organs for profit – the organ market – the system could then reorganize itself around a lower threshold in which self-determination is respected. There would be a new input – the sale factor – which would lower the intangibility value of the body of a living person: the value which rests on the discretionary assessments of the physician, 'objectively' justified, would rank lower.

One might object that the sale of goods does not diminish, rather it increases the value of ownership. But goods can be expropriated.

The availability of organs for sale – I repeat, among living persons – for purposes of solidarity keeps the consensus level on a high-ranking value; it makes it conceivable to 'expropriate' an organ when the situation is extremely severe, such as the case imagined by Calabresi, of a huge Chernobyl calling for a 'compulsory contribution' of bone marrow from all.

Conversely, a principle of 'expropriation' of organs from cadavers founded on solidarity contrasts with the right to die as one wishes – and the right to dispose of one's own body during the terminal stage of one's life – but it would not lower the threshold of the intangibility value of the body in the ordinary context of the physician-patient relationship right until the moment of death.

This is a risk I can see if we accept the notion of commercialization. And it is an example, open to question, no doubt, of the problem of the impact on the system of a 'law for bioethics'.

This leaves a last comment, almost a moralistic observation: ethics for the jurist and the legislator in bioethics.

The problem of the limitations of the letter of the law, of its ability to adapt or not to ethical prescriptions, is an issue which calls for a very high level of intellectual honesty on the part of the jurist.

A judgment of juridical unfeasibility can make a difficult consensus-reaching process useless; it would be unacceptable for a jurist to pass a similar judgment because he is morally against the idea. Conversely, it would be equally unacceptable for a jurist to suggest that a legal solution is possible because he approves of the moral principle it supports, when he knows that it will most likely be sterile as a law, or even produce contrary behaviour.

It is also to this lack of honesty – or to the confused perception of the limits of the law – that we owe the problem of national juridical disciplines whose main objective is to ignore rather than solve bioethical issues. A sort of 'clean hands' policy which allows some countries to proclaim very strict and severe principles, thus forcing their more liberal neighbours to act as shelters.

3. What Rules for Procreation?

What Rules for Procreation?

Alexander M. Capron*

1. Theoretical Framework

Before addressing the specific issues of procreation,[1] I believe it is worthwhile, in this first session on 'Legal Regulation of Bioethics', to raise several basic issues of framework. First, while *Norma Giuridica* is translated in a way that suggests specific focus on law in the form of statutes or judicial decisions, a more liberal reading would serve to remind us of the role that 'norms' play in society. This broader category of public policy (of which formal laws are only one part) encompasses the system of norms that not only underlie and inform judges' articulation of the common law and interpretation of the constitution but that are also embodied in various types of private ordering which include individual agreements and professional societies' standards of conduct. These additional aspects of public policy are particularly important when analyzing the regulation of procreation in the United States – especially when compared to most of the other topics considered during the workshop, such as patenting biotechnology and organ transplantation – because until recently many aspects of procreation (other than abortion and contraception) have been remarkably free from direct regulation by the State.

The second framing issue emerges from the instructions I received from the workshop's organizers, who were hopeful that across all five sessions we would address: at least two extremely legal aspects of [bioethics] ...

(1) **Property rights logic.** Who owns the body, the living one or the cadaveric body, the human organs, the genetic code, etc.?

* Henry W. Bruce, Professor of Law, University Professor of Law and Medicine, Co-Director, Pacific Center for Health Policy and Ethics, University of Southern California, Los Angeles, USA.

1 Although '*la procreazione*' once connoted coital reproduction, for the purposes of this discussion, I take it to have the broader meaning of begetting offspring through any available means, including assistance from medical professionals and individuals who may provide genetic or gestational aid.

Cosimo Marco Mazzoni (ed.), A Legal Framework for Bioethics, 67-77.
©1998 *Kluwer Law International. Printed in The Netherlands*

(2) **Individual choice or social control.** In each of the topics there exists a problem to locate the subject who has the right to choose. On whom is the duty to choose, to dispose? The individual, the society, the owner of the right?

Again, my concerns over this way of framing the issue may be peculiar to the topic of procreation, although I suspect it is not and that such concerns are equally relevant in considering the other areas of the life sciences addressed at the workshop. My basic concern is that the language of 'property' and 'ownership' is more appropriate as one possible conclusion at the end of an analysis, rather than as the starting framework; likewise the separation of 'choice' among 'the individual, the society, the owner of the right' suggests (perhaps too restrictively) a dichotomy between society (the State) and individuals (as persons or as 'owners of rights'), rather than as an array of relationships with varying authority.

Therefore, I would suggest that prior to looking narrowly at legal regulation, we begin by asking what interests various participants might have in procreation and then examine how law does or should protect or restrict those interests. For example, it may or may not turn out that the interests will be ones that are best expressed through the legal device of 'property', which is a particular way of describing a bundle of rights to possess and transfer something and to exclude others from possessing or enjoying it. Likewise, it may or may not turn out that the primary conflicts in the procreative process involve differing individual choices, rather than a conflict of individual interests with those of the state.

2. Parties, Interests and Public Policy

Following the approach just suggested, I would reformulate the object of our discussion to be concerning (1) which *individuals or other entities* (2) have what *interests* that (3) must be taken into account when *public policy* aims either to (a) *directly regulate* private conduct through statutes or judicial rulings or (b) *accept or facilitate* the arrangements made by private parties and professional societies. For the purposes of this discussion, I will limit myself to activities intended to enhance or enable procreation not those (i.e., contraception or abortion) that would curtail it; although I draw on the law as it has developed in the United States, I make no pretence of encompassing every aspect of positive law nor every jurisdiction in the Nation – instead, I plan to illustrate the process of legal regulation through examples of particular cases and statutes. While most children are born as a result of intercourse within a traditional heterosexual union (and the legal rules developed for this situation underlie all the rest of the discussion), I will focus primarily on the regulation of newer techniques – artificial insemination by donor (AID), *in vitro* fertilization (IVF), and so-called surrogate motherhood.[2] These techniques typically involve procreation without coitus and participants besides a single heterosexual couple (at the very least, one or more medical specialists participate in most instances).

Let us turn, then, to the three elements that seem appropriate in defining legal regulation of bioethics: the individual persons and others (including the collectivity) who are affected by procreative efforts, their interests, and the various ways that public policy can respond to procreative efforts in the light of these interests.

A. INDIVIDUALS AND OTHER ENTITIES

Thanks to medical developments, procreative activities today may implicate a staggering array of persons or entities:

- gamete (ovum or sperm), inside or outside the human body
- fertilized ovum or blastomere (prior to cellular differentiation), inside or outside the human body
- zygote or pre-embryo (prior to implantation), inside or outside the human body
- embryo or foetus incapable of surviving outside uterus (non-viable)
- viable foetus (*in utero*)
- child (after birth)
- female source of gamete (genetic mother or ovum donor)
- spouse of genetic mother/ovum donor
- female in whom the embryo grows and becomes a viable foetus (gestational mother)
- spouse of gestational mother
- female who will raise the child (social or rearing mother)
- spouse of rearing mother
- male source of gamete (genetic father or sperm donor)
- spouse of genetic father/sperm donor
- male who will raise the child
- spouse of rearing father
- owner/operator of sperm bank (i.e., *in vitro* facility, etc.)
- obstetrician or other physician (e.g., endocrinologist, urologist) caring for genetic, gestational or rearing mother or father
- physician (paediatric, neonatal) caring for child after birth
- the facilities at which the medical professionals practise
- professional associations of the medical professionals and facility operators

This list probably does not exhaust all the private parties, to which social entities (municipalities, States, and the Federal Government) must be added; but the list may also

2 In the process, the discussion will also take note of the rules relevant to adoption, which does not involve a new reproductive technique.

be artificially long, in that some participants may fall into several categories (e.g., when a 'spouse of rearing mother' is also a 'genetic father' in a surrogate-mother arrangement).

B. INTERESTS

Procreation is such a basic – and, in evolutionary terms, essential – activity that people's 'interest' in procreating traditionally received less attention than the related duties, from the biblical injunction to 'be fruitful and multiply' to the widely recognized responsibility of parents for their children's welfare. In American jurisprudence, the interests involved began to be addressed in this century as a consequence of the use of techniques for *avoiding* birth through sterilization, contraception and abortion. People's interest in *not* reproducing has led to the recognition of *negative* procreative freedom. Although the exact contours and rationale of legal regulation shift with each new Supreme Court decision on abortion, it now appears that the U. S. Constitution recognizes individuals' freedom of personal choice in matters of marriage and family life as an essential element of the personal liberty guaranteed by the constitution.[3] In *Griswold* v. *Connecticut*, the court held that a statute penalizing the prescription or use of contraceptives violated a married couple's 'right to privacy'[4] (a right not enumerated in the U. S. Constitution but widely regarded as a cornerstone of life in a free society), In its famous 1973 abortion decision, *Roe* v. *Wade*, the court held that this right was 'broad enough to encompass a woman's decision whether or not to terminate her pregnancy'.[5]

The legitimacy of the 'right to privacy' and its precise implications for the state regulation of abortion has been one of the most contentious issues of constitutional jurisprudence – and, more notably, of public debate – in the past two decades.[6] For our purposes, what is important is that in the course of expounding on the right to privacy, the court has repeatedly spoken of the constitutional protection for 'the decision whether or not to beget or bear a child'.

Some scholars (particularly Prof. John Robertson) have argued from this that 'procreative liberty' is a fundamental right protected by the Constitution against state interference except to further compelling a societal interest.[7] Although this conclusion enjoys wide acceptance regarding the core aspects of *negative* liberty that have been the subject of the major constitutional rulings, the court has had less to say about *positive* liberty, which involves not avoidance of reproduction but protection of the

3 *Akron* v. *Akron Center for Reproductive Health*, 462 U.S. 416, 427 (1983).

4 381 U.S. 479 (1965). In *Eisenstadt* v. *Baird*, 405 U.S. 438 (1972), the right to be free of governmental intrusion regarding procreation was recognized for unmarried individuals as well.

5 410 U.S. 113, 153 (1973).

6 *See*, e.g., Ronald Dworkin, *Life's Dominion*, New York, Alfred A. Knopf, 1993.

7 John Robertson, *Children of Choice: Freedom and the New Reproductive Technologies*, Princeton: Princeton University Press, 1994.

choice to reproduce – and perhaps to have medical or other aid in doing so. What, then, are the compelling interests that may be arrayed regarding the positive aspects of procreative rights (and duties)?

(1) The Procreators: On the individual side, the interests of those who wish to reproduce (or to aid others in reproducing, such as through surrogacy) may include: first, an interest in creating a family that includes children whom one will rear; second, an interest in having heirs (to pass on a family name, protect other family interests, etc.); third, an interest in passing on one's genes; fourth, a woman's interest in experiencing pregnancy and childbirth; fifth, a psychological interest in possessing the 'normal' human attribute of fertility which traditionally has meant that an act of sexual intercourse could lead to reproduction); sixth, an interest in being treated with respect and concern during the reproductive process; seventh, an interest in privacy and confidentiality and eighth (and most comprehensively), an interest in being informed decision-makers, possessing access to information about the risks and benefits of various methods as well as to the medical services that will enable them to control their reproduction as they wish. Plainly, not every person at all times in his or her life would embrace all these interests in reproducing – as attested by medical science's vigorous efforts to perfect methods to allow patients to avoid reproduction. Also, individuals' interests in reproducing can be threatened by pathological conditions as well as by restrictions imposed by the State.

(2) The Procreated: On the individual side, the 'objects' of procreation – zygotes, embryos, children and so forth – also have interests: first, an interest in life itself;[8] second, an interest in avoiding harm; third, an interest in maximizing their potential well-being (to which some might add, 'within the constraints of their genetic makeup', although increasingly, that is a moving target); fourth, an interest in being accepted into a family that is capable of nurturing them; fifth, an interest in knowing their familial/genetic heritage; and sixth, a possible interest in having their genetic makeup protected against non-beneficial alteration. Individuals in the 'procreated' category are, of course, unable to articulate their own interests, meaning that these interests will either have to be determined and asserted by someone related to them or through a social mechanism (such as a legal presumption).

8 I believe that most commentators who have considered the matter are more inclined to doubt that ova and sperm have either a (theoretically coherent) 'right' – or even an ' interest ' – in being born, whereas it makes sense to say that after conception when the generic identity is set the embryo or foetus does have an interest in being born (recognizing, however, that one-third to one-half of conceptuses abort naturally, frequently because of genetic or chromosomal conditions that are inconsistent with survival).

(3) The State: What interests does the State have that might shape its interaction with these individual interests? First, the State has an interest in seeing that the welfare of individuals who are unable to protect their own interests (such as children or even potential children) are taken into account; second, the State has an interest in the orderly resolution of disputes among individuals with conflicting interests, in a fashion that is consistent internally and with the way that like interests are resolved; and fourth, the State has in interest that individuals are seeking to promote their own interests do not harm or wrong parties outside their immediate transactions and do not undermine important societal values. For example, if Mr. and Mrs. Famille enter into a surrogate mother arrangement with Ms. Fertile in order to further their interests in having a child to raise, in having an heir, and in passing on Mr. Famille's genes, the State will need a means not only to weigh these interests against the interests of Ms. Fertile (should she wish to retain custody of the child) but also to bring into the balance the welfare of any child created through this arrangement and the possible social interest in avoiding commercialization of the parent-child relationship.

C. THE SALIENCE OF INTENTION AND RELATIONSHIP

As may already be apparent in considering the list of participants and their interests, the very contours of those interests and the rights that may flow from them may be shaped by the intention of the parties and their relationship to one another. The importance of intention can be seen in the varying roles that genetic parents may play depending upon their expectations regarding a prospective child. For instance, the woman from whom an egg is removed for IVF might be the 'ovum donor' if she did not intend to bear or rear the child, but the 'genetic mother' if she did intend to rear the child even though another woman gestated it. The few American jurisdictions that have adopted statutes to facilitate a non-commercial surrogate motherhood have captured the importance of intent by stating that the 'intended parents' (who may have no biological relationship to a child) will be treated as the child's natural parents if certain procedures have been followed confirming the parties' intentions.[9] Plainly, such a system is not without its problems, especially if State involvement in confirming the intention of the parties comes only after the birth of a child about whose custody a dispute has arisen.

Similarly, the relationship of the interest-holders may modify their interests and resulting rights. For example, a foetus's interest in life may be sufficient to engender a right of protection from harm issuing from certain parties (i.e., strangers) but not from others with an intimate relationship to the foetus (i.e., the expectant mother) who may

9 *See*, e.g., Nev. Rev. Stat. Ann. 126.045 (2)(1993); N.H. Rev. Stat. Ann. 168B:1-168B:9 (1993); Va. Code Ann. 20-158 (1993).

cause harm as a result of certain choices she makes in her own life (what she eats or drinks, where she works), even to the point of having an abortion.[10]

D. PUBLIC POLICY

In the United States, Despite the flood of legislation (and resulting litigation) on the aspects of *preventing* reproduction, the law has been slow in responding to the new procreative technologies that aim to overcome infertility. Direct controls have been aimed at (1) identifying at least one father and one mother with responsibility for each child and promoting regularity in record keeping about such relationships (by providing certain legal benefits – including protection of privacy – to individuals who use professional services, and then insulating from certain types of liability physicians and other participants in non-coital reproduction); (2) establishing quality-control standards for professionals and institutions involved in procreation (such as licensing laws for physicians, inspection methods for laboratories, etc.); and (3) limiting or prohibiting payment to a parent in exchange for transfer of custody of a child. More extensive standards have been established by various voluntary professional bodies (such as the American Fertility Society), which the State either allows to fill the field or which enjoy indirect validation through reliance on professional norms in resolving disputes in court.

3. Specific Instances of Legal Regulation

In the light of this theoretical framework – the participants, the interests and the forms of public policy – we turn now to specific examples of legal regulation in the United States. Although this is more of a sampling than an exhaustive review, it supports two conclusions that I believe would be reinforced by a more comprehensive survey: first, that no single calculus can be applied to the interests involved across the full range of situations (which is to say that the law has inconsistencies), and second, that in many (perhaps most) U.S. jurisdictions, public policy on most of the new procreative technologies has not taken the form of positive law but has instead been left to private ordering, often in the shadow of professional norms and explicit standards.

10 *See*, e.g., Cal. Penal Code Sec. 197, which includes within the definition of murder any act 'solicited, aided, abetted, or consented to by the mother of the foetus'. In a May 1994 decision, *People* v. *Davis*, the State appellate court held that the State's interest in protecting foetal life (as well as a pregnant woman's interest in her own health and that of her foetus) meant that a party other that the pregnant woman could be charged with murder for killing a foetus that had not reached viability. The Minnesota Supreme Court reached the same conclusion regarding its statute on 'murder of an unborn child', M.S.A. 609.2661, in *State* v. *Merrill*, 450 N.W.2d 318 (1990).

A. INVOLUNTARY STERILIZATION

Involuntary sterilization provides a logical starting point, even though it is not a novel technology; natural fertility is not only one of the basic interests identified above but steps taken to remove fertility provided an early opportunity for the courts in the United States to consider what limits, if any, our constitution places on state action regarding procreation. Early in this century, many States adopted so-called eugenic sterilization statutes, which were applied primarily to persons institutionalized as mentally disabled. Involuntary sterilization of a patient in a state institution was upheld in *Buck* v. *Bell*, in which Justice Holmes uttered his famous dictum, 'Three generations of imbeciles are enough.'[11] The decision is still cited by the Supreme Court even though many commentators doubt that the state interests on which the Court relied (centrally, the avoidance of the burden of caring for abnormal individuals) would be regarded as sufficient today in the light of *Skinner* v. *Oklahoma*. In that case, the court found procreation to be 'one of the basic civil rights of man' and struck down a statute that, in mandating sterilization of only certain criminals, denied the petitioner equal protection of his right to procreate.[12]

B. RESTRICTING IVF AND AID BASED ON THE STATUS OF THE PROCREATOR

Should the status of the person using AID or IVF affect whether the State encourages, permits or restricts use of the technology? This question has received different answers in different contexts, as can be seen by comparing the initial legislative responses to a recent development in IVF with embryo transfer[13] with the laws governing paternity for children following AID.

Over the past four years, several physicians in the U. S. and Europe have been able to assist 50 to 75 post-menopausal women to become pregnant, the oldest being a 62-year-old Italian who became pregnant using donated eggs, fertilized *in vitro* before transplantation. While the first results were reported several years ago, the subject only received widespread attention in December 1993 when a 59-year-old British woman announced that she had given birth to twins with the help of Dr. Severino Antinori's fertility clinic in Italy. As with many biomedical developments, the first reaction (after amazement that anyone that age would want a newborn, much less two) was shock at the unnaturalness of the procedure. Defenders responded that medicine is centrally concerned with altering the natural course of events, from preventing infections to

11 274 U.S. 200 (1927). It was later found that neither the patient in question, Carrie Buck, nor the daughter she bore prior to being sterilized was actually retarded.

12 316 U.S. 535, 541 (1942).

13 A pre-embryo created from an ovum obtained from one woman is placed into the uterus of another woman who intends to carry it to term and raise the resulting child.

replacing failed organs. Moreover, while menopause at 40 made sense biologically when the average life-span was hardly more than that, it makes less sense today when most women can expect to live roughly twice that long.

Some people were offended at the idea that once again women were going to have more choices about becoming mothers, timing the decision to their own convenience, undeterred by the ticking of their ' biological clocks'.[14] The physicians involved reported, however, that most of their patients had tried to become pregnant using other methods for many years. Other critics argued that it was cruel for children to have parents who will have difficulties dealing with rigours of midnight feeding and the other ordeals of having young children – or worse, that they might not live to see the children through their teenage years or college graduation. The fact that this risk already exists regarding men – whose natural capacity to become fathers is typically present, if not undiminished throughout life – came under the heading 'two wrongs don't make a right'.

All of these concerns – from maternal and paternal(health and longevity to the further commodification of children (order what you want, when you want it) – have some force. Indeed, they are among the factors that one would hope would go into the decision of any person – be they prospective mother or father or physician – contemplating reproduction late in life. But should these concerns remain matters of individual conscience, to be weighed according to the particular circumstances of each case, or do they justify limitations on IVF based on the age or other factors, and if so, should regulating be left to medical professionals or undertaken by the State?

Several European countries have responded with proposals or legislation to allow use of 'assisted procreation' (IVF and AID) only by women of 'procreating age' (which appears to beg the issue as medical science in effect extends the age at which women can become mothers). I do not believe that any U.S. State has attempted to limit IVF in this fashion. The present lack of legislation may reflect that public policy now relies on self-regulation by the professionals involved. Physicians offering this technology apparently worry about the genie they have let out of the bottle, because they know they will be faced with requests that they are now able to grant but do not want to. For example, Dr. Mark V. Sauer, Professor of Obstetrics and Gynaecology at the University of Southern California who has pioneered the use of egg-donation for pregnancies after menopause, has set a 55-year cut-off age for patients. 'It's simply that my comfort level

14 Perhaps the most far-sighted criticism was that, like any new technique, this one might become less of an option and more of an expectation. Some people attempt to overcome infertility for years, at great financial and emotional expense. The hope offered by each new method may simply extend their agony and interfere with their concluding 'Enough is enough, already!' In this view, a restriction on the use of a technology could be understood as enhancing people's interest in being informed decision-makers, with a real possibility of exercising choice.

gets stretched beyond that.'[15] However, the American College of Obstetricians and Gynecologists and the American Fertility Society have not yet issued formal guidelines placing an age limit on the use of IVF or embryo transfer.

The standard law on AID in the United States does directly and indirectly regulate access to this procedure. As in most of the world, AID relies upon anonymous 'sperm donors' (the standard term even they are really vendors, paid a small amount for each 'deposit' at the 'sperm bank'). Further, even if the donor becomes known to the parents raising a child conceived through AID or to the child him or herself, the law in most states (based upon the Uniform Parentage Act or like model statute) treats the husband of the woman who bore the child as its 'natural' (and hence legal) father provided the husband consented to the AID (usually in writing).

This leaves open two issues of 'status'. First, what happens when the woman has no husband? Some of the statutes explicitly provide that whenever AID is carried out by a licensed physician, the sperm donor is treated in law as not being the natural father – and hence free of any rights or obligations regarding the child, but in other statutes the exemption of the sperm donor seems to be linked with the existence of a consenting husband to whom the role of natural father can be assigned. On the one hand, it appears that it is in the child's interest to have someone in that role; on the other hand, removing the protection of sperm donors from the role of natural father is likely to reduce the number of men willing to be sperm donors.

The state's interest in promoting safety and in maintaining adequate records of birth and of biological relationships is probably served by encouraging prospective parents to use medical professionals for AID. Yet the procedure is a simple one, and some women prefer to undertake it without medical supervision. Some state statutes do not provide the same protection for such self-administered AID. This is particularly relevant to women who are unmarried or older or who are lesbians since they may have difficulty finding a physician willing to perform AID for them. Thus, the combination of statute and professional practice may place limits upon the use of AID based upon certain characteristics or status of the prospective parents.

C. THE STATUS OF EMBRYOS AND SIMILAR ENTITIES

This issue has mostly been developed in the context of an embryo or foetus *in utero*, focussed on the state's authority to protect an unborn entity from injury by pregnant women and others. The existence of sperm banks and of facilities for freezing embryos gives rise to new problems, as does research on foetuses after abortion. (The latter is covered by federal regulations and by laws in 25 states, half of which apply to foetal remains only after induced abortions; dead foetuses or foetal material is encompassed

15 Elizabeth Mehren, 'Testing the Limits', *L.A. Times*, 6 Feb 1994, p. E-1, col. 2.

within Uniform Anatomical Gift Act.) In *Davis* v. *Davis*, the Supreme Court of Tennessee held that frozen pre-embryos were neither persons nor property but occupy a special category that entitles them to 'respect' because of their potential for human life.[16] In that case, the court concluded that although there was no property in either party (a husband and a wife going through a divorce, who had stored the embryos as part of their participation in a failed attempt to become parents using IVF), both had a right to decide about any disposition of the embryos. (The wife had originally petitioned for them in order to try to achieve pregnancy; by the time of the High Court decision, she was proposing to give the embryos to other infertile couples, to allow them to use the embryos to reproduce.) The right to decide was based on the two-sided right to procreate and to avoid procreation.

16 842 S.W.2d 588 (Tenn. 1992).

What Rules for Procreation?

Christian Byk*

As far as we consider procreation as the process by which a man and a woman generate offspring, we have seriously to wonder 'What kind of rules should such a process obey?'.

The fact that this process has constantly been repeated since the human species appeared on earth does not mean, of course, that procreation – which is therefore viewed as 'a natural process' by some – does not follow some rules. Although our scientific knowledge of human procreation is quite new,[1] in particular regarding genetic issues,[2] we know that procreation is governed by physical rules as well as by the laws of genetics.

Anthropology has also made us aware of the existence of the role played by customs and symbols in human societies. Procreation is therefore a cultural phenomenon which has its own social rules.[3]

But what of legal rules? Does procreation need to be considered in law? If so, to what extent?[4]

* Professor of Law, University of Poitiers, France and Secretary-General of the International Association of Law, Ethics and Science. The International Association of Law, Ethics and Science is an international multidisciplinary network which aims at developing exchange of information and experiences in the field of ethics of sciences. It publishes a quarterly review, *The International Journal of Bioethics* (Ed. A. Lacassagne-Eska, 162 Avenue A. Lacassagne, 69003, Lyon, France).

1 S. Laurent, *Naître au Moyen-Age*, Le Léopard d'Or, Paris, 1989.
2 J.L. Serre, J. Feingold, *Génétique humaine*, Inserm, Nathan, Paris, 1993.
3 D. De Coppet, 'Parenté (Systèmes de)' in *Encyclopaedia Universalis*; F. Zonabend, 'De la famille, regard ethnologique sur la parenté et le mariage' in A. Burguière et Coll. *Histoire de la famille*, Ed. A. Colin, Paris, 1986, I I. p. 15.
4 For a diversified answer to this question: R. Ganghofer (Ed.), *Le droit de la famille en Europe (son évolution de l'antiquité à nos jours)*, Presses Universitaires de Strasbourg, 1992.

Cosimo Marco Mazzoni (ed.), A Legal Framework for Bioethics, 79-87.
©1998 *Kluwer Law International. Printed in The Netherlands.*

In fact, the answer to this question largely relies on the ambiguous nature of procreation, as it is both a private and a social act.[5] Historically, the legal approach to procreation largely took into account this aspect in establishing the fundamental principles of family law and lawyers have always been conscious of the importance of biology, sociology and symbolism in elaborating laws in this field.

Can the emergence of reproductive technologies, which suppose the involvement of physicians and biologists in the intracorporeal process of procreation therefore be viewed as something essentially 'artificial' as opposed to something which should be regarded as mostly 'natural'? Certainly not. It does not mean, however, that the use of these technologies could not affect our representation of procreation. Consequently the law should ensure that what new technologies make possible will not cause fundamental damage to a balanced respect for biology, sociology and symbolism as applied to the image of an evolving family.

Procreation, Law and Fundamental Values

In Western culture – and I chose this example on purpose not by reason of its simplicity, but because it emphasizes the emergence of the conflict between the interests of the individual and those of the community – the fundamental values of law, particular in the family area, have largely been inherited from Greek philosophy, the Roman legal tradition and Judeo-Christian beliefs.[6]

The concept of filiation and the status of the human body largely reflect this influence, although it is apparent that social changes which have recently occurred affect this permanent relationship between fundamental values and their legal expression.[7]

A. THE CONCEPT OF FILIATION

Although universal, because the concept of filiation is drawn from biological, social and subjective grounds, it is deeply rooted in cultural heritage. Therefore it is particu-

5 'Dans les sociétés traditionelles, l'échange matrimoniale institue et structure le social. Il y va d'une question de survie collective'. H. Levy Buchl, 'L'éthologie juridique', in *Ethnologie générale*, Ed. La Pléïade, Paris, 1968, p. 1134.

6 'L'invention de l'homme comme sujet doué d'une personnalité et d'un destin propre auquel il appartient de collaborer en même temps qu'à la maîtrise de l'univers est une création de l'Occident, fruit imprévisible de la rencontre de la philosophie grecque, du juridisme latin et de la foi chrétienne, elle-même enracinée dans la tradition judaïque', M. Th. Meulders Klein, 'La production des normes en matière de bioéthique', in CL. L. Neirinck (dir) *De la bioéthique au biodroit* LGDJ, Paris.

7 'Les quatres logiques du changement', in M. Th. Meulders Klein, *op. cit.*, p. 30; *see also* G. Delaisi de Parseral, *La part du père,* Seuil, Paris, 1981.

larly relevant for us to remember the influence of Greek mythology.[8] It seems that man organized his social life, and the legal rules implied by it, so as to escape the licentious way the gods led their own lives. The central role of the father and the prohibition of incest which govern society are directly derived from the violence of the gods.

1. The Influence of Mythology

Let me remind you how the gods behaved in 'private family life'. Uranus, the original god was dethroned by his son, Chronos, who ate his own children to protect himself from such a rebellion. However, Zeus was able to escape and once he became an adult he fought his father and took over the Universe.

Although Chronos and Zeus disputed the position and authority of their respective fathers, Zeus succeeded in being considered the supreme god, almighty, just and good. He is the father of the living and the dead; holding complete sway over life and death. Consequently, his regulative function is at the origin of the emergence of law in the family as well as in society.

The fact, then, that this law, which appeared during ancient times, largely reflects the mythic role of the father should come as no surprise.

At that time, being a father was already much more a social and legal reality than a biological one and fatherhood was largely a matter of willingness.

The role of the father, however, was even more significant because the father was his family's representative; the legitimate proxy between the family and the authorities: the family and the gods.[9] He spoke for his family but he also spoke to his family on behalf of the gods and the authorities. Thus the 'pater' and the law became confused.

The emergence of the prohibition of incest followed an identical process. Firstly, considering the gods once again, we remember that Zeus married his sister, Hera, but the main story regarding this important issue is, of course, the myth of Oedipus. Laoïs, his father, was warned by an oracle that, if he had a son, that son would kill him: so when his wife, Jocasta, gave birth to a son, Laoïs asked a servant to let his son die. Being full of mercy for the baby, the servant disobeyed. Oedipus grew to adulthood and on his way to Delphi, he killed Laoïs because neither of them would give way on the road to the other.

Following the way to Thebes, Oedipus met the Sphinx, solved the riddle and killed her. He was, therefore, proclaimed king by the Thebans and married Jocasta. When he heard that he had killed his father and married his mother, however, he blinded himself.[10]

8 L. Depret, 'Une origine du droit de la famille en Europe, la mythologie grecque', in R. Ganghofer, *op. cit.*, p. 55.

9 B. This, *Le père: acte de naissance*, Ed. du Seuil, Paris, 1980.

10 J.P. Vernant, *Oedipe et ses mythes*, Ed. Complexe, Bruxelles, 1988.

Secondly, we turn our attention to humans. With very limited exception – the pharaohs, for example – incest was prohibited in ancient times and was penalized. To prevent it, the civil legislations of ancient Greece and Rome determined the degree of consanguinity prohibiting marriage. This prohibition became a recurrent trend in family law throughout history. It can be found in canon law as well as in civil codes and modern family law.

The central role of the father in the social organization of the family and the prohibition of incest have long been expressed in the roots of family law. Could the social transformation of family, which can be observed in family law regulations[11] be interpreted as a renunciation of these fundamental values?

2. The Decline of the Father's Authority in Modern Family Law

It is obvious that the role of the father as the central authority in the family has largely been challenged in Western societies. Parental responsibilities – and I deliberately use the term 'responsibility' instead of 'authority' which is used in the French Civil Code – are nowadays shared equally between both parents. French Civil Code, for example, has posed[12] as a matter of principle, the equal responsibility of the father and the mother in married and unmarried couples and also whether the families are united or separated. Regarding children also, parental authority does not mean any more that this authority is absolute and cannot be challenged.

The State, on behalf of society, is there to ensure that parental responsibilities are used to satisfy legitimate objectives, among which the welfare and best interests of the child are viewed as pre-eminent.[13] It is the result of several phenomena. The first is political and concerns the proclamation, mainly dating from the 18th century, that all men ('men' here means men and women) are born equal. The second is economical and cultural: women during that century had won access to education and the labour market.

A third aspect is probably anthropological: the family within its traditional framework – by framework, I mean marriage – lost its attraction as a model while children have concentrated the interests of society and this has permitted the interference of society with family privacy.[14]

Can these social changes be interpreted as negation of the concept of filiation? And what role are the new reproductive technologies supposed to play in this process?

11 F. G. Dreyfus, 'La Vème République et la famille', in R. Ganghofer, *op. cit.*, p. 203.

12 D. Huet-Weiller, 'De la puissance paternelle à la responsabilité parentale', in R. Ganghofer, *op. cit.* p. 405.

13 As mentioned in the International Covenant on the Rights of Children 1989.

14 M. Th. Meulders-Klein, 'L'évolution du mariage at le sens de l'histoire', in R. Ganghofer, *op. cit.*, p. 215.

Some authors do not hesitate to derive from the fact that the father lost his political status, that the concept of filiation has been superseded. There is no longer a son because there is no longer a father and *vice versa* [...] 'Instead of a structured family there is a kind of mono-generation which includes what we formerly called father, mother, son and daughter and in which all functions can permute.'[15]

Reference to family models is therefore largely substituted by worship of television idols [...] Personality is influenced by the experience acquired within a group of peers and consequently is weak and could be deeply affected emotionally as drug addiction and violence prove.[16] According to this approach, reproductive technologies are just a further step in a process which crosses generations. Firstly, they remove the distinction between sexuality and procreation. Secondly, they make the child no more than an object of the adult's wants. Thirdly, they offer the means of transgressing natural models; giving access to procreation to widows, single people, homosexual couples and menopausal women: allowing surrogacy which includes a grandmother bearing a child for her daughter, or the transfer of an embryo from a white couple into the uterus of a woman of colour.

Faced with such a risk and with the emergence of a 'Brave New World' we can easily understand why those authors would like so much to ban the use of such technologies[17] for the benefit of society and individuals.

We believe, however, that this view is too pessimistic. Although we agree that family values have been affected and even challenged, we do not believe that the family as a structure can be questioned.

We also think that we are in a transitional period which can be characterized by more autonomy of the individuals in the family and an open concept of family.[18]

However, this concept which includes filiation, still serves as a reference when establishing the rules governing 'extra-natural' families.[19]

In adoption as well with children born through gamete donation, the law has created a legal fraction which considers as legal parents the adopting parents or the parent who is not biologically related to the child but who gave consent to the artificial procreation.

15 L. Depret, *op. cit.*, p. 60.

16 T. Anatrella, 'Interminables adolescences: 12-30 ans', *Ethique et société*, Cerf/Cujas, Paris, 4ème éd., 1980.

17 J. Tesart (Ed.), *Le Magasin des Enfants*, F. Bourin, Paris, 1990.

18 This evolution can be observed particularly through the role played by the concept of public policy (ordre public) in French international private law as applied to family matters: *see* D. Alexandre, 'L'intervention de l'ordre public dans le droit de la famille et le droit international privé français' in R. Ganghofer, *op. cit.* p. 105.

19 M. Th. Meulders-Klein, 'Mariage et concubinage ou les sens et contresens de l'histoire' in J. Rubellin-Devichi (Ed.), *Les concubinages dans le monde*, Ed. CNRS, Lyon, 1991, p. 259.

The general trends resulting from legislations passed in this area just confirm that new reproductive technologies are respecting this legal framework.[20] They are only accessible to heterosexual couples, whether married or not – but children out of wedlock have been recognized as having the same status as legitimate children.[21] The couple should be infertile, or, in some legislations, it should carry or risk transmitting to the offspring an incurable disease. Although very few legislations would have defined what is infertility, medical ethics would, in general, regard non-accidental menopausal women as not covered by this indication.[22]

Surrogacy is also prohibited and *post mortem* insemination is rarely admitted[23] as is posthumous marriage.

The major breach to the 'natural family' model would be that in some countries single women could have access to reproductive technologies.[24] But many families are nowadays lone parent families and adoption is permitted to single persons in different legislations.[25]

However, I can hear the vigorous protestations of some of my colleagues at the university. The prevailing role of the concept of filiation that has just been described is nothing other than superficial appearance. The reality is different. Bioethics legislations, although asserting the pre-eminence of legal principles, have in general authorized so largely the exceptions that new laws are but a façade which hides a total abdication of the fundamental values which are supposed to be protected.[26]

The way the so-called 'status of the human body' is defined by those legislations is a good example of the perverted role played by the law when faced with reproductive technologies issues.

B THE 'STATUS OF THE HUMAN BODY'

I often feel, as do my colleagues, surprised and even irritated when I read many papers explaining how new the concept of autonomy is.[27] We could even be troubled when

20 C. Byk, 'Les enfants de la procréation et le droit; disparités nationales et harmonisation européenne', colloque 'L'Europe et les enfants de la procréatique', Bruxelles 30 juin-1er juillet 1994.

21 A. Tisserand, 'De l'apparition aux dernières séquelles du statut d'infériorité de l'enfant illégitime', in R. Ganghofer, *op. cit.* p. 105.

22 *See* the proceedings of the FIGO conference on Ethical aspects of human reproduction, UNESCO, Paris, 6-8 July 1994.

23 Commission de réforme du droit du Canada, la procréation médicalement assistée, document du travail N$65, groupe de communication du Canada, Ottawa, 1992, pp.190 and 197.

24 Atr. 6-1 of the Spanish Act of 22 Nov. 1988.

25 For example, Article 343-1 of the French Civil Code states that 'The adoption of a child can be requested by any person who is older than 30 years'.

26 G. Mémeteau: 'Il faut, dit on, des lois pour permettre l'action sans "risque médico-légal" et non pour créer le droit' in 'A l'abordage I (de l'article 16-3 du Code Civil)' Les Petits Affiches (1994).

27 G. Hottois, *La paradigme bioéthique*, de Boeck, Bruxelles, 1990, p. 190.

hearing Members of Parliament considering that we face new problems for which there are no legal answers.[28]

Lawyers of common or Continental law know, however, that the respect of human integrity, which is encapsulated in all human rights declarations since the 18th century, has served medical law as a basis to declare that without the free, informed consent of the person it is impossible to heal the body.[29]

Consequently, it is obvious that physicians who practised reproductive technologies should ask the consent of the recipient woman as well as the donors of gametes involved. The interest of specific regulations in the field of reproductive technologies, including the respect of autonomy, is obviously elsewhere. From the scientific viewpoint, it is a way of clarifying questions of liability. By incorporating into the regulations aspects regarding the medical practice, the legislator acknowledges that, when respecting these conditions reproductive technologies cannot constitute illegal procedures.[30]

From the individual point of view, those regulations could also be interpreted as a step towards the recognition of advocated new rights: the right to get a child in any circumstances; the right to get a healthy child.

The risk also exists in the present debate on 'should we legislate and how far is it necessary to legislate' that law would become the hostage of members of the medical profession and activists of individual 'rights'.

The development of the concept of privacy in the United States is an example of the exacerbation of individual rights which could conflict with each other with no firm limitations to control them.[31]

In this perspective, the right to autonomy certainly implies the right to dispose freely of one's own body to the point that surrogacy was sometimes considered as legal[32] and facilitating a market for babies was viewed as a normal counterpart of autonomy.[33]

28 'Ce texte (de loi sur la bioéthique) comble les lacunes de notre léglislation dues aux progrès de la science ...' M. Méhaignerie, proceedings of the Senate No. 66, 20 Jan. 1994, p. 92.

29 M. Sommerville, 'Le consentement à l'acte medical', document de travail, commission de réforme du droit du Canada, Ottawa, 1980 and G. Memeteau, *op. cit.*, who reminds us that French (Tribunal correctionnel de Lyon 15 déc. 1859 DP 1859, 3,88) and Belgian (Tribunal civil de Liège, 27 nov. 1989, DP 1891, 2, 281) case law have preceded the decision of U. S. courts (*Schloendorff* v. *Society of New York Hospitals* dates back 'only' to 1914).

30 A good example of the objective of 'bioethical legislations' is given by the French 1988 Act on Biomedical Research on Human Beings. This Act aimed to give, under specific conditions, legal status to experimental procedures with no therapeutic benefit for the person concerned and which were previously regarded as offences.

31 R. Dworkin, *Life's Dominion*, New York, Alfred A. Knopf, 1993; J. Robertson, *Children of choice: Freedom and the new reproductive technologies*, Princeton University Press, Princeton, 1994.

32 New. Rev. Stat. Ann 126 045 (2) 1993; NH Rev. Stat. Ann 168B:1-168B:9 (1993); V2 Code Ann 20-158 (1993)

33 E. G. John Rogertson, *op. cit.* For similar opinion in the field of organ transplants, read R. Hansmann, 'The Economics and Ethics of Markets for Humans Organs', *Journal of Health Policy Politics and Law* 57/85 (1989).

But if this risk exists, its occurrence is not a fatality. Between total prohibition and total permissivity it is possible to set up limits which clearly refer to standing legal principles such as the principle '*res extra commercium*' of the human body. It means that, as far or the human person is living, no distinction could be established between the person an their body. The human body is the human person and obeys to the legal status which protects the human person.

The rule of autonomy is of course one of the most important rules applied to the human person but this rule is not absolute and has its own limits.[34] The explanation for such limits lies in the fact that an absolute right of autonomy could question the legal status of the person. For example, it is the reason why it would be impossible for someone to accept being a slave.

The human person is also entitled to found a family and it is therefore impossible for her to give up parental responsibilities prior to the birth of a child.[35]

These remarks concern the necessity of limits but, on the other side, the reference to common principles and values does not suppose that such principles could not evolve.

Should, for example, gametes donations be still regarded as illegal because third parties interferences in the procreation of an embryo would be a consented and updated form of adultery?[36] Or should we accept as an exceptional procedure – reproductive technologies count for 0.3 per cent of all births – that some people could dispose of significant elements of their body for infertile couples?[37] This is already the case with blood, organs and tissues. The difference with gametes donation is that reproductive technologies are perceived as a way to satisfy with individual desire – those of the commissioning parents but also the desire of celebrity of some physicians – more than to accomplish a medical treatment.

But then, what should we think about the surgeon who amputated an arm with no thought of a prosthesis?

Reproduction is a human function which contributes to the vital integrity of the human being and infertility issues shall be medically considered, including using reproductive technologies in an appropriate and reasonable manner.

Having argued against the pessimistic view of some lawyers, I would like to conclude with a quotation of a philosopher.

34 M. Th. Meulders-Klein, 'Le droit de disposer de soi-même, Entendue et limites en droit comparé', in *Licéité en droit positif et références légales aux valeurs*, Bruxelles, Bruylant, p. 215, X. Dijon, *Le sujet de droit en son corps, Une mise à l'épreuve du droit subjectif*, Bruxelles, Larcier, 1982.

35 In the matter of Baby M, Supreme Court of New Jersey, Feb 3. 1988, A2d 1988 WL 6251 NJ.

36 In 1948, a report to the Archbishop of Canterbury suggested that artificial insemination should become a criminal offence. In 1960, the Feversham Commission appointed by the British Government still condemned AID.

37 As the Warnock report suggested in 1984.

> In the discussion around medical ethics prevails a kind of terror which seizes anyone as it was a fatality that the present use of reproductive technologies should lead to the worst things. And the question to know if a potential use of such technologies to enhance human liberty is not sufficiently considered.[38]

I hope we have now opened the way to such a consideration.

38 Entretien D. Lecourt – RP Driot, *Le Monde*, 1er juin 1993.

What Rules Should Govern Artificial Insemination?

Francesco D. Busnelli*

1. It is Time for Rules on Artificial Insemination: Juridical Rules

We are now at the end of the era when the reluctance shown by legislators to regulate this area of human activity was considered 'cautious wisdom'.

This is the first feeling I am seized by when, invited to open the discussion on the reports that we have jut listened to, I cannot fail to note how dismally 'far' Italy is not only from the European context, as presented by Christian Byk in his report, but also from the North-American experience, on which Alexander M. Capron's paper was based: an unruly Italy (in the sense of being without rules) where the sole beacon to help make one's way is a 'Ministerial Circular', the so-called Degan Circular, which allows a worrying (or stimulating, according to others) gap between public centres, which follow the principle of carrying out only homologous fertilization, and private centres, which follow the opposite principle, without any limitation whatever and without any sort of control; an Italy which has hence become a land where unbecoming records are set.

Alexander Capron mentioned the commotion and sensation caused by the fifty nine year-old English lady who gave birth to twins in Dr. Severino Antinori's Clinic: a sensation which, it is worth adding, prompted the Ministers for Health of the two countries involved to strongly react. Out of sheer coincidence they were both women Ministers. Virginia Bottomley, United Kingdom Health Secretary, vibrantly disapproved of these abnormal forms of 'procreational tourism' and expressed the wish for the European countries to make a joint effort in establishing 'ethical controls' on some 'dramatic achievements in modern medicine'. Maria Pia Garavaglia, Italian Minister for Health, bitterly commented that 'wishes are not rights, and children are not consumer products', and she set up a Committee (of which I had the honour of being a Member) to examine 'the present situation following the use of the PMA methods, also at European level'.

But even more shocking and humiliating is to notice that the sole Italian scholar mentioned by Willy Rothley in his comprehensive and documented Report to the

* Professor of Law, Scuola Superiore S. Anna, Pisa, Italy.

Cosimo Marco Mazzoni (ed.), A Legal Framework for Bioethics, 89-106.
©1998 Kluwer Law International. Printed in The Netherlands.

European Parliament is the Florentine anthropologist Brunetto Chiarelli who had raised quite a stir when he suggested that 'sub-human beings could be produced to be used for repetitive and unpleasant work'.

2. The Report by Alexander M. Capron

The issue being discussed therefore is the problem of choosing between rules, or rather between systems of rules. And in this respect the two speakers had a rather different approach.

The approach adopted by the North-American speaker is what we could call an 'inter-individual' approach, aimed, that is, at listing the individuals involved in reproductive procedures and at comparing their subjective rights: extolling the right to privacy, a real 'cornerstone of life in a free society'; the 'realism' of the solutions proposed; the tendency of the State being 'neutral'; these are the criteria adopted for an inter-individual comparison of rights, in line with the most established trends across the ocean.

The reservations that the European listener has in reaction to such criteria are both of an 'external' and 'internal' order with respect to the rationale of the pattern of interests being conclusively advocated.

An 'external' type of criticism, already raised by Christian Byk, is one that poses the unquestionability of a 'positive procreative liberty', taken as a fundamental right of the individual against any interference by the State and addressed to a new category, 'Children of Choice' according to the significant indication anticipated in the title of a book by John Robertson;[1] and the ensuing alarming statement according to which the interest of the unborn could never justify protective limitations to be imposed on the expectant mother who 'could damage the fetus in making choices she is free to make in her own life (what to eat or drink, where to work), to the point of abortion'.

Of an 'internal' nature is the criticism of inconsistency that within the framework of a view that attributes priority to a rigorous inter-individual comparison of the subjective rights of the individuals involved in the case, and in opposition to the principle of the family as viewed by the Community, can be made against the conspicuous disparity of treatment between 'procreators', whose freedom is over protected and the 'procreated' whose rights instead are under-protected; in the assumption being made here the latter are arbitrarily deprived of the fundamental right of knowing their genetic origin.

Nor are the justifications offered convincing. First of all it is not true that the principle of anonymity of the semen donor would be implemented 'almost all over the

1 J. Robertson, *Children of Choice: Freedom and the New Reproductive Technologies*, Princeton, 1994.

world'. Suffice it to mention the opposite solutions theorized in Germany and embodied in the legislation of Sweden and Austria; and above all the recent referendum held in Switzerland which has introduced in the Constitution the principle according to which 'it is guaranteed that each individual shall have access to the information concerning his/her genetic origin' (Art. 24 *novies*, letter *g*). And debates are now beginning to be held also in the United States on this issue.[2]

On the other hand, considering that with the abolishment of donor anonymity there would probably be a reduction in the number of semen donors, means stepping down from the rigorous level of principles to the empirical ground of considerations based on 'realism': the same 'realism' that induces Alexander Capron to admit almost reluctantly that the so-called semen donors 'are in actual fact traders'.

Hence the focus of the debate shifts to the issue of method: the traditional jurist asks himself, to what point is it acceptable to undermine the internal consistency of theoretical edifices and overturn (or skirt around) general principles in the name of an appeal to the realism of practical solutions?

Related to method are also the reservations raised by the assumptions that the State should have a 'neutral' position, even though it does have 'an interest in the orderly settlement of conflicts between individuals when different interests are at stake', and it is also a party to the 'interest of not having important social values undermined'.

Also with respect to the concept of neutrality the reservations are both 'external' and 'internal'.

From the standpoint of the former, a regulatory system which claims neutrality, hence foregoing the possibility of setting limitations (age, status, health, etc.) to the access to artificial insemination techniques, runs up against the different constitutional vocation of other regulatory systems which defend some values considered to be fundamental and unquestionable by limiting access to these techniques.

From the standpoint of the latter, it is the very concept of 'neutrality' that in such a sensitive area as the rights of individuals can be given dissimilar and at times opposing interpretations, hence revealing its dangerous ambiguity. This point is perfectly illustrated by Cass R. Sunstein in a recent essay where against the more diffused concept of neutrality which tends to put abortion and surrogacy on a par as matters in which there is to be no interference by the State, he offers a 'different and stronger conception of neutrality' in the light of which it is perfectly consistent to 'acknowledge the right to abortion and prohibit surrogacy agreements'; and this assumption is made 'without invoking the interest that the State has in promoting traditional or conventional morality'.[3]

2 *See*, e.g., H.S.W. Swanson, 'Donor Anonymity in Artificial Insemination: Is It Still Necessary?', in *Col. J.L. and Social Problems*, 27 (1993), 151-190.

3 C.R. Sunstein, 'Neutrality in Constitutional Law (with special reference to Pornography, Abortion and Surrogacy)', in *Col. L. Rev.*, 92, (1992), 1-52.

But as any one can see this is a conclusion which is in a hair's breadth of hypocrisy.

3. The Report by Christian Byk

The approach taken by the European speaker could be defined as a 'neo-institutional' approach because it focusses on the centrality of the family and of the likewise institutional principle of respect for the human body, both revisited in the light of '*social changes*'.

The new reproductive technologies are 'a challenge for the law' which had been built up in time around these institutions. And the challenge could prompt some pessimism, a pessimism which is rather widespread throughout the centre of Europe and which has induced the great German philosopher who had set out to find a new ethics for the technological civilization, to inconsolably state that the progress of reproductive technologies occurs 'more under the banner of arrogance than of need'.[4] He convinced an authoritative French scholar to call on 'the resistance of traditional juridical categories' against the alarming process of 'distortion of human nature' by the 'corrosive action of biotechnologies' and have the law say 'no' to the assertion by the latter that 'anything is possible'.[5]

Christian Byk reacts to this wave of pessimism by trying to be optimistic – an optimism dictated by will rather than by reason and by feigning full confidence in the possibility of saving whatever possible of the traditional institutions by opening them up to the new technologies which cannot be ignored by the law.

But the cost that this operation of self-confident 'metamorphosis' demands is not irrelevant, neither in terms of loss of cultural identity of the institutions subject of this 'revisitation', nor in terms of the failure to achieve a new systematic consistency.

A historic overview of the main events concerning the institution of the family to show up how rapidly it has evolved in the last few years is reasonable and imperative, just as it is necessary to mention the process of secularization that has ended up stripping the 'respect for the human body' of any residual sacredness. One of the two French statutes in the area of bioethics focusses precisely on the respect for the human body prompting at the same time the autonomy of the individual in a perspective that tends to identify an individual with his/her body.

Now, the pointing out of these evolutionary processes cannot be the subject matter of interpretations that are more or less consciously subversive interpretations with respect to the principles that continue to underlie the institutions being considered here: the family as an ideal setting for the development of an individual's personality; respect

4 *See* H. Jonas, *Das Prinzip Verantwortung*, Frankfurt am Main, 1979.

5 *See* C. Labrusse-Riou, 'L'enjeu des qualifications: la survie juridique de la personne', in *Droits* 13 (Biologie, personne et droit), 1991, 22 ff.

for the human body as protection of the dignity of each individual, regardless of the full possession of his/her faculties.

And, Christian Byk does not escape the risk of an albeit veiled subversion in his appreciable intent of reconciling *nova et vetera* within a framework that can hence be termed 'neo-institutional'.

Indeed the attempt at reconciling the dogmatic statement according to which 'the family as a structure cannot be questioned' is in the least disputable, by making the mere empirical remark that 'today many families are single-parent families', the corollary then being that the legislations like the Spanish law that allow single women to have access to reproductive technologies do not deny the family institution but, at the most they are in contrast with the traditional model of the 'natural family'.

And the effort of transforming *sic et simpliciter* the principle of respect for the human body – a principle which imposes restraints on the very person who owns the body in not being allowed to dispose of it as he/she wishes, (an example of this is the provision of Art. 5 of the Italian Civil Code) – into a mere principle of self determination (based of course on awareness and information) is even more debatable; and then tracing the risks of an 'exacerbation of individual rights', Byk points out that the right to self-determination 'is not absolute and has self-limitations'.

Ultimately, reconciling *nova et vetera* may at the most be conceived as a political operation, of dubious quality, but it cannot satisfy the jurist who cannot forego the search for systematic consistency, both *de iure condito* and *de iure condendo*. In this latter case the jurist-legislator is capable of identifying a multiplicity of systems whose fundamental choice is to be unveiled and its intimate consistency is to be tested out. Only in this way can the jurist/legislator go about his/her legislative choices, avoiding eclecticisms and ambiguities which ultimately have not been avoided by Christian Byk in his report.

4. The Relationship between Artificial Insemination and the Principle of the Family

The present time is one of great bewilderment (of which the report examined above is in fact a reflection), especially where the relationship between artificial insemination and the 'family principle' is involved, with the latter being viewed in the specific prospect of what the Italian system calls the right (of a minor) 'to be educated in his/her own family'.

In the International Year of the Family disputes are still raging between those who announce the 'death of the family', and those who maintain that it is being relaunched – and the latter then break down into the advocates of the traditional model of the family as 'natural society based on marriage (in accordance with the definition given, for example, in Art. 29 of the Italian Constitution) and the supporters of the multiple forms of the family.

In this atmosphere of uncertainty and contrasting positions, the various ways of viewing the relationship between artificial insemination and the family have produced three fundamental approaches followed by the legislative policy.

5. The Proposal of a *Set of Rules Alternative to the Family*

According to one approach, an 'open' type of regulation of the cases for artificial insemination is the point of arrival of an *alternative system* with respect to that based on the traditional model of the family.

The most crystal clear formulation of this approach has been offered by a 'subversive' but intimately consistent expression of feminist juridical thinking in America.

'The alternative model I am proposing – says Carmel Shalev – should move from the recognition of the individual, without distinction of gender, in determining autonomously all the juridical issues inherent in motherhood and fatherhood before conception'. 'Privacy rules hence replace the traditional rules governing marriage as constitutional principles that protect parenthood relations defined by the autonomy of the parties when they sign the contract; any State rule that restricts the possibility of having recourse to reproduction technology going beyond the general limits set by the regulations governing contracts should accordingly be considered as violation of a constitutional principle'. The basic assumption argued by the author is that 'Such a contractual scheme implies a free market for artificial insemination capable of challenging, if not undermining, the perpetuation of women's position of economic inferiority within a patriarchal system.'[6] For those who support this assumption the ensuing corollaries are irreprehensible.

First of all any disparity in treatment between insemination and surrogacy is not admissible; 'one is the mirror image of the other'.

Therefore, 'equality of treatment between sperm donor and surrogate mother' is desirable: the tie of a woman with her offspring offers a model for criticising the estrangement of the man through the so-called principle of donor anonymity.

Finally, with regard to the interest of the unborn, the basic concern should be that of ensuring that from the time of conception there should be at least one adult (who needs not necessarily be a natural parent) responsible for taking care of him: 'the juridical parent/offspring relationship will thus be based on a voluntary contract, and the natural parent who shuns responsibility for his offspring will be considered as someone who has offered his/her procreative services to the benefit of the social parents'.

6 C. Shalev, *Birth Power. The Case for Surrogacy*, New Haven and London, 1989.

6. The Proposal of a System of Functional Rules Instead of the Traditional Family Model

A second approach prefers a *functional system instead of the traditional family model*, based on 'closed' artificial insemination rules.

Those who criticize this approach and who nurture positions that are very close to the approach examined above, maintain that it is based on a 'prohibitionist rationale' fuelled 'by the ancient fear men have of women's power to procreate without being subjected to the traditional control exercised by men';[7] for those who advocate this position the cry of alarm is: 'L'Europe n'est pas l'Amérique!'.[8]

This approach has been fully elaborated in the heart of continental Europe and it moves from the assumption that there should be no exceptions to the classical model of the family of the 'plénière' type: 'all the psychological and sociological studies show how important the family structure is for the child and therefore also the child resulting from artificial insemination at the time of conception should have a father and a mother'.

On the basis of this precondition which was already spelled out in the 1989 Rapport Braibant, the French Statute on artificial insemination (Act No. 94-654) provided a series of consistent regulations establishing that access to artificial insemination is allowed only to couples consisting of a man and woman, 'alive, in reproduction age, married or capable of providing evidence that they have been living together for at least two years', save that medical assistance 'has the aim of solving a case of a medically diagnosed pathological infertility' or of 'avoiding the transmission of a particularly severe disease to the child' (Art. L. 152-2).

The 'closed' type of regulation of the French Act emerges also in the explicit grading of the different types of medical assistance: whereas homologous fertilization is considered as being a normal act, the law states that one can have recourse to artificial insemination only as last resort when procreation with medical assistance within the couple is unfeasible (Art. L. 152-6).

And finally, consistent with the background approach is the specification made in Art. L. 673/6 concerning the principle of anonymity of a third party who donates the gametes, which is dealt with in more general terms in Art. 16-8 of Act No. 94-653 concerning the human body; the corollary of the principle of the right/duty to respect one's body is confirmed in this latter Act which declares 'the invalidity of any agreement concerning procreation or pregnancy on behalf of others' (Art.16-7).

7 *See*, e.g., S. Rodotà, *Tecnologie e diritti,* Bologna, 1995, 131 ff.

8 *See* Thezeza Meulder Klein, 'Le droit de l'enfant face au droit à l'enfant et les procreations médicalement assistées', in R*ev. Trim. Dr. civil*, 1988, 645-657.

7. The Proposal of a *System Based on Authorizations*

A third approach envisages a system of regulations based on authorizations. This system is neither 'closed' nor 'open' but is made *compatible* with a *family that does not follow any particular model* on a case by case basis.

This is the regulatory system adopted in the United Kingdom by the Human Fertilization and Embriology Act, 1990. This is a system where nothing is prohibited a priori (except limit cases as for instance maternity surrogacy contracts against payment which is prohibited by an Act of 1985), but each case is submitted to a two-tier selective examination: the authorization issued by the health establishments to have the 'therapeutic treatment' specified by law carried out is subjected to a series of conditions (Articles 12-15) and guidelines (Art. 23); the person in charge of a health establishment cannot carry out a therapeutic treatment unless these conditions and guidelines are complied with; in particular he/she is not allowed to 'give therapeutic treatment to a woman if account has not been kept of the wellbeing of the child that may be born as a result of treatment (including the need for the child to have a father), and of any other child that can be affected by the unborn' (Art. 13, para.5).

The hub of this system is the 'Institute for Human Fertilization and Embriology', which even though 'it should not be considered as an arm or as representative of the Crown', it does consist of members appointed by the Health Secretary (Annex I, Articles 1 and 4). The task of the Institute, or rather of the Authorization Committees set up within the Institute, is 'to issue, modify, discontinue or revoke the authorizations' (Art. 9). And in order for an authorization to be revoked, it is sufficient for an Authorization Committee to ascertain that the person in charge of the Establishment 'is not carrying out, or is incapable of carrying out the tasks assigned to him/her ... or he/she has not complied with the guidelines' (Art. 18, c).

8. The Realistic Approach of the Authorization-based System: Criticism

The approach described above meets a very precise basic option: that of providing a realistic approach which, when faced with strong ideological conflicts, does not impose the need to take preset positions and dramatic prohibitions and can deal with concrete problems in the light of mere guidelines which enable the operators to reach the most reconciling and most equitable solution for the case at hand.

A realistic approach can perhaps be explained as an appropriate criterion to skirt around the stalemate, without winners or losers, which had come into being in the United Kingdom in the conflict between the potentially permissive solutions of the *Warnock Report* and the intransigent positions in the subsequent White Paper submitted by the British Government to Parliament; and in any case this method is conducive to the juridical common law traditions and to the well-proven efficiency of

British Institutes and/or Committees called upon by the legislators to carry out important institutional tasks.

Things would be totally different if this very realistic approach were to be adopted in a civil law context where the legislator can assign to others the finding of solutions to highly controversial issues especially when such problems involve the fundamental rights of the individual and therefore are of constitutional importance.

In general, however, apart from the context in which this approach is tested out, there are grounds for expressing doubts that constitutional rights will be reliably protected when such protection is entrusted to the enigmatic mediation of a legislator/suggester who runs the risk of becoming the new Pontius Pilate of artificial insemination. The outcome of such mediation, however, seems to favour solutions of the 'open' regulation type; and so this authorization-based system will tend to become a mere variation of the 'alternative system' (para no.5).

9. The Constitutional Approach of the Alternative System

The 'alternative system' approach, is authoritatively defined as a 'constitutional approach': 'The Constitution protects the right to privacy as fundamental. This right encompasses a right to autonomy in procreative decisions .... Consequently, decisions to use these technologies are likely to be protected by the constitutional right to privacy'.[9]

This is an approach which is closely tied to a given type of Constitution and is strongly conditioned by a certain juridical culture whose most knowledgeable expression – but also most challenging criticism – can be found in present-day American doctrine.

The constitutional model which inspires the approach being examined is characterized by statements, silences and questions which become consistent as a whole in a cultural context that explains and justifies them (albeit not always in a convincing manner, as we shall see).

The 'statements' originate from a fundamental premise: the principle, typical of the North American Constitutional Courts (starting with the 1776 Virginia Declaration of Rights), which places the *Right of pursuit of happiness* as right which underlies any individual's rights. The *Right of privacy*, which has become one of the most absolute rights known to the American legal system is based on this very premise. But, 'if the right of privacy means anything, it is the right of the *individual* married or single, to

9 'Ethical Considerations of the New Reproductive Technologies', The Ethics Committee (1986-1987) of the American Fertility Society in the light of Instruction on Respect for Human Life in its Origin and on the Dignity of Procreation issued by the Congregation for the Doctrine of the Faith, in *Fertil. and Steril.*, 49 (1988), II, Suppl. 1.

be free from unwarranted governmental intrusion into matters so fundamentally affecting a person as the decision whether to bear or beget a child'.[10]

The silences which essentially refer to the unborn are no less significant. 'The fetus is not a person within the meaning of the fourteenth amendment'; or at least 'the unborn have never been recognized in the law as persons in the whole sense'.[11] This silence has been considered by prevailing doctrine as a desirable separation of law from biology and/or religion: 'the legal status that society chooses to confer upon the fetus is dependent upon the goals being pursued';[12] and the goal being pursued here is clearly that of not interfering with the privacy of the woman and with her right to procreate or her refusal to do so. But, especially of late, there have been some criticisms: 'the right to choose the abortion, if indeed it survives, must be based on an approach that allows abortion *even if the fetus is human* – instead of an approach that denies that humanity under cover of the pretense that the definition is none of the State's business'.[13]

The questions always mainly concern the family based on marriage, traditionally intended as being the ideal environment for the education of the child. 'The normative question becomes whether it is better for children to grow up in a home with two parents than in a home with only one'. And the answer is often unclear because of the 'tendency towards easy dissolution of the nuclear family':[14] forecasts suggest a progressive dejuridification of marriage and of an ensuing 'assimilation of legal marriage to cohabitation at a new, low level of regulation'.[15] But there are also those who point out bitterly that while it is true that American law has come to consider marriage as 'a relationship that exists primarily for the fulfilment of the individual spouses' it is likewise true that 'other stories are still vigorous in American culture ...; stories about taking on responsibilities and carrying them through, and about parenthood as an awesome commitment'.[16]

Though being widely advocated in the US non-juridical doctrine, this form of 'community' culture is less popular in the area of law: 'our Constitutional law in recent years has subordinated community to liberty'.[17] 'Libertarianism' prevails in this field and more specifically 'a scientific, not moral outlook on sexuality': 'clear thinking

10 *Eisenstadt* v. *Baird*, 405 U.S. 453 (1992) (Brennan, J., concurring).
11 *Roe* v. *Wade*, 410 U.S. 164 (1973).
12 *See*, e.g., D. E. Johnsen, 'The Creation of Fetal Rights: Conflicts with Women's Constitutional Rights to Liberty, Privacy, and Equal Protection', *Yale L. Journal*, 95 (1986), 599-625.
13 *See* S. L. Carter, *The Culture of Disbelief. How American Law and Politics Trivialize Religious Devotion,* New York, 1994, at 257.
14 R.A. Posner, *Sex and Reason*, Cambridge (Mass.), 1994, at 188, 266.
15 M.A. Glendon, *State, Law and Family. Family Law in Transition in the United States and Western Europe*, Amsterdam-New York-Oxford, 1977, 202 ff.
16 M.A. Glendon, *Abortion and Divorce in Western Law*, Cambridge (Mass.), 1987, at 108.
17 D.P. Kommers, 'Liberty and Community in Constitutional Law: the Abortion Cases in Comparative Perspective', *Brigham Young Un. L.R.* 371 (1985), at 409.

about sexuality – this is the *leitmotiv* of one of the founders of the modern economic analysis of law[18] – is obstructed by layers of ignorance, ideology, superstition, and prejudice that the acid bath of economics can help us peel away'.

10. The Different Constitutional Approach of the Functional System

Moral and religious ideas are instead the foundation of the system that we have defined as being functional to the traditional family pattern.

It would, however, be a mistake and misleading to speak of this as the 'Vatican's approach'. Here as well the approach is constitutional and can be opposed to the one examined earlier, with the latter being referred to as 'alternative' to the system being considered here.

The statements, silences and questions which were mentioned earlier as being characteristic of the constitutional pattern that the 'alternative' approach draws its inspiration from, are matched by just as many silences, statements and underpinnings that characterize the constitutional model that we are going to discuss in the following and whose most significant expression – but also conspicuous contrasts and/or inconsistencies – can be found in the recent legislative measures adopted in Europe.

The modern European Constitutions say absolutely nothing about the individual's right to happiness; privacy (a word which does not exist in the languages of Continental Europe) is not high on the list of fundamental values, which instead is headed by the inviolable principle of the dignity of the person; the attempt at tracing the profile of a positive and/or negative *procreative liberty* is bound to be totally unsuccessful.

The national normative systems instead all confirm the 'protection of the life of the unborn' as a 'goal of constitutional importance' and at the European level this is matched by the Recommendation to work out a definition of the 'biological status of the embryo'.

The recognition of the 'family as natural society founded on marriage' is clearly underlined in the Constitutions; and a sharp distinction is made between the latter and cohabitation *more uxorio* on the basis of a distinctive criterion – recently confirmed by the Italian Constitutional Court[19] – which takes into account and respects the greater space to be attributed, in cohabitation, to the individual subjectivity of its members; and vice versa, in the relationship between the spouses greater importance is to be attached to the objective needs of the family as such, namely as a *stable supraindividual institution*.

18 R.A. Posner, *op cit.*, at 3, 437.
19 Corte Costituzionale, 11 gennaio 1996, no. 8.

But in Europe there are also those who call for the rewriting of the list of values so as to guarantee the full expansion of those that we can concisely indicate with the terms 'freedom' and 'democracy'; those who call for an ethics at the service of the happiness of individuals; those who advocate that artificial insemination is be considered as a *sub specie* of the right of personality; those who, with regard to the problem of the juridical nature of the embryo paradoxically defined as being as simple as it is fundamentally unresolvable, oppose the lay model to the religious model; and finally those who support the anthropological assumption which considers the family founded on marriage as being an absolutely circumstantial and the least representative cultural model of human organization.

But globally, the European juridical culture is still strongly tied to the ancient tradition of Christian Humanism. And as was recently pointed out 'one of the most important features of the law of our century ... is the rediscovery, perhaps unaware and in the forms possible nowadays, of the aspects typical of this tradition'.[20] A recent and significant expression of this is the popular *referendum* held in Switzerland which, with a wide majority, approved the introduction into the Federal Constitution of a rule (Art. 29 *novies,* 2) which calls upon the Confederation to 'issue regulations on the use of human germinal and genetic heritage' taking measures 'in this area to protect *human dignity, human personality and the family*'.

11. Contrast Between the Systems as a Consequence of the Difference in the Constitutional Approaches

However, going back to the issues related to the various approaches brought up at the end of para. 4, an attempt can be made at this point to draw a first conclusion.

The contrast amongst the different legislative policies that is found in the various systems for regulating artificial insemination is the inescapable reflection of a contrast amongst radically different Constitutional approaches, and more precisely of the contrast between the model of a Constitution based on the *Right of Privacy* and a model of a Constitution which places human dignity and the family at the top of its list of values.

This is a contrast which cannot be easily avoided unless one indulges in the oversimplification typical of the zealous supporters of human rights or one hides behind 'a dangerously hazy language, generating delusions and false claims that will never be fulfilled'.[21]

20 *See*, e.g., G. Zagrebelsky, *Il diritto mite. Leggi diritti giustizia*, Torino, 1992.
21 M. Villey, *Le droit et les droits de l'homme*, Paris, 1994, at 154.

On the contrary, it is more appropriate to enhance as much as possible the differences because this is the only way in which we can achieve clarity and become aware of the difficulties that exist.

Once positions have been clarified, a fundamental choice needs to be made. However, this fundamental choice needs not mean a categorical assertion of the values underlying the constitutional model one follows and consequently strictly sacrificing the values of the other model, and moreover each constitutional model reflects only the more consolidated and diffused orientations of a cultural debate which is and must go on being the expression of the pluralism of ideas, customs and traditions.

It is the specific task of the jurist, and first and foremost of the jurist/legislator, to plan and test laws which, within the fundamental choice he has made, will seek to counterbalance tendentially opposing constitutional values.

In carrying out this task, which is undoubtedly a difficult one, the jurist must not fall into the authoritarian temptation of a postulated 'tyranny of values' (or even worse, of one value), and he must also escape the mirage of a demagogic 'coexistence of values' entrusted to a mere 'compromise of possibilities'.

Ultimately, the counterbalancing of values, while on the one hand it does not offer solutions if the equilibrium is only apparent (in that it is under the tyranny of one or more overriding values), on the other it should not lose consistency with the fundamental choice and the consistency of the solutions achieved.

12. Differences in the European Legislations: the 'Liberal Legislations'

In the light of these investigation criteria, it is possible to look at the most significant European legislative experiences in artificial insemination, unveil the underlying fundamental choice and test its consistency hence furthering the distinction between the more liberal legislations of Spain and Great Britain, and the stricter regulations of countries like Sweden, Norway, Austria and France.

As concerns the 'liberal legislations', the investigation criteria adopted here allow for a critical evaluation from the standpoint of the fundamental options which are either not explicitly spelled out by the legislator or do not appear to be consistent with the constitutional model to which they are to be referred.

The first assumption concerns the United Kingdom with regard to which remarks were made earlier (see para no. 7 and no. 8). Suffice it to add here that the failure to spell out the fundamental choice makes the practical results unpredictable and in any case variable: in theory they could turn out to be *too* liberal, hence promoting forms of 'procreational tourism' in a direction which is the reverse of that disapproved of by the British Health Secretary in the case of the patient assisted by Dr. Antinori (see para no. 1); but paradoxically they could also turn out to be *too* restrictive if the obligation of 'taking into account the wellbeing of the child (including the child's need to have a father) and of any other child that may have to endure the effects of the birth of another child' were to be interpreted in a strongly selective way.

The second example concerns the Spanish Law whose fundamental choice – 'eliminating any limitation that may restrict a woman's wish to procreate' – does not appear to be in accordance with the constitutional model that it is to refer to. The 1978 Spanish Constitution, which follows the Italian model and especially the German model has adopted from the latter the principle which envisages 'the social economic and juridical protection of the family' (Art. 39, 1); and the main interpretation of the regulation is consistent with a constitutional confirmation of the *verdadera familia* based on marriage, and already considered as '*institución natural*' by the *Fuero de los españoles*.

Perhaps this inconsistency in the fundamental choice explains also the discrepancies that are found in the solutions adopted by the Spanish Law.

Indeed, the rule that sets forth that the contracts of surrogacy, with or without remuneration, are absolutely null and void (Art. 10) is not consistent with the legislator's intention of admitting in line of principle pregnancies arising from the sheer desire of motherhood; but consistency can be re-established if reference is made directly to the principle of the dignity of the person assumed by the Spanish Constitution as the 'foundation of public order and of social peace' (Art. 10, 1).

Likewise there is inconsistency in recognizing a woman's absolute right to artificial insemination and then denying the offspring thus begotten the no less fundamental right of knowing his/her origins within the framework of an 'inter-individual' evaluation of a person's rights (see para no. 2). But the principle of the anonymity of the donors of gametes, confirmed by Art. 5, 4 of the Spanish Law, may be justified if directly related to the recognition in the Constitution of the *verdadera familia*.

13. Differences in the European Legislations: the 'Strict Legislations'

'Strict legislations' at times are evidence that the fundamental choice is consistent with the Constitution that they refer to; at times they surprisingly express an anomalous fundamental choice.

The former concerns the legislations issued in France and Austria and the one being developed in Switzerland.

However, only the French Law (see para no. 6) matches the consistency of the fundamental choice with a general consistency of the solutions adopted.

The Austrian Law, by attributing the right to have access to all the information concerning the donor (Art. 20) to the 'minor begotten with the sperm of a third party after his fourteenth year of age', is inconsistent with the constitutional recognition of the principle (of the stability) of the family, that the law itself embodies when it sets forth in Art. 2 that 'artificial insemination is allowed only for couples that are married or that cohabitate'. Here we find the same type of inconsistency noticed in the Spanish Law, but reversed.

In the Swiss system, the inconsistency lurks in the constitutional provision of Art. 24 *novies* which at first confirms the protection of the family in the sphere being considered here (para 2), and then declares that it follows the principle of allowing an individual access 'to the information (para 2, g) concerning his genetic origin'.

The third example concerns the Norwegian and Swedish legislations. For legal systems that are often quoted as examples for their open-mindedness for the various forms of hetero- and homosexual cohabitation, the fundamental choice of selecting the heterosexual, stable family as the 'ideal milieu for the growth and development of the child' may appear to be extravagant. Indeed, access to artificial insemination is restricted to 'married women' only or to 'couples that are married or that cohabitate only if it is possible to presume that the child will be able to grow up in a favourable environment'. There is significant awareness of the difficulties in dealing with the issue of the dubious compatibility between protection of the development of the child within the family and the respect for the right of the latter to be informed about his biological origin.

It is quite likely that underlying this 'extravagant' choice is the tendency, detectable especially in Sweden, to enhance the responsibility of procreation. But it is enlightening to notice that the enhancement of responsibility occurs by going back to the traditional family.

14. The True Fundamental Choices and Internal Consistency

But the most significant profile which reveals the true fundamental choices and tests out the consistency which they are applied is undoubtedly the legal statute of the embryo.

Now if the fundamental choice is to tie the statute of the embryo to the principle of the dignity of the person with the assumption of protecting human life right from its beginning, then for the sake of consistency: 1) embryos should be formed artificially only to produce a pregnancy; and 2) supernumerary embryos should not deliberately be formed.

This is a consistency that is very hard to demand and in practice it is imposed only by the German Law on the protection of the embryos.

What are found more frequently are the normative solutions that mitigate the fundamental choice: a) by reconfirming item sub 1 but allowing the conservation of supernumerary embryos formed as an exception to item sub 2 only for fertilization purposes; and b) reconfirming item sub 1 but allowing the conservation of the above-mentioned embryos for research purposes, within limitations to be set.

Mitigation sub a) draws inspiration from an evident need to counterbalance some fundamental personal rights – the human dignity of the embryo and protecting the health of the woman that could be endangered if submitted to repeated biopsies for harvesting the oocytes – and it does not affect consistency between the solution adopted and the fundamental choice. Instead, mitigation sub b) does raise some doubts because it ends up counterbalancing interests of different rank, namely the human dignity of the embryo and the social interest of research.

These doubts are further enhanced by the remark that the Spanish Law as well (Art. 15) reaches the same solution based on the mitigation of sub b); the preconditions are rather different in that it is the sole case in Europe that formally accepts the distinction between 'embryo' and 'pre-embryo', hence breaking the conceptual unity of the life-giving process, and enabling as a consequence a more consistent counterbalancing of interests (protection of the pre-embryo interests pursued by research).

Paradoxically in the Spanish Law we find an opposite inconsistency: in fact once the debatable (and debated) concept of 'pre-embryo' is accepted there are no longer grounds for categorically prohibiting the 'fertilization of human oocytes for any purpose other than human reproduction' (Art. 3). But, again, the Spanish system seems to reveal the contradiction between the liberal approach of the Law and the constitutional choice founded on the dignity of the person (see para no. 12).

What instead does emerge clearly is the true fundamental choice made by the British Law, that is not explicitly spelled out in other respects (see para no. 12). Indeed, subject to authorization, it is allowed to produce and/or use embryos 'for the purposes of a research project specified in the authorization', provided that the utilization does not occur 'after the appearance of the *primitive streak*', saving that 'it is assumed that the *primitive streak* appears in the embryo by no later than the fourteenth day from the fusion of the gametes (Art. 3, 3 and 4; Annex 2).

From this point of view, the English Law is authentically and consistently liberal. But it is also the only one in Europe.

15. The Common Factors in the European Legislative Experience

Having shed light on the differences that can be found amongst the most significant European laws, we must now reconstruct the features that we have in common.

One aspect that all these legislative experiences do seem to share, or in any case that brings them closer, is the central position of the protection of health which is of critical importance not only for the *quomodo* of the implementation of the various artificial insemination techniques, but also for the *cur* of the access provided to such techniques.

This is evident in the 'strict legislations' where the basic aim of artificial insemination is that of providing a remedy to the infertility of the couple when it is impossible or extremely difficult to treat the infertility in any other way. Under the umbrella of the protection of health comes also the other additional aim of artificial insemination, namely preventing the transmission of severe disease to the unborn.

But also in the 'liberal legislations' the freedom of the woman's access to artificial insemination does not take on the features of an absolute and unquestionable right to (assisted) procreation, but is always targeted to the protection of health. This can be inferred from the Spanish Law which in Art. 1 para 2, states the medical purpose of the techniques of artificial insemination; in the English Law such techniques are referred to as 'therapeutic treatment' (Art. 13, and in Annex 2).

Therefore, nothing could be more remote from the European legislative experience than the emblematic assumption of access to artificial insemination (with preservation of the embryo) or to surrogacy by a busy professional woman who has no intention of having her professional life hindered by an untimely pregnancy.

Another strongly cementing factor is the prohibition to enter into surrogacy agreements. The prohibition is absolute and constant across the 'strict legislations'; it appears in the same terms as we saw earlier (para no. 12) in the Spanish Law whereas is the English Law it is restricted to the cases where compensation is envisaged.

This prohibition takes us back to a general principle of the respect for the human body which in turn is an expression of the constitutional principle of the dignity of the person.

Finally, there are factors that, as we saw earlier (para no. 13 and no. 14), seek to aggregate the 'strict legislations' and, at times to bring the 'liberal legislations' closer to them.

This is a principle which seeks to protect life from its very beginning and it ranges from the 'strict legislations' to the Spanish law, albeit with some limitations; and the principle of the stable heterosexual family which is assumed as precondition by the 'strict legislations', but simply 'suggested' by the English law.

16. Are we Moving Towards a European Approach to Artificial Insemination?

Now at the very time when the legislative experiences appear to be outlining a 'European approach' to the regulation of artificial insemination, which is tendentially homogeneous in its constitutional approach and sufficiently consistent in the solutions it adopts, 'in Europe the individualist ideological fervour of the American culture seems to be gaining an increasingly warm approval, and is viewed as a model to be imitated'.[22] This is a difficult (or excessively easy) paradox to explain.

It is to be hoped that the explanation is not that given by Amitai Etzioni during a recent interview: 'Unfortunately in Europe there is a craving to follow the tendencies of the United States. If something happens here it is easy to expect it to be picked up

22 F.D. Busnelli, 'Law and the New Frontiers of Human Life', in A. Pizzorusso (ed.), *Italian Studies in Law,* II, Dordrecht, 1994, at p. 73.

in Europe after some time. For this reason, during the Reagan administration I used to invite my European friends to come and see how things were faring in America: so that they would understand what the social experiments that were being carried out here would lead to, so that they would not repeat them'.

Licensing Parenthood and Regulating Reproduction: Towards Consensus?

Derek Morgan*

Do we Need Rules for Procreation?

- whether 'natural' or 'assisted'?
- what reasons are there for regulation?
- what form should these rules take?

The existence of a few specialist clinics has revealed a global market for assisted conception services. The techniques and trappings of assisted conception, AID, IVF, GIFT, cryopreservation of gametes, eggs and embryos, gamete and embryo donation, surrogacy, and other developments in assisted conception challenge traditional views of procreation and parenthood. This challenge has legal as well as ethical implications.

If the family, by definition, consists of an adult or adults bringing up children, then the new techniques of assisted reproduction raise many issues. Some of them are often phrased in terms of rights; they concern amongst many other things: which adults should be permitted to make use of assisted conception; what rights and responsibilities should gamete donors or surrogate mothers have in relation to the embryos and children created; what interests might the State or society have in regulating and controlling these techniques, and what should be the rights of children themselves? If the 'wrong' embryos are given to two women patients[1] – i.e., they receive non-genetically related gametes – should this be treated simply as a breach of contract by the clinic, or does it raise more profound questions (can a woman be assaulted by an embryo?) regarding our attachment to the genetic basis of parenthood? Does the easy availability of surrogacy or gamete donation reinforce an increasing tendency to view reproduction as the commodification of human life, or perhaps the alienability of reproductive labour

* Cardiff Law School, Cardiff, Wales, UK.

1 As reported, for example in the *Observer* 8 August 1993.

Cosimo Marco Mazzoni (ed.), A Legal Framework for Bioethics, 107-115.
©1998 *Kluwer Law International. Printed in The Netherlands.*

and the commodification of children was more apparent when women were regarded as having no role outside marital motherhood, or when abortion first became legalized. Addressing these questions may lead us to a clearer picture of what it is that we mean by family and what it is in family that we value.

Part of the reason why it is commonly said that assisted conception techniques and medical technology generally outstrips ethical and legal debate is because there exists no consensus about the complex ethical issues which arise. Part of the reason for the apparent despair is that society has chosen, for a variety of reasons, to avoid attempts at reaching a moral consensus. Some of the regulatory mechanisms can be applied to some but not all of the technologies with equal ease or facility, others can be applied in different ways and subject to different, varying or temporal limitations and exclusions. In such a field, Government sometimes acts wisely in refusing or failing to regulate (by law) in order to allow debate and discussion to proceed, and, perhaps for some moral consensus to emerge. 'Where matters of morality and medicine are concerned, society is best served not by policies based on fear, ignorance, prejudice, or raw emotion, but by the emergence of moral consensus.'[2]

James Watson writing in 1971 suggested of the possible developments in human reproductive research that different societies are likely to view the matter differently and that it would be surprising if all came to the same conclusion. We must, he said, assume that techniques for the *in vitro* manipulation of human eggs are likely to be of general medical practice, capable of routine performance in many major nations within some 10 to 20 years.[3] He argued that international agreement was the preferred method of control and that on some matters 'a sufficient international consciousness might be apparent to make possible some forms of international agreement 'before the cat is totally out of the bag'.

In each country of Europe, including Central and Eastern Europe, similar questions arise with respect to law, medicine and bioethics. But there are differences of a philosophical, economic, social, political and even geographical nature which are not easily (even if desirably) bridged. The parallel between explosive political change within and across Europe and the rapid developments in bioethical sciences and their impacts on the fields of law, ethics and human rights give rise to challenges at least three levels.[4]

2 Arthur Caplan, 'Introduction', in Dianne Bartels, Reinhard Priester, Dorothy Vawter and Arthur Caplan (eds), *Beyond Baby M: Ethical Issues in New Reproductive Technologies*, Clifton, New Jersey, Humana Press, 1990, pp. 5-6.

3 James Watson 'Potential Consequences of Experimentation with Human Eggs', Paper presented at the 12th meeting of the panel on Science and Technology Committee on Science and Astronautics, United States House of Representatives, Washington DC, January 28, 1971.

4 Following Mme Catherine Lalumiere 'Allocutions d'Ouverture', in *Europe and Bioethics*, Proceedings of the 1st Symposium of the Council of Europe on Bioethics, Strasbourg, 1989, pp. 12-14.

I. Human rights

What is the meaning, for example, of a 'fundamental right to human life', and in what way(s) is this question metamorphosed by biotechnology? What is meant by the European Convention on Human Rights' guarantee (in Article 12) of the right to 'marry and found a family' and how do substantive and procedural barriers to access to biotechnology impinge on that 'right'? Reconciliation of advances in medicine and science with values expressed through human rights is necessary to preserve the bioethical balance; to ensure that the risks to patients, providers and the subjects of biotechnology are minimized. Laws, administrative regulations and professional codes of conduct must be carefully scrutinized to elaborate the effects they set out to achieve, whether they achieve those and only those ends, and whether there are other, unintended, unforeseen or unforeseeable effects.

II. Democracy and public choice

How should these difficult issues be mediated; towards consensus, a toleration of moral pluralism, or within the dictates of one dominant philosophical approach? What is the fulcrum of the bioethical balance? What institutional structures are used, proposed or necessary to articulate and effect these determinations of public choice? Is there a difference between, and are there advantages to, standing national ethics councils charged with parliamentary accountability (such as the Danish Council on Ethics, or the French and Portuguese Councils), compared with either the voluntary committee such as recently instituted in the United Kingdom under the auspices of the Nuffield Foundation or a statutory regulatory body such as the Human Fertilisation and Embryology Authority?

III. The rule of law

A fundamental question which arises for any jurisdiction is whether there is any existing law which regulates biomedical practice, research and development and whether it is satisfactory in assisting our responses to dilemmas posed by biotechnology; is it too accommodating or too hostile?

In each case, again, it is necessary to consider the relationship between

- the international community
- the nation state
- 'individual' parents
- individual resultant children
- medical practitioners
- the resulting 'social practices' with respect to kinship and the relationship between people

For example, attention has focused upon the desirability (or otherwise) of 'procreative tourism'. Sometime United Kingdom Health Secretary Virginia Bottomley intimated that the regulation of assisted conception has a global dimension. Commenting on the birth to a 59-year-old British woman of twins following fertility treatment at an Italian clinic which she had been refused in England, Bottomley said 'We cannot stop people going to any country in the world for treatment but maybe we'll renew our efforts to have discussions with other countries as to the examples we set and how they can establish ethical controls over some of the dramatic achievements in modern medicine.' (see the *Independent,* 28.12.93; *The Guardian,* 28.12.93, reporting an interview on the Today programme 27.12.93.)

Almost immediately the French junior Health Minister Phillipe Douste-Blazy announced his government's intention to introduce legislation to prohibit *in vitro* fertilization of post-menopausal women (*The Guardian* 5.1.94) although this was followed by howls of protests from various parts of the political spectrum and different interest groups (*The Guardian,* 5.1.94). And the Italian Health Minister Mariapia Garavaglia was quoted as saying that 'desires are not rights, and babies are not consumer goods,' announced the imminent establishment of a commission to establish controls over the treatment of sterile and post-menopausal women (*The Guardian* 6.1.94).

As the generation of women who have chosen to postpone child birth until later in their lives comes of age, the question of a 'natural' span of child birthing is one which is being challenged, both in its logic and its limits. And with an increasing number of second or third relationships seeking to enjoy the pleasures and pains of mutual family life, women and their partners are renegotiating boundaries which previously seemed set as much by convention as constitution. The consequences of this we have hardly begun to hazard at. As Marilyn Strathern has suggested:

> The new reproductive technologies and the legislative and other actions to which they have given rise seek to assist natural processes on the one hand and the social definition of kinship on the other. But this double assistance creates new uncertainties. For the present cultural explicitness is revolutionizing former combinations of ideas and concepts. The more we give legal certainty to social parenthood, the more we cut from under our feet assumptions about the intrinsic nature of relationships themselves. The more facilitation is given to the biological reproduction of human persons, the harder it is to think of a domain of natural facts independent of social intervention. Whether or not all this is a good thing is uncertain. What is certain is that it will not be without consequence for the way people think about one another.[5]

The question, 'Who do you think you are?' will have new and dramatic significance for the second millennium.

5 Marilyn Strathern in Meg Stacey (ed.), *Changing Human Reproduction,* London, Sage Publications, 1992, pp. 148-169 at 167-168.

Regulating Reproduction

Here there are a number of different questions:

1. What is meant by regulation?

   With respect to professional activities and those of professional bodies and particularly those of medicine and health one may distinguish between:
   1. formal (State) law; specially formulated legal principles and norms applied to the subject matter in question, or to the processes which are the subject matter;
   2. formal (State) law which is of general applicability;
   3. informal, general or specific law; such as professional codes of practice or discipline which may be either promulgated under a general state law which regulates professions, or professionals of a particular kind, or subject to special and specific qualifications or which may be adopted voluntarily by the professional body concerned and which may be either of a general directive kind or specific mandatory provisions which cover certain defined activities rather than (say) providing only the conditions of good professional practice;
   4. moral suasion;
   5. the market.

And in respect of each type of approach, to whom or to what are 'the rules' of the regulation directed?

There is, of course, a further complicated relationship. It is that between morality – or bioethics in this context – and law. Once you have decided on the ethics or morality of a particular issue, it does not then follow necessarily that this has to be translated into legal language. That will depend on what we see to be the relationship, if any, between law and morals. Questions about whether an activity is right or wrong, morally innocuous or repugnant and the arguments supporting those views belong to moral philosophy. We have identified above only three of the many possible approaches which can then be brought to bear in this analysis. The question of whether we should then have laws governing any particular issue, and what shape and rationale those laws might take, belong to legal and political philosophy. There is no necessary, simple connection to be made between the rightness, wrongness or moral indifference to an act or practice, and the propriety or desirability of having a law which requires, permits or forbids it. Of course, we may have a position which holds, for example, that any conduct which is morally repugnant should be and is unlawful. Similarly, we may hold that because conduct is prohibited by legal *fiat* endorsed with sanction – whether criminal or civil – that it is therefore morally imperative not to break that law. We could hold this latter position simply because we felt that whatever was unlawful was necessarily immoral, or because, whatever our judgement of the morality of the particular law, we placed a particular moral primacy on obeying the law, even if we find it to be morally repugnant.

We can put this another way. That there is no general direct connection between law and morality can be tested straightforwardly. One may consider that an act may be wrong, and wrong *only* because it was against the law. If one decided that then there would be a direct connection between the morality and legality of an act. But generally we do not believe that to be the case. We look for some background, justifying moral reason for the law to be the way it is. Debate in legal philosophy then turns on whether morals and law should be co-extensive and co-terminous, or whether there should be some acts which are 'not the law's business'.

Of course, while it does seem to follow from this that the scope of moral debate need pay no necessary attention to law, the question for lawyers has been the extent to which the law is or should or indeed can be co-terminous with moral positions, and if so, with which one(s).

2. What Sorts of Consequences do We Want to Create or Achieve?

In terms of:

- the types of assistance that we want to encourage or discourage and what sort of family relationships we want to make available and to whom?
- what do we want to make available by way of changing family forms? What precedence do we want to give to social, biological or genetic parentage?

Marilyn Strathern and her colleagues have shown how the deployment of reproductive technologies is affecting assumptions which we bring to understandings not only of family life but to the very understanding of family itself and cultural practice;[6] '... the way in which the choices that assisted conception affords are formulated, will affect thinking about kinship. And the way people think about kinship will affect other ideas about relatedness between human beings.'[7] And, we would add, the way in which we think about relatedness between human beings will affect the way in which we think about the relationship between individuals, groups and the State.

6 Marilyn Strathern, *et al.*, *Reproducing the Future: Kinship and the New Reproductive Technologies*, Manchester, Manchester University Press, 1993. And *see* Marilyn Strathern 'The Meaning of Assisted Kinship' in Meg Stacey (ed.), *Changing Human Reproduction*, London, Sage Publications, 1992, pp. 148-169. This essay is a succinct introduction to cultural and linguistic concepts deployed in arguments about the family, demonstrating in her use of examples the way in which what are taken as natural facts are themselves social and cultural constructs. For developments of this sort of argument, applied to various intellectual disciplines, *see, inter alia*, Michel Foucault, *The Order of Things*, London, Tavistock, 1970, and Keith Thomas, *Man and the Natural World,* Harmondsworth, Penguin, 1983.

7 Marilyn Strathern in Meg Stacey, *op. cit.* at 149.

The most radical challenge to understandings of the family has been presented by assisted conception, or what Singer and Wells have called the 'reproduction revolution'.[8] The legal, biological and social constructs of parenthood have all faced vigorous re-examination, and new definitions and new family forms have become available. Even where families are created without assisted reproduction, parenthood is not a straightforward matter. As John Eekelaar has written of the United Kingdom parenthood can be broken into three distinguishable elements: biological parenthood, legal parenthood and the holding of parental responsibility,[9] in such a way that 'the resulting structure of parenthood in English law is one in which a mediaeval land lawyer would have taken pride.'[10]

The tensions between genetic and social parenthood, for example, have led Ruth Macklin to suggest that a number of different determinants of what is meant by 'family' can be drawn. In addition to the 'traditional' biological vector, she suggests that law, custom and what she awkwardly calls 'subjective intentions' (more simply what people choose to do despite law or accepted custom) can all be factored to produce an understanding of what family is, or how we understand it or them to be composed. She concludes:

> The effect of artificial means of reproduction on our understanding of the family will vary, depending on which of these three determinants is chosen to have priority. There is no way to assign a priori precedence to any one of the three. ... there is no simple answer to the question of how artificial means of reproduction affect our understanding of family. We need to reflect on the variety of answers, paying special attention to what follows from answering the question one way rather than another. Since there is no single, univocal concept of the family, it is a matter for moral and social decision just which determinants of 'family' should be given priority.[11]

The role of the family, and conceptions of personal identity and human nature are underlined in many ways by programmes of assisted conception, especially in the way in which rational women will use and pursue infertility programmes even when they know that the success rates are low. This has been most critically studied by Lene Koch who has observed that even where women entering IVF programmes felt deprived of correct and realistic information, it did not seem to have affected their decisions to

8 Peter Singer and Deane Wells, *The Reproduction Revolution*, Oxford, Oxford University Press, 1984. A comprehensive consideration of the issues and questions involved is presented in the two volume final report of the Canadian Royal Commission on the new reproductive technologies, *Proceed with Care*, Ottawa, Minister of Government Services, Canada, 1993.

9 Eekelaar, 'Parenthood, Social Engineering and Rights', in Derek Morgan and Gillian Douglas (eds.), *Constituting Families*, Franz Steiner Verlag, 1994, citing the Children Act 1989 for the introduction of the third important element.

10 *Ibid.*

11 'Artificial Means of Reproduction and our Understanding of the Family', *Hastings Center Report*, 1991 5 at 6.

commence or to continue in an IVF programme after one or more failed attempt.[12] In seeking to provide an explanation for this apparently 'irrational' behaviour Koch reformulates the starting point of the rational inquiry not as one from an external, impartial observer, but as one which is taken from and constituted by the women's own experiences.

Thus, as she pertinently observes, the wish to have a child is seen as part of what Helen Homans has in another context called part of the woman's reproductive career.

> To want a child and to try to have it is an exercise of the reproductive freedom that the feminist movement has argued for since its very beginning. The decision to have a child at age 30 may be seen as a natural succession to the decision to contracept at 18, to have an abortion at 20; in other words to avail oneself of the medicotechnical services of the health system – first to avoid having a child, later to have one.[13]

Thus she concludes, the wish for a child is an authentic wish and does not become less strong – nor less authentic because it is, as some critics of IVF and other reproductive technology programmes have argued, socially constructed. As Frances Price has commented, it is only after failing to satisfy the initial stages of socially sanctioned authentic wishes (unassisted conception) that the use of reproductive technology is introduced as evidence of inauthentic wishes.[14] As Koch comments:

'The fact that infertile women want children, want to have a so-called normal family, is part of the explanation of why they do not hear the feminist critics. ... infertile women do not consider prevention of infertility a relevant alternative to IVF. This is an option for future generations – not applicable to their situation.'[15]

And then in an important step she argues that the apparent irrationality of women in IVF programmes can be shown to make sense if the view of the 'infertile' woman is seen as belonging to a culture structured by its own rationality, one which is removed from, or supplements any notion of 'universal rationality'.

From this it follows that women who experience infertility do so as a loss of control, which is often reinforced by social stigmatization. 'The decision to try IVF – may be considered an attempt to liberate oneself from the powerlessness of infertility – if only to realize that a child of her own is no longer an issue.'[16] Hence the purpose of the IVF trials may be quite different for the infertile woman compared with what an external, 'objective' or 'rational' observer might afford. Participating in an IVF programme may be one way of negotiating access to infertility; a woman is able publicly to admit to herself and to others that she is infertile once she has followed and exhausted all the

12 *See* Lene Kock, 'IVF – A Rational Choice?', *Reproduction and Genetic Engineering: International Journal of Feminist Analysis*, 3, 1990, pp. 235-242.

13 *Ibid.* at 238.

14 in Derek Morgan and Robert Lee (Eds.), *Birthrights: Law and Ethics at the Beginnings of Life*, 1989.

15 *Op. cit.* p. 239.

16 *Ibid.* at 240.

acceptable rites of passage, including IVF, the choice for which, if seen solely as the choice for a child, would be regarded as an irrational one, given the paucity of the take home baby rate measure of success.

> IVF may be considered a way to prove to others that you are infertile – and is a precondition to a final resolution of infertility. ... As each new reproductive technology enters the market, the definition of infertility changes. Infertility can only be defined as the condition that no reproductive technology can resolve. Thus, IVF virtually becomes an imperative, even for those women who might otherwise have been ready to accept their infertility. Human identity is closely affected by parental status and childlessness is an identity which is hard to obtain and must be fought for in a pronatalist society, since no doubt must exist as to the certainty of the condition.[17]

The discovery of the structure of DNA and the mapping of the human genome has given us a plot of human life, Aldous Huxley has even given us a title to the fabulous world which might be entered, and with which we can advertise the project. What we appear to know about the intimate structure and workings of gametes and embryos, foetuses and babies enables us to speak almost of a quantum theory of reproduction, to be set alongside a theory of general relativity – in which we factor the social, environmental, cultural, and emotional aspects of fertility, parenthood, individuation and society.[18]

There are those who believe that work in present biotechnical research and associated infertility treatment services is like playing alchemy in the crucible of the genetic future. They suspect the danger that the atoms will enter new and unforeseeable trajectories and take on vectors and forces which cannot now be understood. In parallel with this are doubts which have consistently been voiced about the wisdom of investing resources so heavily in the 'reproduction revolution.' The question, 'Who do you think you are?' will have new and dramatic significance for the second millennium, but the social problems may not derive from individual choices themselves, but the anthropological consequences of the summation of those individual choices.

17 *Ibid.* at 241.

18 *see* Derek Morgan, 'Undoing What Comes Naturally – Regulating Medically Assisted Families', in Andrew Bainham and David Pearl (Eds.), *Frontiers of Family Law*, London, Chancery Publishing, 1993, pp. 94-121.

4. Genetic Information

Bioethics and Law[1]

Dorothy Nelkin*

In a futuristic novel, *A Philosophical Investigation* (1992), Philip Kerr described a society in 2013, obsessed by an epidemic of violent crime. Efforts to control criminal behaviour were organized around the belief that male criminals were genetically predisposed to violence – a belief that had been strengthened by 'the failure of schemes which claimed to ameliorate the environment.' All men in Kerr's scenario carried identification cards with their DNA profiles. The key weapon against crime was the 'Lombroso Program' designed to screen men for their innate predisposition to violence. (Lombroso stood for 'Localization of Medullar Brain Resonations Obliging Social Orthopraxy'). Clinics used a scanning machine, resembling Positron Emission Tomography, to identify men whose brain lacked a Ventro Medial Nucleus (VMN), and were, therefore, likely to become criminals. The idea was to track the individual offender 'before he offended at all'. In Kerr's society, it was considered a measure of public health to screen all men and socially responsible citizens were expected to comply. Though screening was not 'mandatory', it was a condition for employment and insurance.[2]

Kerr's fictional world, organized around the use of biological testing for purposes of social control is futuristic, yet it is grounded firmly in the 1990s, when assumptions about genetic determinism and the predictability of inherent traits are having practical consequences for insurance decisions, employment practices, and, I will suggest today, the American legal system. The problems of genetic discrimination are often discussed in the context of insurance or work, but I would like to mainly focus on law, suggesting

* Professor of Sociology, New York University, New York, NY, USA.

1 This paper brings together material that is further developed in D. Nelkin and L. Tancredi, *Dangerous Diagnostics*, Univ. of Chicago Press, 2nd ed., 1994; R. Dreyfuss and D. Nelkin, 'The Jurisprudence of Genetics, *Vanderbilt Law Review*, 45, March 1992; and D. Nelkin and S. Lindee, *Supergene: DNA in American Popular Culture*, W.H. Freeman Press, 1995.

2 Philip Kerr, *A Philosophical Investigation*, New York: Farrar Straus, Giroux, 1992.

Cosimo Marco Mazzoni (ed.), A Legal Framework for Bioethics, 119-129.
©1998 *Kluwer Law International. Printed in The Netherlands.*

that legal decisions are increasingly influenced by assumptions about genetic determinism.

As a broadly accepted science-based concept, assumed to be impersonal, rational, and value-free,[3] the idea of genetic determinism is becoming a resource for the courts as a way to resolve ambiguous and difficult problems and anticipate future risk. Courts are drawing on genetic concepts in custody disputes and in criminal cases where judges are using biological expertise in sentencing decisions. The science of genetics seems to promise that DNA, if comprehensively known and accurately understood, could largely explain an individual's past performance and could be used to predict future behaviour.

As genetic assumptions enter the legal arena, they will have important implications for genetic discrimination in other contexts as well. Thus, I will begin by describing some ways in which genetic information is influencing legal reasoning in two areas: first, in decisions about family relationships; second, in interpretations of criminal responsibility and culpability. I will then turn to a broader consideration of the concepts of genetic predisposition and prediction and their implications for discrimination and social control.

Decisions in Family Law

In legal disputes over the custody of children, American courts are increasingly invoking genetic explanations to guide complex decisions. The courts have rarely interfered in family relationships; its goal has been to maintain stability, assuring children continued contact with the significant people in their lives. Adoption laws, for example, have been largely shaped by social concerns aimed at protecting the integrity of ongoing family relationships. To create a shield of privacy between the family and society, the law has fostered a legal fiction of natural birth, and, in most jurisdictions, original birth certificates and adoption records were permanently sealed.[4]

Similarly, the courts have generally adjudicated custody disputes on the basis of judgments about the psychological best interests of the child. The goal has been to preserve 'existing affection relationships'.[5] Guided by psychoanalytic theory, custody procedures have considered emotional ties as the most important factor in decisions

3 Yaron Ezrahi, *The Descent of Icarus: Science and the Transformation of Contemporary Democracy*, Cambridge: Harvard University Press, 1990. For cases that illustrate this pattern, *see* Dorothy Nelkin (ed.), *Controversy: The Politics of Technical Decisions*, Newbury Park, Ca., Sage Publications, 1992.

4 *See* Melissa Arndt, Comment, 'Severed Roots: The Sealed Adoption Records Controversy,' 6 *Northern Illinois University Law Review*, 103, 104-15 (1986).

5 Peggy C. Davis, 'There is a Book Out: An Analysis of Judicial Absorption of Legislative Facts,' *Harvard Law Review*, 100, 7, May 1987, 1539-1604.

involving children. This has permitted courts to intervene in the biological family in order to protect the child, and especially to avoid disrupting the emotional bonds between children and their psychological parents.

However, when the person is reconceptualized as a genetic entity and forging genetic relationships becomes a goal in itself, legal protection for social interests is weakened. This has become apparent during the 1980s and 1990s, for example, in changing adoption procedures. Encouraged by a popular belief that genetic relationships are the essence of individual identity and that knowing one's roots is prerequisite to becoming a functional adult, most agencies have now opened adoption records.[6] Twenty years ago, adoption agencies discouraged adoptees from searching for their birth parents. Today, confronted by increasing requests to locate genetic relatives, they facilitate searches for 'natural' parents, for 'biological roots' even though such searches may dismay the adoptive family and violate the biological family's interest in confidentiality. These new practices rest on the belief that knowing genetic connections is so important and so critical to a person's identity and emotional health, that it overrides norms of privacy and confidentiality. Recent custody disputes also demonstrate the increasing legal sympathy for genetic ties, and the use of such ties to explain decisions that could be justified in other ways. The decision in the 1991 California custody dispute, *Johnson* v. *Calvert*, over a child born to a surrogate mother provides a graphic example. The Calverts had donated their gametes (both egg and sperm) and hired a surrogate, Anna Johnson, to carry the fertilized egg to term in her womb. The dispute was described by the press as a contest; ('genetics vs. environment').[7] It began after Anna Johnson refused to relinquish the baby, Christopher, at his birth. When DNA tests confirmed that the Calverts were Christopher's genetic parents, the judge awarded them sole custody.

For our purpose in this seminar, the significance of this decision lies in how it was framed. The judge could have simply enforced the terms of the original contract. He could also have used the traditional standard of the child's best interest and weighed Johnson's claim as a single mother against the value of placing Christopher with two parents who could provide more for him. Alternatively, he could have considered the biological processes of pregnancy and birth as a legitimate basis for a motherhood claim and awarded custody or, at least, visitation rights to Anna Johnson. Instead, the judge linked the child's proper place to his genetic constitution and justified his decision in terms of the child's genetic endowment:

> We know more and more about traits now, how you walk, talk and everything else, all sorts of things that develop out of your genes, how long you're going to live, all things

6 *See* Elton B. Kilibanoff, 'Genealogical Information in Adoption: The Adoptee's Quest and the Law,' 11 *Family Law Quarterly* 185, (1977), 193.

7 Seth Mydans, 'Surrogate Denied Custody of Child', *New York Times*, 23 October, 1990. pp. A14.

being equal, when your immune system is going to break down, what diseases you may be susceptible to. They have upped the intelligence ratio of genetics to 70 percent now.[8]

The judge noted the 'tremendous need out there for genetic children',[9] and cited popular beliefs about the importance of genetics. He called Anna Johnson, the surrogate mother, a 'genetic hereditary stranger' to the child. The California Supreme Court affirmed in then appeal, defining genetics, not gestation, as the 'natural' basis of a mother-child relationship. In effect, the courts defined the child as a genetic entity – a packet of genes – and assumed that shared genes are the essence of identity and the basis of human relationships.[10]

Assumptions about the importance of genetic relationships are also appearing in disputes between genetic and adoptive parents. In a 1989 case, *Coburn* v. *Coburn*, the former husband of Mrs Coburn petitioned for visitation rights with his daughter Angie Lee, who he had nurtured for ten years. The court dismissed the petition when genetic tests revealed that the child was not, in fact, his biological daughter. The decision was later reversed on appeal, because the appellate court considered the effect of 'chaos on the emotional wellbeing of the child'.[11] But several justices still adopted a biological perspective, declaring, for example, that 'knowledge of one's biological parents and hereditary history is crucial in ordering one's affairs and making life's decisions.'[12] The court approved the use of DNA tests to assure the child knowledge of her biological father, but it did not consider the danger that this genetic information might pose to the relationship between Angie Lee and the man she had long considered to be her father in her day-to-day life.

Decisions are by no means consistent, but regardless of how a case is resolved, courts commonly feel compelled to address the relative importance of genetic and emotional bonds and the validity of 'genetic rights'.[13] This was the issue debated in the widely publicized dispute over 'Baby Jessica'. The legal circumstances of this case indisputably favoured the claims of her biological father, and though he had never seen

8 *Johnson* v. *Calvert*, No. X 63 31 90 (Cal. Super. Ct. Oct. 22, 1990).

9 *Johnson* v. *Calvert*, *op. cit.*, p. 11.

10 The influence of genetics is highlighted by the fact not mentioned by the court, but evident in the illustrations in the press that the Calverts were white and Johnson was black. Johnson appealed the decision and in May 1993, the California Supreme Court denied her appeal on grounds that genes were 'a powerful factor in human relationships.' *See* Janet Dolgin, 'Just a Gene: Judicial Assumptions about Parenthood,' *UCLA Law Review*, 40, 1993, pp 637-694.

11 Commonwealth *ex. rel. Coburn* v. *Coburn*, 558 A.2d 548, 553 (Pa. Super Ct. 1989). *See* also John Lawrence Hill, 'What does it mean to be a Parent? The Claims of Biology as the Basis for Parental Rights,' 66 *New York University Law Review*, (1991) 353 .

12 Judge J. Crillo, (concurring), decision, *ibid.*, p. 554.

13 In a Vermont adoption case involving a nine month old baby, the court worked out a settlement between the biological father and adoptive parents. *See* 'Pact reached in Vermont Adoption Case'. *New York Times*, 23 August, 1993.

the child, she was handed over to him. Popular sentiment, however, strongly favoured leaving the child with the DeBoers who had raised her for two years. Nature versus nurture framed the legal discourse.

The relative importance of genetic and emotional bonds were also debated in several cases in which teenage children have gone to court to 'divorce' their biological parents. In 1992, twelve-year-old Gregory Kingsley went to a Florida court to end the parental rights of his genetic mother and to allow his foster family to adopt him. Gregory had been living with this foster family for two years, after years of abuse and neglect by his biological parents. In this case, the court considered the indisputable evidence that Gregory had been abused as overriding the biological connection, and allowed the child to sever connections with his mother. The decision, however, was controversial, criticized as a 'dangerous precedent' threatening 'the preservation of the family'. To critics of the decision biological connection appeared more important than the social context experienced by the child.[14]

The concept of genetic rights remains contested, but privileging biological connections is attractive as a way to clarify ambiguities and resolve complex situations. Judges can avoid the difficult task of assessing the emotional pain of a child or interpreting the motives of the parents making claims. Genetic ties define difficult family dilemmas as molecular problems, permitting the resolution of disputes on the basis of scientific testing. Similarly, ideas about genetic predisposition have been incorporated into criminal law where they are guiding complex decisions about responsibility, free will, and their bearing on appropriated punishment of criminal offenders.

Criminal Law and Punishment

The American legal system is built on the premise that responsibility, necessary to attribute culpability, rests on volition or on free will. To be responsible in the legal sense, a person must be able to freely exercise choice and to control his or her behaviour. This definition of responsibility underlies the insanity defence. And often, when scientific research suggests the biological origins of problematic behaviour – origins that may preclude the free exercise of choice – the research becomes the basis of new legal defences. The influence of sugar (the 'Twinky defence'), Pre-Menstrual Syndrome, Post-Partum Depression, and an extra Y chromosome have all been used by defence attorneys to argue that their clients acted involuntarily and they were, therefore, not properly subject to punishment.[15] In this context, the legal significance

14 Anthony Depalma, 'Custody Decision Dividing Experts', *New York Times*, 27 September 1992.

15 Rochelle Dreyfuss and Dorothy Nelkin, 'The Jurisprudence of Genetics', *Vanderbilt Law Review*, 45, 2 March 1992, pp. 321.

of genetic explanations lies in their bearing on free will. Those who defend themselves on genetic grounds, defining genetic predisposition to addiction or to violence as the cause of a criminal act, anticipate that this will be viewed as a full defence, or, at the very least, that it will mitigate punishment. As in family law, scientific, that is apparently definitive explanations, appeal as a way to resolve complex decisions about culpability. Thus, a criminologist, writing on the insanity defence, claims that new genetic and imaging technologies will provide 'direct scientific evidence of the defendant's brain ... and we need not rely on verbal reports and questions such as "Did the defendant know right from wrong?"[16]

The influence of genetic information on decisions about punishment can be illustrated by comparing two similar cases considered by the Supreme Court of California in 1990: *Baker* v. *State Bar*[17] and *In re Ewaniszyk.*[18] Both were disbarment proceedings against attorneys who had misappropriated client funds and had admitted the allegations. Both attorneys attributed their crime to substance abuse, and both had apparently learned to control their addiction. Yet Ewaniszyk was disbarred while Baker, who claimed a 'genetic predisposition' to alcoholism, was merely placed on probation. Why should the genetic factor matter if both attorneys posed similar dangers to their clients and demonstrated equivalent capacity for rehabilitation? In effect, Baker's genetic endowment mitigated his punishment because the court assumed that predisposition precluded free will. Driven by his genes, Baker could not be held responsible for his actions.

As images of 'criminal genes' or 'alcohol genes' shape popular understanding, claims of genetic predisposition are likely to enjoy greater public and legal acceptance. If so, cases like *Baker* and *Ewaniszyk* raise a broader question: how will society adequately protect itself from those who constitute a genetic threat? Logically, the California court could have made the opposite choice, disbarring the genetically addicted Baker, but not Ewaniszyk. Since substance abuse was not part of Ewaniszyk's genetic constitution, perhaps he was more capable of complete reformation than Baker, whose genetic predisposition could doom him forever to battle his own nature. If this interpretation were to guide such decisions (as it did in Kerr's fictional society), information about genetic predisposition could be used to argue for *enhancing* rather than mitigating punishment. Indeed, attributing behaviour to a genetic cause does not necessarily dictate the way institutions will use such information. Genetic information can serve quite different social agendas.

Sentencing decisions are often based on predictions of dangerousness, that is, on the probability that the defendant will continue to constitute a threat to society. Most

16 C.R. Jeffrey, *Attacks on the Insanity Defense Biological Psychiatry and new Perspectives on Criminal Behavior*, Springfield, Ill., Charles C. Thomas, 1985, p. 82.

17 781 P. 2d 1344 (Cal. 1989).

18 788 P.2d 690 (Cal. Ct. App. 1990).

courts have used social indicators, such as the nature of past behaviour or the criminal's family context, to make such predictions.[19] But the availability of genetic information suggests the added importance of biological predisposition – an apparently permanent risk. Just as those acquitted of crimes by reason of insanity can be removed from society for longer periods of time than the maximum sentence for their offences, so the genetically disordered could be permanently isolated. Though not wilfully responsible for their actions, their liberties may be circumscribed; for if violence reflects a genetic predisposition, rehabilitation may have minimal effect on the deterrence of future crime.

The past failures of rehabilitation schemes, rising costs, and the politicization of penal policy in the climate of scepticism about social welfare have all contributed to a decline in the rehabilitation ideal.[20] The terminology in this policy arena has changed from 'rehabilitation', building on assumptions about the importance of 'nurture,' to 'incapacitation', implying that criminal tendencies are fundamental and hard-wired. A psychologist, writing in a popular science magazine, explained this changing view: the criminal is 'a different species entirely' and this has implications for his rehabilitation: 'There is nothing by which to rehabilitate a criminal. There is no earlier condition of being responsible to which to restore him.'[21]

Growing public fears of crime and concerns about the administration of criminal justice are shaping the institutional uses of genetic essentialism in the 1990s. According to a National Academy of Sciences report, the United States is no more violent today than it has been at many times in the past. But the level of public fear has significantly increased, outpacing the actual rates of violent crime.[22]

Perceptions of crisis can sanction suspension of rules and rights, as control may come to seem more important than civil rights. There are, indeed, many calls for drastic actions. For example, in a 1992 letter to the editor of JAMA (the Journal of the American Medical Association), a physician insisted that 'Drastic times require drastic cures ... We cannot let such matters of conscience as the Second Amendment or preservation of personal freedoms stand in the way of public safety.'[23] And a columnist in the *Washington Post* suggested that, in the context of the crisis over crime, identifying genetic predisposition could justify social intervention. After all, he wrote: 'It seems pointless to wait until the high risk prospects actually commit crimes before

19 David Garland, 'Of Crime and Criminals' in Mike Maquire, Rod Morgan, and Roland Reiner (eds), *Oxford Handbook of Criminology*, 1994.

20 David Garland, *ibid.*, observes that there is often a difference between the discourse and the reality, for in fact treatment programmes do persist.

21 Jake's Page, 'Exposing the Criminal Mind', *Science 84*, September 1984, pp. 84-5.

22 National Research Council, *Understanding and Preventing Violence*, Washington, D,C., National Academy of Sciences Press, 1993, Chapter 1.

23 To the Editor from Roger Nemendez, *MD JAM*, 2 December 1992, p. 3070.

trying to do something to control them.' But he also recognized that genetic information about predisposition could not really be considered the equivalent of an actual act of violence: 'It seems both unconstitutional and unconscionable to convict them of the predisposition absent of any evidence of actual criminality.'[24]

A crisis mentality shaped the creation of the Bush administration's Violence Prevention Initiative which was – and still is – located in agencies dealing with matters of public health: the Department of Health and Human Services and the Centers for Disease Control. The programme was based on the assumption that crime must be approached as a public health problem and treated as if it were an epidemic. Preventing the spread of infection required the identification of 'natural carriers' assumed to be 'biologically prone' to criminal behaviour. Thus the program focussed on early detection of those at risk, especially in 'epidemiological cachement areas' (the inner cities). It called for screening about 100,000 inner city children to identify potential criminals. They would then be sent to special day camps where they would participate in remedial behavioural modification programs to help them avoid their 'fate'.

Applied to crime control, the public health model suggests that, as in the case of epidemics, individual rights must be suspended in order to protect the safety of the larger society. As novelist Kerr put it in his futuristic scenario of crime control in 2013: 'Determinism is not considered to constitute a menace to freedom in the new century. A pragmatic assumption of order … can hardly be questioned.'[25] Resonating with the popular acceptance of deterministic explanations, genetic information could offer opportunities for social control of unprecedented power as predispositions are employed to predict and avoid potential risk.

Prediction, Discrimination, and Social Control

The power to predict criminal tendencies, and therefore to control crime, has been a subject of journalistic speculations. A writer for *Science Digest* wondered whether children who are suspected of being genetically prone to criminal behaviour should be isolated or operated on just as defective cars are recalled to the factory.[26] Travellers on American Airlines could read in the free magazine, *The American Way*, that 'there are some who believe rape could be reduced greatly if we had a way to determine who was biologically predisposed to it and took preemptive action against them.'[27]

In some contexts, predispostions are already perceived as equivalent to being diseased. Investigations of genetic discrimination have found many cases in which

24 Whilom Rasberry, 'Criminal Types', *Washington Post*, 22 November, 1985.

25 Kerr, *op. cit.*, p. 44

26 Lawrence Taylor, 'The Genetic Defense', *Science Digest*, November 1982, p. 44.

27 Joel Keehn, 'The Long Arm of the Gene', *The American Way*, 15 March, 1992. pp 36-8.

'predisposition' was interpreted as determinative of disease.[28] For example, in 1992, a middle-aged man discovered that he had a genetic predisposition to a neuromuscular condition. He had experienced no obvious symptoms, and, in particular, he had never had an automobile accident or traffic violation in 20 years of driving. But when his insurance company learned through his medical records about his predisposition, it refused to renew his automobile insurance policy.

Many institutions and organizations – schools, motor vehicle bureaux, immigration authorities, sports teams, organ transplant registries, adoption agencies, the military, even university tenure committees – have significant interest in predictive information. Pressured to maintain economic viability, efficiency, and accountability, such institutions need to anticipate future contingencies and to avoid future risks. Genetic tests can differentiate individuals on the basis of ostensibly natural categories by identifying predispositions. They appear to resolve ambiguities while limiting the role of arbitrary interpretation.[29] And they can define the competence of individuals, controlling their access to social services, educational programs, insurance, or jobs. But while predictive information can be useful to institutions, it can be devastating for the individuals involved.

Genetic information can extend discrimination to new categories of persons. Those who carry the traits for certain disorders can be reconceptualized as the 'predisposed,' as 'persons at risk,' whose potential condition differentiates them from 'the normal,' and labels them unsuited for normal opportunities.[30] If an employer, educator, or insurer can make the case that the future, predicted status of their clients matters, then discrimination – the denial of opportunity for medical care, work, or education – can occur with impunity. Indeed, predictive genetic typing may create an underclass consisting of individuals whose genes seem to have marked them for the 'nowhere track.'

Medical institutions, and especially insurers, face economic pressures that encourage interest in predictive information. Genetic information can help health care providers conform to the reimbursement constraints of third party payers, control access to medical facilities, and plan for future demands in a system increasingly preoccupied with cost containment and economic accountability. Insurance underwriters, favouring 'preferred' customers who are expected to incur fewer medical expenses, welcome genetic information as a means to cut their costs. They can

28 Paul R. Billings *et al.*, 'Discrimination as a Consequence of Genetic Testing,' *American Journal of Human Genetics* 50, 1992, 476-482

29 Dorothy Nelkin and Laurence Tancredi, *Dangerous Diagnostics*, New York, Basic Books, 1989.

30 Abby Lippman argues that 'disorders and disabilities are not merely physiological or physical conditions with fixed contours. Rather, they are social products with variable shapes and distributions.' Abby Lippman, 'Prenatal Genetic Testing and Screening: Constructing Needs and Reinforcing Inequities', 17 *American Journal of Law & Medicine*, 15, 17 (1991).

incorporate genetic information into their underwriting methodology; people discovered to have a genetic predisposition to a costly disease may be denied insurance coverage or pay exorbitant rates.[31] Some health insurers have already tried to refuse coverage for children born with birth defects when the mothers, warned through prenatal testing, refused to abort.[32]

The right of access to genetic information is disputed. Insurers, for example, argue that their underwriting policies, involving distribution of known risks, require access to all known information about their clients. A 1992 public opinion survey by the March of Dimes Birth Defects Foundation suggests that many Americans do not regard genetic information to be 'private.' Most of those surveyed seemed to believe that genetic information is public property, and that those with a right to information about a person's genetic characteristics include not only those family members who might be immediately affected, but insurers and employers as well.[33]

Genetic information is rapidly becoming available for a growing number of diseases and conditions, reflecting the intersection of commercial interest in developing genetic tests with the policy and institutional stakes in predictive information. Demands for genetic information also reflect the appeal of scientific explanations that seem to justify social agendas. The promise of genetics is especially seductive because of its implications for social control. In recent years, growing perceptions of risk have encouraged the development of several fields of study – technology assessment, risk analysis, social forecasting, and even 'futuronics'[34] – devoted to predicting and, therefore, controlling risks. Actuarial reasoning has become a guiding principle, a way to anticipate future contingencies. The appeal of genomics research, which promises, according to its advocates, a 'blueprint of destiny', a 'medical crystal ball', lies in its image as a predictive science, a means to uncover predispositions.

Predisposition, however, is a malleable concept, easily exported from genetics to law and social policy.[35] In the quest to identify genetic predispositions, the statistically-

31 Benjamin Schatz, 'The AIDS Insurance Crisis: Underwriting or Overreaching?', 100 *Harvard Law Review*, 1782 (1987); Katherine Browkaw, 'Genetic Screening in the Workplace and Employer's Liability, ,23 *Columbia Journal of Legal and Social Problems*, 317m 327 n.49 (1990) cites cases in which genetic diseases have been excluded from coverage as 'pre-existing conditions'.

32 Larry Thompson, 'The Price of Knowledge: Genetic Tests that Predict Conditions Became a Two Edged Sword,' *Washington Post*, 10 October 1989.

33 Natalie Angier, 'Many Americans Say Genetic Information is Public Property', *New York Times*, 29 September 1992. *See also*; Louis Harris & Associates, 'Genetic Testing and Gene Therapy: National Survey Findings', *March of Dimes Birth Defects Foundation*, September 1992. This survey also found 40% of respondents approved the use of gene therapy for the enhancement of physical and behavioural traits as well as the treatment of disease.

34 Theodore Modis, *Predictions: Society's Telltale Signature Reveals the Past and Forecasts the Future*, New York, Simon and Schuster, 1992.

35 Laurence Tribe, 'Trial by Mathematics: Precision and Ritual in the Legal Process', 84 *Harvard Law Review*, 1329 (1971).

driven concept of correlation is often reduced to 'cause.' In science, terms such as 'predisposed' or 'at risk' are understood to mean that the individual is vulnerable to a disease that may or may not be expressed in the future. But institutions often interpret 'predisposition' as equivalent to current status. A genetic predisposition to alcoholism, for example, becomes an 'alcohol gene'. And an individual 'at risk' may be regarded as deserving differential treatment even before it is known whether or not the risk will materialize. Thus, people diagnosed as predisposed to a behaviour or disease may find themselves treated as if it were certain to be expressed, even when the relationship between genotype and phenotype – between a genetic mutation and its manifestation in actual behaviour or disease – is conditional, uncertain, and poorly understood.

Research in molecular biology is yielding powerful new information that may reduce ambiguity in some areas and define meaningful constraints in others. Institutions are understandably attracted to the predictions promised by a genetic 'map' and to the certainties implied by genetic explanations. But the institutional universe in which research is applied is never very neat, and science can rarely offer complete answers to complex real-world problems. While such applications may help institutions control uncertainty and contain costs, they can also have drastic effects on individuals as biology becomes a standard for opportunity and a justification for discrimination.

In the rush to incorporate the latest research into institutional decisions, the highly complex and poorly understood relationship between genetics and environment, between nature and nurture, may be grossly oversimplified. And in the urgency to find unambiguous solutions for social problems, important values such as equal opportunity, personal privacy, individual and family autonomy may be compromised or obscured. Assumptions about the importance of genetic information can change the meaning of choice and beliefs about free will. Screening to identify the genetic basis of intelligence or predisposition to learning or behavioural problems can affect the right to work. If social problems are located in the genes, reforming education, providing support through welfare programs, or opening opportunities through affirmative action would have limited effect. If proper families are defined as molecular families, this has implications for the thousands of successful family arrangements based on social and emotional ties. If crime is genetic, hard-wired, and inevitable, efforts to rehabilitate prisoners will be of no avail. And placing responsibility for social problems on the genetic predispositions of certain individuals can justify policies of exclusion in the interests of managing social problems, enhancing efficiency, or maintaining social control.

Bioethics Markets and Morals: The Case of Biotechnological Patents

Marco Ricolfi*

The field of moral reasoning, which usually is referred to as bioethics, is specifically linked with the kind of choices which have appropriately been characterized as tragic[1] to show that a conflict between ultimate values is involved in them. When one of the most authoritative scholars in the field[2] in recent times tried to give 'a first account of the areas in which choices at the frontiers of life are made', he presented a catalogue which indeed appears exemplary: 'to procreate or not; to intervene on the procreative process or not; to be informed of one's own genetic characters or not; to extend the term of life or not; to live or to die'. It is by no means a chance that around a list of this kind the structure of this conference has, so to say, shaped itself of its own accord.

In each of the areas encompassed, the conflict, it may be easily seen, concerns values or – in other terms – moral perspectives. Accordingly, it appears appropriate to speak about 'moral dilemmas' whenever a choice has to be made between such values: e.g. in connection with the situations in which a child is claimed simultaneously by the 'surrogate mother' and by the couple who has so to say 'contracted'[3] for it, a choice

* Professor of Law, University of Turin, Turino, Italy.

1 For the use of this terminology *see* G. Calabresi and P. Bobbit, *Tragic choices*, it. ed. *Scelte tragiche*, Giuffré, Milano, 1986.

2 S. Rodotà', *Repertorio di fine secolo*, Bari, 1992, 214. The chapter concerning bioethics is significantly devoted to 'The frontiers of life' (p. 210 ff.).

3 (3) *See*, for Italy, Trib. Monza, 27 October 1989, in *Foro It.*, 1990, I, 298 ff., and, for the U.S., New Jersey Court of Appeals, 31 March 1987 (*in re* Baby M.), in *Foro It.*, 1988, IV, 97 ff. with note by G. Ponzanelli, *Il caso Baby M., la 'surrogate mother' e il diritto italiano,* and New Jersey Supreme Court, 3 February 1988 (in the matter of Baby M.), in *Foro It.*, 1989, IV, 293 ff. with comments of G. Ponzanelli, *Ancora sul caso Baby M.: l'illegittimità dei contratti di 'sostituzione di maternità'*, and with comments of R. Clarizia, *Inseminazione artificiale, contratto di sostituzione di maternità, interesse del minore*.

Cosimo Marco Mazzoni (ed.), A Legal Framework for Bioethics, 131-142.
©1998 Kluwer Law International. Printed in The Netherlands.

between the 'right to parenthood' of the couple and the 'right to motherhood'[4] of the surrogate mother or, in connection with terminal patients, between the professional duties of the physician and the rules against the 'unproportionate use of therapeutic means'.[5]

I am not certain, however, that we are faced with a merely moral dilemma when we consider questions as the ones just referred to; and even more so, when we consider the range of problems which is linked to organ transplants. Even though one of the most adamant supporters of the liberalization of the rules governing this area[6] has endeavoured to establish the exquisitely moral character of the dilemma, there is enough evidence to support the conclusion that, on the recipients' side, strong claims are made not only in the name of a value which is indeed embedded in the Western tradition, the 'right to life', but also on behalf of well organized economic interests and well established markets (in the field of medical services and allied industries); and the significance of both for the debate cannot be neglected, except by those intellectual approaches which, under the cover of banning 'ideology', may have chosen to jettison in bulk all the legacy of realistic thought.

What seems beyond dispute is, however, that there is at least a single area – the one concerning the question of patentability of life forms – in which the heart of the matter lies not at the 'noble' level of the conflict between moral values but at the even more significant and dramatic, albeit 'lower', level of a conflict between ethical imperatives on the one side and interests on the other, or, if one prefers, between morals and markets. In this case, we are faced with a specific problem: we have to seek a trade-off between ultimate goals (values; moral perspectives) on the one side and a different goal, the quest for optimal allocation of resources in scientific and technologic innovation, on the other side, which surely is of paramount importance for our societies but clearly is only subordinate, in that allocative efficiency belongs to the realm of means and not of ends.

I shall try to outline the contours of this conflict; to set forth the legal techniques which are available to solve it and, finally, to examine the institutional background – under EEC law, Italian legislation being subject to it – against which the question has to be looked at.

It is well known that in the last decades biotechnological research has proved remarkably successful in various directions and has been moving along lines foresha-

4 I here use the word right in its wider (and, for those who reserve the term to the classic instances of *jus perfectum*, ambiguous) meaning, illustrated and discussed by N. Bobbio, *L'età dei diritti,* Torino, 1990, XVI e segg.

5 In the terminology adopted by the Sacra Congregazione per la dottrina della fede in its *Dichiarazione sull'eutanasia* of 1980. *See also* S. Rodotà', *Repertorio*, cit., 228 ff.

6 H.T. Engelhardt Jr., *Il corpo in vendita: dilemmi morali della secolarizzazione*, in (a cura di S. Rodotà'), *Questioni di bioetica*, Bari, 1993, 123 ff.

dowing advancements in the areas of genetic engineering in connection with plants, animals and man which seem very promising indeed. Virus resistant and insect repellent plant varieties have been developed;[7] by appropriate genetic manipulation sheep have been turned into 'animal factories' for the large scale production of an important chemical as human factor VIII (essential in the treatment of haemophilia).[8] In the human field biotechnology has enabled large scale production of insulin by means of RDNA, the preparation of interferons against cancer and leukaemia, of vaccines, of tissue plasminogen activator (TPA) against heart attacks; in recent times promising perspectives seem to have been opened up in the therapy of diseases like adenosin-deaminase (ADA) and perhaps also of sickle cell anaemia, cystic fibrosis and muscular dystrophy.[9]

It is not difficult to single out the main actors of this extraordinary momentum in biotechnological advancement. Surely, public research institutions have not abdicated their pivotal role in basic research; but to a large extent a tight web of allegiances between the private sector and public research has dictated the timing and the priorities even of the latter.[10] Therefore it might be accurate to say that, in this domain more than in others, it has been private businesses, both large and small, which dominated the process. In the agricultural field, while the role played by traditional plant breeders has been extremely limited, the leadership has passed into the hands of agro-chemical and veterinary firms;[11] in the human field, multinational firms active in the chemical and pharmaceutical areas, along with a panoply of small but highly innovative firms, have taken the lead.[12]

Private business as the ones just indicated have certainly not shied away from posing one of the most appropriate questions relating to any innovative process: what is the kind of legal protection available to those who obtain first access to a new technology? It is also hardly surprising that in the Western world and in Europe[13] the reply favoured by those asking the question has been found in the resort to the patent

7 For a review of this kind of innovation *see* A. Albertini, 'Biotecnologie e paesi in via di sviluppo', in *Questioni di bioetica*, cit., 289 ff.

8 R. Whaite-N. Jones, 'Biotechnological Patents in Europe: The Draft Directive', in 5 *EIPR*, 1989, 145 ff. at 146.

9 *See* Y. Ko, 'An Economic Analysis of Biotechnology Patent Protection, in 102 *Yale L. J.*', 1992, 777 ff., at 783-4, where, at notes 46-8, additional references, and R.M. Henig, 'Gene Therapy: Medicine's New Frontier', in *Dialogue*, 1992, 51 ff.

10 *See*, also for additional references, Y. Ko, *op. cit.*, 794 and n. 115 and, in a critical perspective, R.C. Lewontin, 'The Dream of the Human Genome', in *New York Review of Books,* 28 May 1992, 31 ff., at 38.

11 According to A. Albertini, *op. cit.*, 299, 'the twenty larger agrochemical and veterinary firms have invested in 1990 sums in the range of 300 million dollars in biotechnological R. & D.'.

12 *See* Y. Ko, *op. cit.*, 794-5 and n. 120.

13 *See* the *Joint Position* adopted by the EEC Council concerning the Draft Directive on legal protection of biotechnological inventions issued on 23 February 1994.

system, which, after all, is traditionally considered capable of providing an incentive to industrial research through the temporary monopoly afforded by patentee's exclusive rights.

However, the idea of extending patent protection to biotechnological innovation has immediately raised serious questions. As these fall into two categories, the one intrinsic to the logic of the patent monopoly, the other extrinsic to it, it appears advisable to keep them analytically separate.

For the present purpose, it appears sufficient to observe that the problems falling in the first category are rooted in the circumstance that the patent system originates from the mechanic field and, while it has adapted itself with some twists and turns to new areas as chemical and pharmaceutical innovation, it now seems to face greater difficulties when called to extend its reach to situations in which the protection should cover living and self-reproducing matter.[14]

The problems falling into the second category, which are directly relevant to the questions raised above, have to deal with the fact that the extension of patent monopoly to biotechnology may conflict with:

(a) the preservation of biological and genetic diversity existing in nature;
(b) the need of greater fairness in the industry/agriculture and North/South relations;
(c) the right of the individual – and of the future generations – that human genetic characteristics are not tampered with.

What are the forms taken by the conflict between patent protection of technology and the values and constraints listed above?

A. The environmental balance of our planet is based on the preservation of genetic diversity in the vegetal field.

Such diversity has been kept through the centuries by agriculture and, more specifically, by local agricultural techniques employed in cloistered areas in the Third world and by plant breeders. It is presently fostered by legislation on plant varieties protection (1961 UPOV Convention) which, in the effort of providing a protection mechanism compatible with the characters of living matter, grants a research exemption[15] and the right to protection to whomever may breed a new variety even though the same is obtained from matter for which another subject has obtained prior protection.

14 For an overview *see* also my paper 'La brevettabilità della materia vivente: fra mercato e nuovi diritti', in *Giur. It.*, 1993, IV, 292 ff. and, with specific reference to patentability and infringement, Y. Ko, *op. cit.*

15 *See* Art. 5 (3) of the UPOV Convention of 1961. The relevant rules have been modified in a more restrictive direction by Art. 14 (5) of the new Convention signed on 19 March 1991.

According to the views held by scholars with different academic backgrounds[16] and shared by environment protection groups,[17] the extension of patent protection to biotechnology would increase the dependence of agriculture on chemical industry and would lead to a drastic erosion of genetic diversity. There is some empirical evidence confirming this alarming prospect: it may be easily proved that 'the stock of vegetal species necessary to sustain genetic diversity decreases, as plant varieties marketed by multinationals replace, in ever increasing lots of land, local cultivars of undeveloped countries and thereby homogenize the genetic characters of harvests';[18] and it is easy to see how such homogeneity of the harvests enhances their 'vulnerability to parasites and pathogens':[19] it is well known that bio-diversity is a form of self-insurance against epidemics and famine.

More arduous it may seem to explain why access to patenting for genetic engineering relating to plants should increase the dependence of agriculture on chemical industry and thereby contribute to the erosion of bio-diversity. In this regard, some characters of the patent system should be considered: for patent purposes, it is sufficient that one character of a certain seed or seed group is transformed by chemical or genetic means for the patent monopoly to extend to the altered seed at large and its offspring.[20] In turn, in its present form the patent system does not provide for a mechanism equivalent to the research exemption afforded by the UPOV Convention in connection with those situations in which the new plant variety is generated on the basis of a patented plant or seed instead of a plant variety protected under UPOV. Therefore, resort to patent protection may prevent plant breeders, who are believed to give a substantial contribution to bio-diversity through their cross-breeding efforts,[21] from

16 Among others J.J. Hardon, 'Industrial Patents, Plant Breeding and Genetic Resources: A Plant Breeder's View', in *Patenting Life Forms in Europe*, Proceedings of an International Conference at the European Parliament', Brussels, 7-8 February 1989, Barcelona, 1989, 34 ff.; P. Kennedy, 'Preparing for the 21st Century: Winners and Losers', in *New York Review of Books*, 11 February 1993, 32 ff., at 42 and A. Albertini, *op. cit.*, 298 ff.

17 *See* the positions expressed in this respect by H. Hobbelink for the GRAIN group in 'European Parliament, Public Hearing on the Legal Protection of Biotechnological Inventions', 11 May 1990, PE 141.102 (55/89), 34 ff. and by the Genetics Forum in the brochure 'Patent Concern. Patenting of Plants and Animals', London, 1990, 3.

18 A. Albertini, *op. cit.*, 299.

19 *Ibid.*

20 *See* G. Ghidini-S. Hassan, *Biotecnologie, novità vegetali e brevetti,* Milano, 1990.

21 It should, however, be noted, that the views on the impact of plant breeders on biological diversity differ widely. According to the Report of the EEC Commission and to the statements of the AIPPI (in the *Nouveau Rapport revisé établi par le Bureau del l'OMPI, Comité d'experts sur les inventions biotechnologiques et la proprieté industrielle. Quatrieme session*, Geneve, 24-28 October 1988, Biot/CE/IV/2, 46), the research exemption might have an adverse impact as it is apt to divert plant breeders' investments towards small variations of pre-existing plant stock and not towards true basic improvements. An opposite opinion is expressed by AIPH (*ivi*, 49 e 65) as well as by R. Whaite-N. Jones, *op. cit.*, 145, 146.

marketing their new varieties unless consent by patent holders in the originating variety is obtained – which, it is submitted, is not forthcoming short of the payment of possibly substantial licensing fees or royalties.

B. The extension of the patent mechanism might well lead to an additional form of 'unequal exchange' between the North and the South of the world.

A moment ago reference was made to genetic engineering carried out in connection with seeds or plants. It should now be added that usually the process entails insertion of genes obtained by biotechnological research onto spontaneous germoplasm or, in other words, vegetal species preserved in their pristine forms by the most backward and sheltered agricultural systems. Presently no constraint is foreseen on the free use of preserved germoplasm. Therefore, a situation may arise in which, while Third World countries have no way to oppose the free exploitation by the rest of the world economy of the germoplasm preserved by them, its patenting in a genetically modified form gives birth to a monopoly which the patentee may enforce as a barrier against agricultural exports incorporating the patented characteristic even though they originate from the same Third World country which preserved the corresponding germoplasm. It is therefore hardly surprising that Third World countries, hit by a severe deterioration of the overall trading terms of their production,[22] are considering to resort to germoplasm embargo.[23]

Such an adverse impact of the extension of patent protection to biotechnology on the terms of North/South trade is the ultimate outcome of a mechanism whereby the protection available to patentees concerns not only propagating material (seeds, genes) but also the products deriving therefrom,[24] including – according to the provisions of draft legislation pending[25] – all subsequent generations of protected living matter.

22 For some recent data *see* F. Praussello, "E' possibile un commercio 'equo e solidale'", in *Il mulino*, 1994, 125 ff., especially at 127 ff. and S. Zamagni, *Sviluppo, efficienza e solidarietà: per un mondo non ineguale, Il mulino*, 1993, 394 ff. and the data and estimates at 399.

23 'A Report on Germoplasm Embargoes, Rural Advancement Fund International', 1988, quoted in *Patent Concern*, cit., 3 e 6. *See also*, in the same direction, J.P. Chiaradia Bousquet, 'Plant Genetic Resources: Protection of Rights', in *Patenting Life Forms*, cit., specially at 47. Recent information on the subject are to be found in C. Grande, 'Variabilità genetica, Non rubare i semi d'altri: in pericolo troppe specie locali', in *La Stampa, TuttoScienze*, 14 October 1993, p. 3.

24 As provided by patent law (*see* Art. 1 of Royal Decree n. 1127 of 29 June 1939 and subsequent amendments, as revised by Presidential Decree n. 338 of 22 June 1979) but not by plant variety protection legislation (*see* Art. 4 of Presidential Decree n. 974 of 12 August 1974, as amended by Presidential Decree n. 338 of 22 June 1979 and by Act n. 620 of 14 October 1985).

25 Art. 10 of the *Joint position*.

C. Genetic engineering relating to germ cells not only affects the individual concerned but also his (or her) offspring; its patenting risks therefore to collide with the – individual and collective – right to freedom from genetic manipulation.[26]

When we rest for a moment to consider the kind of conflict arising in the above situations from the perspective of a purely ethical judgement, we cannot escape the conclusion that only one of the conflicting terms should prevail. While it is beyond dispute that there is a collective interest that biotechnological research is fostered and there may be a reasonable – albeit not unchallenged[27] degree of consensus on the appropriateness of the patent monopoly to attain such a goal, there is no way to refute the argument that, at least for purposes of ethical reasoning the underlying quest for optimal allocation of resources has a lower ranking than claims, as the ones referred to in lett. A) and C) above, which, according to an eminent scholar,[28] belong to the third and fourth 'generation' of fundamental rights and the value of distributive justice, as described in lett. B). In case of conflict, efficiency should give way to claims and values of such a standing.

26 On this kind of issue *see*, in addition to the brief but remarkable notes by N. Bobbio, *L'età dei diritti*, cit., XV, the outstanding pages by W. Rothley, *Report Problemi etici e giuridici della manipolazione genetica e della fecondazione artificiale umana, Parlamento Europeo, Commissione giuridica e per gli affari dei cittadini*, Luxemburg, 1990, 27 ff. specially at 36 ff. and S. Rodotà', *Repertorio*, cit., 223. The final resolution of the fifth Conference on bioethics of the seven most industrialized countries (1988) states: 'the delegates have established that at this stage there are neither medical grounds nor moral reasons which warrant intentional genetic manipulation of human germ cells.' In connection with the – indeed sinister – possibility of the pursuit of goals of 'enhancement engineering' *see* R.M. Hennig, *op. cit.*, p. 54 and, in much stricter terms, F.D. Busnelli,'Opzioni e principi normativi per una disciplina normativa delle biotecnologie avanzate', in *Riv. crit. dir. priv.*, 1991, 283 ff. at 291-2. 'Suggestions favourable to a more flexible approach in this regard are made by J. Harris, 'Regolazione bioetica e legge', in *Questioni di bioetica*, cit., 331, specially at 335 and by M. Mori, *La 'novità' della bioetica, ivi*, 397 e segg. at 412.

27 Indeed, three decades ago prof. F. Machlup (*An Economic Review of the Patent System*, Study n. 15, Subcommittee on Patents, Trademarks and Copyright of the Committee of the Judiciary, U.S. Senate, 85th Congress, Second Session, Washington D.C, 1958) reached the conclusion that it is not possible to establish whether the allocative costs of the patent system outweigh its benefits. For a more optimistic view *see*, however, in specific connection to biotechnology, F.K. Beier-J. Straus, *Patents in a Time of Rapid Scientific and Technological Change*, in the OCSE Report (edited by F.K. Beier, R.S. Crespi and J. Straus) *Biotechnology and Patent Protection. An International Review*, 1985, 15 and, in general terms, M. Lehman, 'Property and Intellectual Property: Property Rights as Restrictions on Competition in Furtherance of Competition', in 20 *I.I.C.*, 1989, 1 ff.
An excellent discussion of economic literature in the field is in E. Kaufer, *The Incentives to rift für die gesamte Staatswissenschaft- Journal of Institutional and Theoretical Economics, 1986, 210 ff.* and now in Y. Ko, *op. cit.*, 791 ff.

28 N. Bobbio, *L'età dei diritti*, cit., XIV f. It easy to understand that claims relating to the environment are amenable to a variety of philosophical foundations: for a persuasive perspective *see* now S. Maffettone, 'La questione ambientale: metafisica e politica', in *Questioni di bioetica*, cit., 235 ff. and, for a fascinating account, H. Jonas, *Il principio responsabilità. Un'etica per la società tecnologica*, Torino, 1990.

To be sure, in connection with the area which I referred to under C (patenting of genetic engineering on germ cells) there has been dispute both on the status of the claim to genetic integrity and on the very possibility that it may conflict with patent protection.

It seems, however, that the argument that claims to genetic integrity may be waived by the free consent of interested parties[29] misses the point that intervention on germ cells affects not only the party directly concerned but also his (or her) offspring and, *a fortiori*, the future generations. In such a situation, it seems appropriate to doubt that decisions may be made by (present) political majorities,[30] let alone by the immediately affected individuals.

The argument has also been put forward that patenting of genetic engineering relating to germ cells does not conflict with any value because it does not entail by itself authorization to its actual use: after all, patenting of weapons is clearly admissible because the very limited circumstances in which they may be employed are painstakingly defined by law. It should nevertheless be noted that, while certainly there are instances in which resort to weapons may be legitimate (e.g., use by police in given circumstances, self-defence and even hunting), no such exceptions are to be found in connection with manipulation of germ cells; and we cannot easily forget that a rule in favour of patenting would provoke a flow of financial resources in the field of research on genetic engineering relating to germ cells large enough to ultimately endanger the preservation of prohibitions to its use.

It seems therefore reasonable to stick to the conclusions previously reached on both counts. However, it is apparent that the legislative process leads to an outcome at variance with the choices mandated by ethical reasoning: in short, market interests systematically prevail over moral values.

This result is hardly surprising in the European matrix: except in exceptional cases – which may present themselves when extraordinary mobilizations transform values into interests[31] – a legislative process which confers law-making powers on executive bodies like the EEC Commission and the Council and marginalizes the Parliament, the reasons of power are bound to prevail over the powers of reason.

In making the last point, I do not want to suggest that ethical reasoning is of no relevance in this field. On the contrary, the question of the patenting of biotechnology seems to hold in store a wider lesson concerning the difficulties to be found when a

29 Put forward, for instance, by B. Lemennicier, 'Le corps humain: propriété de l'Etat ou propriété de soi', in *Droits*, 13, 1991, 112. For a critical evaluation of this perspective *see* F.D. Busnelli, *op. cit.*, p. 286.

30 For a similar point *see* S. Rodotà, *Introduzione* a *Questioni di bioetica*, cit., XI, who rightly remarks that in this event the decision might turn out to be irreversible even though a subsequent majority might change its mind.

31 As envisaged by A. Pizzorno, 'Sulla teoria dei movimenti collettivi', in *Le radici della politica assoluta e altri saggi*, Milano, 1993, 129 ff.

coordination between markets and morals is attempted. It seems that, when the ones conflict with the others, it is not enough to show that the moral principles invoked are valid (are rationally founded) and overriding (have an axiologic priority over the market interests) but an additional step is to be made, to prove that the relevant principles are implemented through the choice of the one alternative among all theoretically possible competing approaches which minimizes the potential for adverse impact on efficiency.[32]

How can such a condition be satisfied? In principle, this may happen to the extent the values referred above under letters A, B and C are implemented through means consistent with market mechanisms and specifically with the functioning of the patent system.

The task thus set is to show in detail which particular solutions may satisfy the criterion just set forth in each of the conflict areas previously described.

A first step towards the setting up of rules favouring the preservation of bio-diversity (lett. A above) may be made by establishing a *legal licence* mechanism in favour of any party who may wish to incorporate a biotechnological patent into a new vegetal variety.

The corresponding rule may have a positive impact on bio-diversity in that it plays a role similar to the research exemption in the UPOV system and avoids that plant breeders who contribute to biodiversity by creating new plant varieties are placed at the mercy of holders of blocking biotechnological patents.

To achieve this aim, the rule enables plant breeders to incorporate a biotechnological invention into their (new) varieties even before obtaining the patent holder's consent, provided they pay the latter a royalty at a rate set by legislation and proportional to the end-sale price of the patent incorporating plants or seeds. While the corresponding amount may be easily transferred forward by the well known cost-translation mechanisms,[33] the flow of remuneration to patentees thus generated would at the same time provide a reasonable reward for biotechnological research.

It has to be stressed, however, that this kind of outcome may be obtained only through a genuine *legal licence*,[34] as the same entails that the need for patentee's authorization to plant breeders is replaced by payment of the flat royalty rate. This

32 Accordingly, arguments in this kind of areas may not resort to the traditional techniques of demonstrative reason and must fall back on those categories of proofs which, by an approach which simultaneously rejects moral rationalism and the application of analytical tools to ethics, are indicated as 'non demonstrative': for the initial highliting of the roads accessible to non demonstrative reason for purpose of normative choices *see* C. Perelman-L. Olbrechts-Tyteca, *Trattato dell'argo-mentazione. La nuova retorica*, Vol. I, Torino, 1976, 3 e segg.

33 As illustrated, for instance and with specific regard to patent licensing, by M. Wheeler, 'A Re-examination of Antitrust Law and Exclusive Territorial Grants by Patentees', in 119 *U. Pa. L. Rev.*, 1971, 642 ff. at 655.

34 In accordance with the wording advanced at n. 36 of my work *La brevettabilità*, cit.

purpose is not achieved, on the contrary, by the compulsory licence provisions of the present text of the draft directive,[35] as past experience shows that this latter mechanism is of no practical avail[36] as its smooth functioning rests on the heroic assumption that the parties be in principle prepared to reach an agreement on the terms and conditions (including royalty rate) of the licence.

If we pass to consider the questions connected with biotechnolgy patents' impact on North/South 'unequal exchange' (lett. B above), we must at the onset note that problems of this import may not be dealt with by simple adjustments of characters and scope of patent protection. However, a few steps in the right direction may be made also in this very limited perspective.

If we consider that in this connection the aim is to prevent that patents are exploited to build additional artificial barriers to the flow of trade originating from Third World countries, we readily realize that a few rules may be fashioned to approach this goal.

First of all, the rules concerning the exhaustion of the patent right should clarify that patent monopoly does not extend to those generations of living matter which do not keep the essential characters for which patent protection was granted in the first place.

Additionally, an extension by international Treaty of the legal licence mechanism – as described in the previous paragraph – from the EEC level to plant varieties originating from Third World countries would certainly contribute to keeping the gates open to agricultural trade.

Solutions of this kind are certainly tentative and of low profile. They certainly must be supplemented by a comprehensive array of additional measures of Third World countries, which supply germoplasm free of charge to the rest of humankind.

Such measures are currently being debated at international level. Moreover, the steps I just described seem to me to be mandated by the Rio de Janeiro Convention and specifically by the third and fifth section of Art. 16.[37] The first provision establishes that developing countries which 'supply genetic resources' should have 'access to technology intended for the exploitation of said resources... including patented technology'; the second is intended to prevent that patents may be used to create 'obstacles to the achievement of the objectives of the Convention' including, *per* Art. 1, 'the fair and equitable apportionment of the advantages flowing from the exploitation of genetic resources'.

I should add that failure to adopt corresponding measures – including the first steps I described above – would not just mean an obtuse entrenchment in the present *status*

35 Art. 14 of the *Joint position*, cit.

36 *See*, with specific regard to the field, R. Whaite-N. Jones, *op. cit.*, at 151 and 153.

37 The text of the Convention on Biologic Diversity of 5 June 1992, which is being adopted also by the EEC, is attached to the 'Council's proposal' relating to the adoption of the Convention published 21 December 1992, in COM(92) 509 def.

quo but would amount to behaviour warranting resort to germoplasm embargo by Third World countries under Sec. 4 of Art. 21 of the Convention itself.

A straightforward and clearcut solution seems appropriate in connection with the questions above indicated under lett. C.

In this regard, it should be provided that: 'Inventions relating to human germ cells, genetic engineering processes relating thereto and any and all kinds of means whereby genetic identity of future generations may be altered are not patentable'.

Such a rule entails an absolute and unconditional ban on patenting of any form of genetic engineering relating to germ cells. In this regard, the argument – underlying the text accepted by a Resolution of the European Parliament[38] – whereby patentability should be admitted when genetic engineering, albeit concerning germ cells, has therapeutic aims and respects human dignity,[39] seems unsound: treading on the downward slope of 'therapeutic' aims we are bound to meet, sooner or later, the sinister claims of 'enhancement engineering' (e.g., in the so-called 'cure' of depressions) which ring an ominous bell to those who believe in liberal values.

We are now in a position to perceive that in pursuing goals which go beyond allocative efficiency the alternatives selected appear, on each of the counts considered, consistent with the basic features of the market oriented patent law system. It is true that in some instances the rules have been fashioned after the example set by the UPOV Convention: but this approach, which certainly is appropriate when protection concerns living – as opposed to inanimate – matter, also leads to provisions (relating to legal licences and exhaustion) which are consistent with the patent law system and the doctrines which marked its evolution in the centuries.

More specifically, both the provision of a legal licence and the simultaneous resort to the same and to a redefinition of exhaustion, while seeming apt to strike a balance between the legitimate interest of the patent holders and collective goals as the preservation of biodiversity and fairness in North-South exchange, are taken from the traditional tools to which intellectual protection has made resort when confronted with novel realities. In turn, the ban on patenting of genetic engineering relating to germ cells is not repugnant to a body of law which, in the area of patent protection, has recurrently incorporated significant limitations to patentability for reasons of public interest.

It appears, therefore, that the proposals here put forward may be able to satisfy the requiremets set before and that, at least in the instance before us, nothing prevents that

38 Doc. A 2-327/88, n. 25. *See* however the appropriate critical remarks by S. Rodotà', 'Modelli culturali e orizzonti della bioetica', in *Questioni di bioetica*, cit., 421 f.

39 Such is the proposal advanced by the Amendment of Representativa Merz at the European Parliament (PE 150.463/Em. 44 Or. PAN) and adopted 20 January 1992 by the Commission for legal Affairs and Citizens' Rights of the same European Parliament and thereafter by lett. b) of n. 3 of Art. 2 of the *Joint position*.

aims framed in terms of justice may be achieved through means which are compatible with the constrainsts posed by the search for efficiency. It might well be said that it is not impossible that the same set of rules is able to apportion different categories of public goods – here optimal allocation on the one side, environmental balance, distributive fairness and genetic integrity on the other side – in accordance with the logics which pertain to each of them.[40]

Normative approaches as the one here advocated are usually countered by the objection that they lead to forms of protection to inventors which are weaker than the ones presently afforded to technological advances by the North American and Japanese legal systems.

A similar line of reasoning disregards that the boundaries of patent protection are quite uncertain also for the other legal systems and moreover ignores that increased protection at the EEC level would certainly benefit more American and Japanese firms than their European competitors.[41]

More to the point, it should be remebered that, in the area we are considering, the goal of legislation is not confined to creating a competitive advantage on behalf of European firms over their American and Japanese counterparts. Such a narrow approach would run counter the provisions of the Rome Treaty setting up the EEC, which provide that the aims of the Community include, *inter alia*, 'a harmonious development of economic activities' and 'an accelerated raising of the standard of living' (Art. 2) and clarify that resort to competitive efficiency is but one of the means designed to reach those purposes (Art. 3, lett. f).

In this perspective, the task of EEC legislation is not just to engage in a sterile competitive race and to bring down our relevant rules to the level set by U.S. and Japanese standards but to use of all the imagination and of all the realism we are capable of in the search for solutions – as the ones here suggested – which may prove apt to combine fairness and efficiency while respecting the moral values underpinning our societies.

40 For the corresponding theoretical framework *see* M. Walzer, *Sfere di giustizia*, Milano, 1987, 15-60 and 312-20.

41 In accordance to data presented by I. Kretschmer ('Biotechnologie: Vorschlag einer EG-Richtlinie', in *GRUR*, 1988, 890 e segg., 892), patent applications at the pending at the UPO were, at the time, originating at 45% from the U.S., 15% from Japan and only 10% from Germany.

5. Markets for Human Organs

Markets for Human Organs

Henry Hansmann*

Each year, many thousands of people die who could have lived if suitable organs had been available for transplantation. At the same time, many potentially transplantable organs go unused. In the United States, for instance, of the roughly 20,000 persons who die each year under circumstances that make their organs suitable for transplantation, only about 15% actually have their organs 'harvested' (as the medical jargon puts it) for transplants.

From opinion surveys, it appears that this low percentage is not a reflection of strong and widespread objections on the part of the deceased individuals, or their families, to organ donation. Consequently, one might be tempted to attribute the low donation rate to the particular legal requirement that prevails in the United States, which requires that either the deceased or his family expressly give consent before organs can be removed. In Europe, in contrast, most countries have adopted a rule of 'presumed consent,' under which organs are assumed available for transplant unless an objection is registered, either by the decedent prior to death or by the next of kin. Yet none of the European countries have notably better donation rates than does the United States, apparently because even strictly construed presumed consent laws function in practice like the American régime under which explicit approval is required.[1]

Moreover, even the relatively few organs that are extracted are often not transplanted to the persons who need them most or to whom they are best suited. In the United States, for example, organs are generally transplanted to patients at the hospital that extracts them, or at another hospital served by the same local regional transplant center, even if there is a more suitable recipient (or a more able transplant team) located elsewhere. This is not because the organs cannot be transported, but because the

* Professor of Law, Yale Law School, USA.

1 *See* B. Gerson, 'Refining the Law of Organ Donation: Lessons from the French Law of Presumed Consent', 19 *New York University Journal of International Law and Politics* 1013 (1987).

Cosimo Marco Mazzoni (ed.), A Legal Framework for Bioethics, 145-159.
©1998 *Kluwer Law International. Printed in The Netherlands.*

hospital that extracts them, and the regional transplant center, have little incentive to do otherwise.

Clearly there is substantial opportunity for saving lives by improving the systems by which transplantable organs are obtained and distributed. It is natural to ask whether such improvement might come if we were to offer compensation to organ donors. Since 1984, however, it has been a federal crime in the United States 'for any person to knowingly acquire, receive, or otherwise transfer any human organ for valuable consideration for use in human transplantation.' Consequently, any effort to develop a compensation system – what we might loosely call a 'market for organs' – has been ruled out as a possible solution in the United States, as it apparently also has been throughout Europe. Unfortunately, this prohibition has been adopted casually, without serious examination of the potential advantages or disadvantages of compensation systems. Because so many lives are at stake, the subject deserves the most thoughtful and careful consideration. In this essay, I offer a survey of the issues involved.[2]

Cadaveric Organs

Most transplantable organs that are vital to life – including hearts, lungs, and livers – cannot be taken from a living donor, but only from cadavers. Kidneys are the important exception. Since humans have two kidneys, yet only one is needed for normal functioning, a living individual can donate a kidney with little risk to their health. When speaking of markets for organs, therefore, we must be careful to distinguish between organs from cadavers and organs from living persons. Because cadavers are the most important source of organs (including kidneys), I shall focus first on the potential for markets for cadaveric organs, leaving the question of living donors to be dealt with separately below.

What Kind of a Market?

Before we can judge the potential advantages and disadvantages of a market system for procuring or allocating human organs, we must have some idea of what that market would look like. Obviously one cannot purchase an organ from a person who is already dead. Also, since persons who die suddenly – such as young persons who die of head injuries in motor vehicle accidents – are the best source of transplantable organs, it is

2 A more detailed discussion of some of the issues discussed here appears in Henry Hansmann, 'The Economics and Ethics of Markets for Human Organs', 14 *Journal of Health Policy, Politics, and Law* 57-85 (1989), reprinted in James Blumstein and Frank Sloane, editors, *Organ Transplant Policy*, Duke University Press, 1990, upon which I have drawn for portions of the exposition here.

infeasible to wait until a prospective donor is about to die before seeking to purchase their organs. Finally, it seems unwise to seek to purchase organs from the families of deceased individuals: even if legislation were adopted that conferred the property rights to a person's organs to their next of kin upon death, the brief hours following an individual's death provide a period of time that is too short, and too consumed by shock and grief, for the family to engage in commercial transactions concerning the use of the corpse.

Consequently, the most promising method for establishing a market in cadaveric organs is to structure it as a futures market, in which the right to harvest a person's organs upon his death is purchased from him far in advance, while he is alive and well. There are a variety of ways in which such a futures market might be structured. In countries, like the United States, in which health insurance is privately purchased, a promising possibility is to integrate the purchase of rights to organs with the sale of health insurance. For the sake of concreteness, I shall briefly describe such a scheme here. In countries such as Italy, in which most individuals do not purchase health insurance, other purchasers of the futures would need to be found – a point to which I shall return below.

Purchasing Organs Through Insurance

Health insurance companies would be natural purchasers of future rights to organs because these companies are already involved in the types of actuarial calculations and financial transactions that would be involved. Insurers might simply insert in their annual premium statements a provision (a check box would probably suffice) by means of which policyholders could indicate that, in case they were to die during the period (generally the coming year) covered by the premium statement, the insurance company or its assignees would have the right to harvest any of the insured's organs that were suitable for transplantation. In return for checking this box, the insured would receive a specified reduction in their insurance premium. (Alternatively, the insured could be required to check a box if they did *not* want to assign to the company the rights to their organs, in which case a specified amount would be added to their insurance premium. Both to take advantage of inertia, and for the psychological framing issues we shall discuss below, this would probably be the more attractive approach.) Individuals would be free to change their mind about being an organ donor annually, or at whatever interval their insurance policy is renewed.

Each insurance company would submit to a central national registry the identification of each of its insureds who had elected to be donors. The registry could be governmentally run or, perhaps better, organized as a cooperative owned by the insurance companies that purchase the organ futures, much as the MasterCharge credit clearing system is owned cooperatively by the hundreds of local banks that sell MasterCharge credit cards. Hospitals would be required (or induced by the offer of payment or the threat of financial liability) to check this national registry upon the death of any patient whose organs are potentially suitable for transplantation. If the patient were currently enrolled in the registry, the hospital would indicate to the registry which of the patient's organs were available, and suitable recipients would be located through a national matching network connected with the registry. A recipient of one of the deceased's organs (or the recipient's health insurer) would then be obliged to pay the deceased's insurance company, or their assignee, the latter's specified price for an organ upon accepting it for transplant. Any individual who had not sold such a futures contract for their organs prior to their death would be conclusively presumed to wish not to have their organs made available for transplant.

A country with publicly financed health care would need to turn to institutions other than health insurance companies to purchase organ futures. One natural choice would be sellers of other types of insurance, such as automobile insurance, life insurance, or property insurance, although a variety of other institutions, including public utilities that provide telephone, electricity, or gas service, could also easily serve this role.[3] Indeed, subject to modest regulation, the right to purchase organ futures could be left open to potential entrants of any type. The initial purchasers of the futures probably would, in any case, immediately resell the rights to a smaller number of firms that specialize in holding such contracts.

Prices

The price (or premium reduction) that an insurance company would pay for the future right to cadaveric organs would depend on the price that they could obtain for those organs at the time of removal. Since the insurance business is reasonably competitive, presumably insurance companies would be able to take only a market rate of return for their efforts as intermediaries in such transactions; the rest of the (expected) price received by the insurance companies for the harvested organs would be passed through to their policyholders in the premium reductions offered them.

How would the price for the harvested organs be determined? One possibility, discussed briefly at the end of this essay, would be to establish a market in harvested organs and let the forces of supply and demand determine the ultimate price. The system would also be perfectly workable, however, if the price that an insurance

3 Another possibility is to have the State purchase the rights. For example, it has been seriously proposed in the United States that states offer a reduction in the fee for issuing or renewing a driver's license to individuals who sign an organ donation form. Of course this scheme, like all other compensation schemes, would clearly violate current federal law criminalizing the purchase of organs.

company could obtain for a cadaveric organ were set administratively by the government rather than by the market.

For example, such a scheme could be employed in the context of the system for organ procurement currently employed in the United States. Under that system, organs are harvested and distributed through a network of roughly 70 regional nonprofit organ procurement agencies that effectively have local monopolies on the supply of organs. These agencies charge prices for the organs they procure that are, on average, just sufficient to cover their costs. At present these agencies do not charge, nor do they pay, any amount for the organ *per se*; rather, all charges are for the doctors' services and other personnel and equipment involved in harvesting and transporting the organ. If a futures market such as the one described here were implemented, these agencies could continue to function much as they do now; the only necessary change is that they would have to pay administratively determined prices for organs to holders of the rights to those organs – prices that the agencies would then pass on the recipients of the organs or their insurers along with the other costs of the transplant.

As an alternative, the market elements of the scheme could be even further attenuated by requiring that the insurance companies resell the organ futures to the Government, immediately upon purchasing them, at a price set by the Government. The Government could then simply allocate the organs through the existing organ procurement and distribution system without financial charge.

Regardless of the method employed to determine the price for harvested organs, an insurance premium reduction system of the type described here would be practical only if the price were sufficiently high to make the value of the future rights to a policyholder's organs large enough to cover the costs to the insurers of administering the system and still have enough left over to provide a premium reduction to policyholders sufficient to induce their acquiescence. If $100,000 is the average aggregate price of the organs that can be harvested from each of the 20,000 Americans that die every year in circumstances that make their organs suitable for donations, and if we assume that half of the population is too young, too old, or too infirm to have organs suitable for donation if they should die, then the value of the rights to harvest the organs of the remaining half of the population would be about $20 per year. This would then be the largest average annual premium reduction than an insurance company could offer. If, alternatively, the average of the total prices for the organs that can be harvested from a suitable cadaver were $1,000,000, then the maximum premium reduction would be about $200 per year. We need to ask, then, whether the offer of compensation of these magnitudes would be likely to bring a substantial increase in the rate of organ donation.

Supply Response

As already noted, most individuals are evidently not in principle opposed to donating their organs; presumably they fail to donate only because of inertia, mild doubts about their preferences, a slight distaste for considering the subject, or the inconvenience involved in completing or carrying a donor card (which in the United States is the principal current method for indicating one's willingness to donate). In this context, it is possible that a relatively modest financial incentive would improve donation rates substantially. The proffered premium reductions would serve to focus the attention of potential donors on the issue and would give them an incentive – or perhaps simply an excuse – for resolving their doubts in favour of donating. Put differently, the premium reductions might not serve primarily to compensate people for giving up something of value to them, but rather simply to make it worth their while to incur the transactions costs, both material and psychic, involved in making a decision to donate. In addition, and perhaps of equal or greater importance, because there would be a set of institutions – the insurance companies – with a strong incentive for soliciting donations, solicitation would presumably be far more extensive than at present.

Reducing Altruism

A common objection to providing compensation in contexts such as this is that it will drive out voluntarism – that is, that individuals who would otherwise be willing to donate out of a spirit of altruism will actually be less willing to donate if payment is offered. If this effect were serious and widespread, then the introduction of payment might produce little or no net increase in organ supply. The issue has been much debated in the context of blood donation. The limited empirical evidence is ambiguous even as regards the supply of blood, and arguably does not carry over well to the context of organ donation in any case. Thus, we can only say that neither logic nor data permit us to conclude at this point that a payment scheme, such as the premium reduction plan described above, would be counterproductive because of interference with altruistically motivated donations. Only experimentation will provide clear answers.

Note, however, that whether the type of payment scheme described here would be perceived by prospective donors as inconsistent with their altruistic inclinations would presumably depend in considerable degree on the way in which the issue is framed. For example, is the question whether the typical individual would be willing to sell the rights to his organs for (say) $40 per year? Or is it whether the individual is willing to pay an extra $40 per year in health insurance premiums for the privilege of refusing to make his organs available to save several other persons' lives after he has died? Putting the question the latter way – which would be the tendency if the presumption were in favour of donation, and one had to check off a box and pay an extra premium each year to retain the rights to one's organs – then a compensation scheme might actually make it appear *more* selfish not to donate than it appears at present, and hence actually *increase* altruistically motivated donations.

We should note, too, that under an insurance premium reduction scheme organ donors could be permitted to designate that their premium reduction be donated to a selected charity rather than paid to them personally, hence appealing even further to altruistic motivations.

Making Decisions at the Right Time

An important advantage of the future contracting approach is that it would encourage decisions to donate when they are least problematic – namely, when they are made by the person whose own organs are involved and at a time when that person is healthy and has the opportunity to reflect at leisure on the matter and discuss it with family, friends, and advisers. In contrast, the existing systems, and most of the reforms currently proposed for them, rely heavily on persuading an individual's family to agree to donate the individual's organs immediately following death. An unfortunate detriment of this approach is that it imposes considerable psychological pressure on both the family and the physician. Although it is sometimes suggested that putting a price on human organs would in some way be offensive to our values (an issue to which we shall return below), any such moral objections to markets must be compared to the morality of routinely inflicting distress on families by forcing them to make an emotionally difficult decision in the minutes and hours immediately following the death of a family member and subjecting them to considerable psychological and social pressure to make that decision in favour of donation. Indeed, it is something of a misnomer to call existing organ procurement systems 'voluntary'; it is more accurate simply to call them 'uncompensated.'

Purchasing Organs from Living Donors

In theory, it would be much simpler to employ compensation in procuring organs – in particular, kidneys – from living donors that it would be in procuring cadaveric organs. Payment is already routinely made to living donors for replenishable body products such as blood, sperm, skin, and hair. Strong controversy has arisen, however, over proposals to extend payment to kidneys. In fact, the existing legal bans on organ sales seem to have been inspired primarily by the adverse reaction to such proposals.

The Virtues of Compensation

A great advantage of using living donors for kidneys is that they could easily satisfy 100 per cent of the demand for transplants. The supply of cadaveric organs, in contrast, is ultimately inelastic; since only a limited number of individuals die each year under circumstances permitting their kidneys to be harvested, there will be a point beyond which raising the price for organ futures (or pursuing any other strategy to encourage donations of cadaveric organs) will not appreciably increase supply. Moreover, widespread use of living donors could substantially increase the quality as well as the quantity of kidneys available for transplant. Careful matching of tissues between donor and recipient can improve the long-term success rate of kidney transplants. With the limited supply of cadaveric organs, close tissue matching often cannot be achieved. With a large pool of potential living donors, however, nearly universal close matching could presumably be accomplished easily. Moreover, transplants from living donors eliminate the critical problems of timing that affect transplants of cadaveric organs, which require that a recipient be located and prepared, and the transplant undertaken, within hours of the (often unexpected) death of the donor.

Moreover, for a large fraction of the population, selling a single kidney might be a reasonable decision at prices in a range that demand could support. Donation is evidently not highly hazardous to the donor's health: it has been estimated that the increased risk of death to a healthy 35-year-old from giving up a single kidney is about the same as that involved in driving a car sixteen miles every workday.[4] Many individuals willingly (and, most of us would probably conclude, reasonably) incur risks on this order to achieve savings in personal expenses or to obtain higher wages. Moreover, the fact that living individuals commonly donate kidneys to their relatives also suggests that such transactions are efficient in the economic sense – that is, that the organ is worth more to the recipient than it is to the donor – and thus that there will commonly be a price that will make both donor and recipient better off even in the absence of altruism.

Why, then, is there so much opposition to the idea?

Paternalism

It is often argued that the poor would be the principal sellers in a market for organs, and that therefore such a market would unacceptably exploit the poor for the benefit of the rich. The classical objection to this argument is, of course, that it is a perverse kind of paternalism that prohibits a class of transactions simply because the poor are

4 Hamburger and Crosnier, 1968.

likely to be the principal sellers, since the result of the prohibition is to leave the poor worse off by their own lights: any individual who would agree to sell would evidently rather have the money than have the slightly greater chance of avoiding death or illness that would result from keeping the kidney. Thus, if society is not willing to give the poor sufficient assets so that they are not inclined to sell a kidney, then it is inconsistent for society to refuse to let the poor sell one of the few assets that they have. And, after all, society does not prevent the poor from accepting pay for jobs such as coal mining and meat packing that carry substantial risk of injury or death.

There are, however, at least two reasons why selling kidneys might be thought of as distinguishable from selling one's labour to a meat packing plant. For one thing, taking a job as a meat packer is a day-to-day decision that can be abandoned at any point that one thinks better of it. The sale of a kidney, in contrast, is a one-time act that is to a degree irreversible (although the possibility that a donor can get a transplant himself if his remaining kidney fails considerably reduces the degree of irreversibility). This means that the possibility of making a mistake in selling a kidney is much larger than the possibility of making a mistake in taking a job as a meat packer. One might therefore be concerned that those individuals who would sell a kidney for commercial motives would (as compared with those who held jobs as meat packers) contain a disproportionate number of individuals who had acted improvidently – whether from lack of education or intellect or because circumstances made them temporarily and irrationally desperate – and who will come to regret their act.

Kidney sales may also be different from risky jobs in another sense. Suppose that the market-clearing price for kidneys from living donors would be high enough – say, $15,000 – to be a serious temptation for a large number of poor people, but still not quite high enough to induce most poor persons to agree to sell. In such circumstances, many of the numerous poor who decide not to sell may feel themselves considerably worse off after making that decision than they would have if never faced with the decision at all. These individuals must, after all, live with the knowledge that they have refused to give something of themselves in return for funds that would be valuable to their family. Conventional economic analysis assumes that persons are always made better off by having more choices, but that is not always true.

In any event, a market for kidneys from living donors would need to be regulated in some fashion to guard against improvident transactions. Presumably one would not want a situation in which an unscrupulous doctor could induce a drunk to come in off the streets and yield up a kidney on the spot for $50. Many forms of regulation would be possible. A heavily regulated régime, for example, might require that only governmentally licensed agencies be able to purchase kidneys (and might also require that the agencies be nonprofit); that there be a six-month waiting period between the time that the agreement of sale is entered into and the time the kidney is removed, at any time during which the transaction can be rescinded; that sellers must be at least 25 years of age, be examined by a physician and a social worker, and be approved by a consultative panel unconnected to the purchasing agency; that the price not be below a stated minimum sum; and that the contract of sale include lifetime insurance guaranteeing the donor a free kidney transplant if his remaining kidney should ever fail. The question, then, is whether a commercial market for kidneys, even with an appropriate degree of regulation, would so harm the poor and improvident that such a market would be socially unacceptable. Or, as a further way to test one's sensibilities here, consider a system under which the poor would simply be barred from selling their organs – for example, by prohibiting purchases from individuals whose average income for the last three years was not at least 80 percent of median family income in the nation as a whole (thus excluding from the market persons in the lower 40 percent of the income distribution).

Moreover, it is important to recognize that the poor and improvident are quite disproportionately represented among those who suffer from kidney failure. If commercial purchase of kidneys from living donors would substantially increase the supply available for transplantation, these groups would therefore gain much of the benefit. The net result might therefore be quite beneficial to the disadvantaged, even if we allow for some improvident sales.

In sum, although the issues are difficult, it is not at all obvious that concern for the poor and improvident is a sufficient, or even a substantial, reason to reject purchases from living donors. And the same is true with respect to exploitation of the Third World. Again, as a way of focusing on the problems, we can imagine a scheme in which organs can be purchased only from citizens of the country, or only from citizens of other countries in Europe or in the North Atlantic community.

Commodification

It is frequently said that the commercial sale of human organs, and particularly organs from living donors, should be prohibited because it would tend to 'commodify' them. It is difficult, however, to find a clear statement of precisely what is meant by commodification or why it is undesirable.

Perhaps an important part of the underlying problem here is that – to oversimplify a bit – as a society we tend to put most transactions into one of two distinct normative categories, which we might label 'market transactions' and 'non-market transactions.' In market transactions, a good or service is exchanged for cash or other consideration under circumstances in which the parties to the transaction enter into it in the expectation that they will be personally better off after the transaction than before. In non-market transactions, on the other hand, an individual's willingness to enter into the transaction is governed not by the assurance of immediate personal gain but by a variety of other-regarding social mores or norms that the individual feels obliged to observe. Transactions involving the acquisition and care of automobiles tend to be put in the first category; transactions involving the acquisition and care of children tend to be put in the second category. For those transactions that are in the first category, social mores not only permit but encourage individuals to be strongly self-seeking. Thus, if one sells one's used car to a stranger for less than its full market value, one is likely to be called a fool rather than an altruist. For those transactions that are in the second category, on the other hand, narrow calculations of personal advantage are considered inappropriate. If one tires of one's child, it is not deemed acceptable, much less praiseworthy, to stop giving it food or to sell it to the highest bidder.

One important characteristic that commonly distinguishes market transactions from non-market transactions is that the latter involve substantial external costs or benefits. When selling a child, for example, there is a third party whose interests are heavily at stake – namely, the child himself. And, owing to such factors as the child's inability to borrow against future earnings and his imperfectly developed rationality, he is in no position to enter into transactions to protect his own interests. Parents must therefore be led to internalize a set of norms that induce them to provide care for their children whether or not they feel that what they get in return yields them adequate compensation.

A second reason for using norms of right and obligation rather than market exchange to govern a set of transactions is that the cost of employing market mechanisms would be high relative to the value of the transactions involved. Thus, small transactions among individuals who interact frequently, such as those among friends, family, or workers within a firm (including those between managers and their subordinates), are often not mediated by markets but rather by shared norms, since establishing prices for all such transactions would be unduly complex and time-consuming.

These two reasons for using morals rather than markets to govern any given set of transactions are fundamentally the same. The question in either case is ultimately whether it would be unduly costly to develop market mechanisms adequate to internalize to the decision-makers involved all of the important costs and benefits of the transactions.

As has often been remarked, it is advantageous to assign as many transactions as possible to the category of market transactions since this 'economizes' on morality. Where the 'invisible hand' of the market works well in advancing social welfare, there is no reason to expend the substantial social effort necessary to develop and inculcate a (possibly very elaborate and perhaps rather rigid) set of norms to guide transactions.

Perhaps because our cognitive capacities are limited and because the social costs of inculcating norms are high, the psychological categories to which transactions are assigned tend to be broad and crude. It is not easy for us to consign one set of transactions to the non-market category and another seemingly closely related set of transactions to the market category. Moreover, substantial forces of inertia make it hard for us to rearrange our categories. Sometimes changes in technology or social institutions render it feasible to move a set of transactions from the second category to the first – that is, to use markets to handle transactions that were formerly guided by norms mandating a degree of altruism. But the process of undertaking such a shift may be difficult and highly contentious. If individuals were previously socialized to think it immoral to approach a set of transactions from a strongly self-regarding stance, then at first they are likely to find it deeply offensive to see the same transactions subjected only to the mores of the marketplace. Norms, by their nature, are not easily changed.

This inflexibility in our normative categories may help explain the reflexively negative moral response that commonly greets proposals for marketing human organs. There are a number of reasons why individuals might commonly be inclined to feel that giving up a body part to another individual belongs in the category of altruistic non-market transactions: There have previously been no markets here to which individuals might become accustomed. To those who have not thought closely about the risks involved, yielding up a vital organ such as a kidney while still alive may seem like the kind of life-threatening sacrifice (such as attempting to rescue a drowning person in heavy seas) that cannot easily be made the subject of market transactions and that have therefore always been governed primarily by other-regarding norms. For the past twenty years, for good reasons or bad, our society has sought to deligitimate markets and encourage norms of altruism in the seemingly analogous area of blood donation. And for 30 years we have also been trying to encourage norms of altruism in the area of organ donation itself.

Moreover, an important reason for assigning kidney donations to the non-market realm in the past involved family relationships. Prior to the development of effective immunosuppressive drugs, kidney transplants were likely to be rejected by the donor's body unless there was a close match between the tissue types of the donor and the recipient. This meant that transplants of kidneys from living donors within the same family were often the most successful. Most intrafamily transactions, however, are and must remain non-market transactions, and thus we are socialized to think that the self-interested calculus of the market is inappropriate among family members. Introducing market considerations into one very significant type of intrafamily transaction – transfers of kidneys – might therefore strain the whole moral fabric of the families involved. You cannot extract a high price from your mother for one of your kidneys and then expect her to happily continue cooking your meals for free.

Moreover, it may not be possible to employ market transactions only for kidney transplants *outside* the family without putting severe strains on intrafamily relationships. For example, an individual might feel deeply resentful if subjected to moral pressure to donate a kidney to a family member without compensation when a substantial payment would be forthcoming if the organ were transplanted outside the family. In short, it may be very difficult here to draw lines, whether between transfers of kidneys within the family and other types of intrafamily transfers, or between intrafamily and interfamily transfers of kidneys.

It follows that, when most kidneys had to come from family members, it may have been wise not to try to develop market transactions for kidneys, even among strangers. The rapid development of immunosuppressive drugs, however, has now made transplants among unrelated individuals relatively safe, and perhaps nearly as safe as transfers between family members. The need for intrafamily donations has therefore substantially declined. The result is that the costs of using market transactions among living kidney donors – in the form of moral strain on family relationships in general, and perhaps also in the form of reduced intrafamily kidney donations – have also declined, and may no longer be important.

Arguably, then, recent changes in technology have made it timely for us to redraw the lines between market and non-market transactions where transplantable organs are concerned, just as other transactions have been recategorized when technological changes have made market mechanism more advantageous. For example, we are now quite accustomed to proprietary institutions marketing nursing care for the elderly and matchmaking ('dating services') for the young. And, to take another example much closer to the subject at hand, after several decades' experience our society has accepted a thriving market in human sperm brokered by proprietary firms. It would be easy to characterize such a market as deeply offensive to fundamental values involving paternity, sexual relations, responsibility for and identity with one's offspring, and the need to make both children and their parents feel that their relationship with each other transcends that of mere commodities. And there was in fact substantial ethical resistance to a commercial market for human sperm when it was first introduced. Yet over time we have chosen are to redraw the symbolic lines between our normative categories so that market transactions in human sperm are not perceived as undermining non-market norms in those areas of sex, reproduction, and child care where such norms continue to play a strong functional role.

Given the inertia that characterizes normative categories, it is understandable that, whatever the ultimate merits of a market for human organs, the initial reaction to a proposal for such a market is commonly one of strong moral opposition. The proscription of such markets enacted in the United States in 1984 presumably reflects precisely this type of reflexive reaction. Ironically, but perhaps expectably, this ban was enacted just when such a policy was apparently becoming anachronistic, not only for cadaveric organs but perhaps for organs from living donors as well. Before markets for organs were feasible, there was little reason to outlaw them. Now that such markets seem feasible, the idea of having them offends the norms that developed to make up for their absence, which in turn has led us to ban them.

Will Social Costs Increase?

One might think that paying compensation for transplantable organs would have the unfortunate effect of substantially increasing the already high cost of organ transplants, thus further increasing the already large portion of society's wealth that is spent on health care. But for the most part payments for organs would simply be transfer payments involving no real social costs. Indeed, if administered through medical insurance as described above, the net change in the cost of health care might be negligible for most individuals, since they would find their insurance premiums increased to cover the increased cost of organ transplants, but reduced by a nearly equal amount to compensate them for their organs.

Pressure on the Allocation System

If a system for compensating donors were introduced and were to have the desired result, namely a substantially increased supply of organs (whether from cadavers or from living donors), it would have the paradoxical consequence of placing severe strains on the existing systems for allocating the available organs among potential recipients.

Organ transplants are extremely expensive in their use of medical resources. At present, even in the United States, public funds pay for most transplants. Because the supply of transplantable organs is so limited, there is no effort to limit the number of transplants performed; all available organs are transplanted. And because demand substantially exceeds supply, the available organs must be rationed among potential recipients. Generally an effort is made to give the organs to those who will benefit the most from them – such as those who are young, provident, and otherwise healthy. As a result, it is arguable that, despite their high cost, most transplants performed today are socially valuable in the sense that their social benefits exceed their social costs. But this might not remain the case if the potential supply of transplantable organs were to increase significantly. Then society would either need to spend enormous amounts of resources providing transplants even where their overall benefits are modest, or else find a way to deny transplants to many individuals even though organs can be found for them.

So long as the supply of organs remains severely limited, this painful choice can be avoided. Perhaps this is another reason why there is some reluctance to consider methods, such as paying compensation, that might substantially increase the number of organs available.

Markets for Allocating Organs

So far we have been speaking of the use of market mechanisms to increase the supply of transplantable organs. In addition, market mechanisms might be used to decide who will receive the organs that are supplied. This is only feasible, however, where health care in general is allocated through a market, as it is in the United States. Where, as is generally true in Europe, health care is publicly provided at no direct cost to the user, market allocation is necessarily ruled out. Moreover, even in the United States kidney transplants (though not most other types of organ transplants) are provided almost entirely at public expense, making market allocation of the kidneys themselves unworkable. Consequently, although the issues are interesting, I shall not address here the prospects for using markets to allocate the available organ supply, or to equilibrate total supply with total demand (that is, to determine how many organs will be transplanted in total).[5]

It is important to realize, however, that one can use markets – or, more precisely, compensation schemes – to encourage the supply of organs without using them to determine either how many organs will be supplied or who will get them.[6] In particular, even a thoroughly nationalized health care system could employ a compensation scheme to increase the supply of cadaveric organs without making other important changes in the mechanisms by which health care, including organ transplants, are produced and distributed.

Conclusion

It is understandable that, upon first consideration, policy-makers have been appalled at the notion of using market mechanisms to acquire human organs, and have reacted by simply prohibiting them. But the issue of organ transplants is far too important to be left to unreflective moralizing. And, when we probe more thoughtfully into the practical and moral problems involved, a ban on all forms of compensation for transplantable organs is difficult to justify. Rather, because so many lives and so much suffering is at stake, thoughtful experimentation with compensation schemes seems well worth pursuing.

5 For further discussion, *see* Hansmann, *supra*.

6 The reverse is also true: one can use markets to allocate scarce resources without using markets to determine how much of that resource will be consumed or where it will come from. *See*, generally G. Calabresi and P. Bobbitt, *Tragic Choices* (1978).

Marketing of Human Organs?

Erwin Bernat*

1. Introduction

The question as to whether human organs may be seen as commercial objects can be viewed in three different ways. First, there is the question as to what the current laws have to say about this problem. Then, it would seem appropriate to examine the answers that a given moral order would provide. Only when this second normative level has been examined can the question be regarded from the third perspective: ultimately, in all problems of bioethical regulation the question should be that of recognizing whether legislative action should be taken or whether existing laws suffice to cover new biomedical circumstances. These three levels of discussion thus are highly interrelated. Discussion level one shows how existing legal regulations are to be evaluated, discussion level two shows how an ideal norm for the resolution of existing bioethical problems could look, and at discussion level three, an attempt is made to formulate a legal norm that would update or supplement current law. The normative content of the 'ideal norm' at discussion level two is not necessarily congruent with the legal-policy suggestions that are worked out at discussion level three.[1] For one thing, not every ethical postulate should be understood to be a demand for modification of existing laws. It is often emphasized in the realm of bioethics that legal rules are simply an 'ethical minimum'.[2] It is not the task of the law to establish binding standards that cannot possibly be met by those to whom they apply. For another thing, discussion on level two usually produces a number of ideal norms, all of which can appear to be valid. This dilemma usually confronts the legal policy-maker when it is a matter of estab-

* Professor of Law, University of Graz, Austria.

1 Bernat, E., 'Biotechnologie, Rechtsethik und Gesetzgebung', *Ethik und Sozialwissenschaften* 3, 1992, pp. 294-297.

2 Deutsch, E., 'Theorie der Aufklärungspflicht des Arztes – Ethische und rechtliche Grundlagen der Information des Patienten -', *Versicherungsrecht* 32, 1981, pp. 293 f.

Cosimo Marco Mazzoni (ed.), A Legal Framework for Bioethics, 161-171.
©1998 *Kluwer Law International. Printed in The Netherlands.*

lishing norms to cover biomedical situations. As far as the outcome is concerned, it sometimes makes a big difference whether the 'ideal norm' found at discussion level two has been reached via a metaphysical,[3] individualistic,[4] utilitarian[5] or intuitive[6] route. As a rule, discussions at level two will lead to very different ideal norms, each of which can be rational in itself, but which are in complete and irreconcilable disharmony with the others. What meaning does this then have for legal policy? If one comes to the conclusion that the prevailing laws are inadequate with respect to the evaluation of the biomedical situation, the existence of a number of ethical ideal norms will lead to the conclusion that the legislature will have to create a fair compromise within the context of the basic legal standards that takes into account values-related convictions that are often socially polarized.[7] The legislative decision thus remains rational when the legislature openly admits the advantages of what may simply be a 'formula for compromise'. Of course – and this must be emphasized here – the compromise on which the legal solution is based must itself have a rational basis. If legal 'formulas for compromise' are contradictory in themselves, then they will usually not be satisfactory and may even be unconstitutional, as they fail to fulfill a basic requirement of the total legal system, i.e. the requirement of objectivity. Seen this way, the path from 'ideal' to 'practical' norm, i.e. the (new) legal norm, must always be one that the person to whom it applies can always follow objectively. The individual affected by the norm must be able to understand why the legislature deviates from certain ideal norms and must be able to comprehend the thinking that led to the practical norm and the suitability of its contents.[8]

2. Marketing of cadaver organs

The organs of a deceased person can be sold for profit either by relatives of the deceased after death or by the donor himself prior to his death. The theoretical possibility of a donor's organs being sold during his life time by relatives need not be discussed here as it clearly violates *bonos mores*. This may be seen in sec 879 (2) no. 3 of the Austrian

3 *Cf.*, e.g., Spaemann, R., *Die Unantastbarkeit des menschlichen Lebens. Zu ethischen Fragen der Biomedizin*, Freiburg/Basel/Vienna, Herder, 1987.

4 *Cf.*, e.g., Nozick, R., *Anarchy, State, and Utopia*. New York, NY, Basic Books, Inc. 1974.

5 *Cf.*, e.g., Singer, P., *Practical Ethics*, 2nd ed., Cambridge, Cambridge University Press, 1993.

6 *Cf.*, e.g., Thomson, J. J., 'A Defense of Abortion', *Philosophy & Public Affairs* 1, 1971, pp. 47-66.

7 Birnbacher, D., 'Gefährdet die moderne Reproduktionsmedizin die menschliche Würde?', in: Leist, A. (ed.), *Um Leben und Tod. Moralische Probleme bei Abtreibung, künstlicher Befruchtung, Euthanasie und Selbstmord*, Frankfurt/Main, Suhrkamp, 1990, pp. 266 ff. (279).

8 Bernat, E., 'Bioethische Regelungsprobleme im Spannungsfeld von Gewissensfreiheit und Sachlichkeitsgebot', in: Bednaříková, J./Chapman, F. C. I. I. (eds.), *Essays in Honour of Jan Štěpán on the Occasion of his 80th Birthday*, Zurich, Schulthess, 1994, pp. 81-87.

General Civil Code, (ABGB) which clearly states that a contract is void if someone sells an inheritance he expects to receive from a third party while that person is still living. By extension, sale of organs by relatives during the donor's lifetime is invalid. German law shows the same valuation, as expressed in the prohibition in sec. 312 (1) of the German Civil Code, corresponding to sec. 879 (2) no. 3 ABGB.[9]

A. The sale of cadaver organs by relatives

1. The current law

What, now, is the situation in the case of practical interest in which the relatives have obtained a promise of payment for the release of an organ for the purpose of transplantation from the physician who will perform the transplant or from the recipient himself? First, a decision must be reached as to whether the legal system involved has adopted an opting-out or a modified opting-in system with respect to donation of cadaver organs.[10] If a pure opting-out system is in effect, the deceased must during his lifetime have objected to organ removal in order to prevent that any of his organs will be explanted after death. In legal systems with an opting-out system, the relatives have no way of preventing organ removal if the deceased has not objected to it in his lifetime. This radical form of opting out was enacted in Austria with an amendment to the Hospitals Act (KAG) (1958) in 1982;[11] sec. 62a (1) says:

> 'It is permissible to explant single organs or parts thereof for the purpose of saving another person's life or restoring another person's health by means of their transplantation. An explantation is inadmissible if the physicians have before them a pronouncement by means of which the deceased, or, before his death, his legal guardian, has expressly objected to an organ donation. An explantation must not result in a disfigurement which offends piety.'

The teleology of this norm alone indicates that sale of cadaver organs by relatives is forbidden under Austrian law. As they cannot even object to an organ explantation, they also have no right to receive compensation for explanted organs. The Austrian legislature says this expressly in sec. 62a (4) KAG: 'A deceased person's organs or parts thereof may not be the object of transactions aiming at profit.'

Disregard of this regulation is a regulatory offence and carries an administrative fine of up to ATS 30,000.

9 Thus Maier, J., *Der Verkauf von Körperorganen. Zur Sittenwidrigkeit von Überlassungsverträgen*, Heidelberg: CF Müller, 1991, pp. 69 f.

10 For a comparative survey cf. Bernat, E., 'Opting-in, Opting-out, and Necessity: The Law of Organ Transplantation in Germany, Austria, and Switzerland', *International Journal of Bioethics* 5, 1994, pp. 101-106.

11 Official Gazette no. 273/1982.

If a legal system has adopted a modified opting-in system, the question as to whether relatives can sell the organ of the deceased cannot be answered so clearly. The modified opting-in approach is based on the anticipated consent of the deceased, but it differs from the 'pure' opting-in approach in that it allows the relatives to decide if the deceased has not given consent while still alive. There are variations: in one case, the relatives have to consent to an organ explantation; in the other, they have to object, if the explantation is to be averted. These two models play an important role in the German discussion on a statutory solution. Furthermore, the prevailing opinion among academics and the judiciary upholds the modified opting-in approach to be unwritten current law.[12] In Germany, relatives could get the idea that they could make their agreement to the performance of an organ transplantation dependent on payment for the organs by the hospital or recipient. Is this sort of compensation agreement permissible? As there is no expressive prohibition, as in Austria, this question can only be answered with consideration of the general goals of orderly policy that in Germany have led to the establishment of the modified opting-in approach. Decisive for the inclusion of the relatives in the decision-making process related to organ explantation when the deceased himself has not agreed to it is the belief that the relatives quasi as representatives of the deceased should be involved in order to respect his postmortal personality rights. Most authors assume that the position of the relatives within the context of organ explantation is only that of a trustee, and that the trusteeship can only be exercised in accordance with the presumptive wishes of the deceased.[13] Although a person's legal capacity ceases to exist at death, acknowledging the postmortem right of personality does not stand for more than 'acknowledging a living person's right to make binding directions – in exercise of his/her personal autonomy – which are to become effective only after the person's death.'[14] From this point of view, the position of the relatives as derived from the general personality rights of the deceased with respect to the question of the permissibility of organ explantation is very closely related to their right to look after their dead. This right is also understood to be a 'non-market right'. As the name suggests, it covers the care of the dead. The payment of a sum of money for the 'release' of the deceased's organ would be a service not to his but rather only to his relatives' advantage. And it is surely the case that the relatives could be tempted not to try to determine what the deceased most likely wanted, but rather to let their own – pecuniary – considerations inform the decision, if the payment of a fee for

12 For a comprehensive survey of the legal situation in Germany cf. Hirsch, G./Schmidt-Didczuhn, A., *Transplantation und Sektion. Die rechtliche und rechtspolitische Situation nach der Widervereinigung*, Heidelberg, CF Müller, 1992.

13 Buschmann, A., 'Zur Fortwirkung des Persönlichkeitsrechts nach dem Tode', *Neue Juristische Wochenschrift* 23, 1970, pp. 2081 ff.; Westermann H. P., 'Das Persönlichkeitsrecht nach dem Tode seines Trägers', *Zeitschrift für das gesamte Familienrecht* 16, 1969, pp. 561 ff.

14 Hirsch, G./Schmidt-Didczuhn, A., *op. cit.*, p. 47.

permission to explant organs were permissible. Based on all of these considerations, according to current German law, commercial exploitation of cadaver organs is prevented by a general normative concept derived from the post-mortem personality rights of the deceased that is a component of cogent law.[15]

2. The moral point of view

From a moral point of view, these results derived from current German and Austrian law can be seen to form a consensus, as supported by two considerations that have already been taken into account in the official commentary to the government bill introducing sec. 62a into the Austrian Hospitals Act.[16] For one thing, reasons of piety forbid profit making on the basis of release of cadaver organs. For the other – and this seems even more relevant to me – commerce in organs between relatives of the deceased and the hospital or recipient would be impermissible on the grounds that the relatives would be being paid for a service that they should not be able to render to satisfy their own interests, but only to satisfy those of the deceased.

In my opinion, there is no legal-ethical need for a change in the current laws here.

B. The sale of organs by the donor him/herself prior to death

Finally, there is the possibility that the potential donor would 'sell' his organs during his lifetime. Here again, a distinction must be made between legal systems that recognize an opting-out approach and those that have approved a modified opting-in approach. What is the legal significance of 'sale of an organ' by the donor in the event of his death in Austrian law which, as we know, has adopted the opting-out approach? From a technical legal point of view, within the context of this sort of contract the donor would be paid to refrain prior to his death from objecting to a postmortem organ explantation which then might be indicated. This sort of agreement is not covered by the prohibition in sec. 62a (4) KAG, as it forbids only profit-oriented sale of an organ from an already deceased person. In the case at hand, the donor is of course still alive when the contract is made. The Austrian literature views the sale of an organ by the donor in the event of his death as an infringement of *boni mores* and thus as invalid.[17] This valuation is actually significant within the context of an opting-out approach.

Austrian law generally views as violating *bonos mores* those parts of a contract that lead to an impermissible limitation of personal freedom because they infringe on freedom of choice in highly personal matters. This means that contracts regarding

15 Thus Maier, J., *op. cit.*, p. 67.

16 969 of the *Appendices to the Shorthand Records of the National Council* (lower house of Parliament), 15th legislative period.

17 Kopetzki, Ch., *Organgewinnung zu Zwecken der Transplantation*, Wien/New York, Springer, 1988, p. 260.

changes in or commitment to a religious faith, obligations to leave a place of residence, promises never to change one's profession or never to practice a certain profession and those forbidding marriage are all seen as void.[18] The obligation not to object to an organ explantation would seem to fall into this category. If such a contractual agreement were in effect, as between a dying person and a certain hospital, it would limit the freedom of choice of the individual that is part of the general personality rights and also infringe upon basic legal positions that sec. 62a KAG expressly intended to guarantee by providing a chance to object.

The evaluation is not much different with respect to German law, which recognizes a modified opting-in approach. In such a case, the sale of an organ would mean agreement to removal of an organ for payment of a fee. Such contracts are overwhelmingly rejected in the German literature[19] and in general, the same arguments are mentioned as were discussed with respect to Austrian law under the heading, 'limitation of freedom of choice in highly personal matters'.

3. Marketing of organs from a living donor

A. THE CURRENT LAW

The questions as to whether under current law a living donor could be permitted to sell bone marrow or a kidney, etc., and to put them at the disposal of the recipient while the donor is still alive is much more controversial than the sale of cadaver organs. Even the question of the general permissibility of the living donation does not receive the same evaluation in all legal systems. Some legislatures forbid living donations unless they are for certain defined blood relatives. I would like in this context to refer *pars pro toto* to the English Human Organ Transplants Act (1989), whose sec. 2(2) lists those relatives who are admissible as donor or recipient. On the donor side these are biological parents and children, full or half children, full or half uncles and aunts and full or half nephews and nieces. The basic idea here seems to be that the genetic bond between certain relatives should be the decisive factor. This could on the one hand be because the English legislature assumes on the basis of the medical circumstances that the recipient will tolerate the kidney, for example, of a relative especially well. On the other hand, the restrictions in the English law could have been devised under the assumption that there will be a special emotional bond between the persons mentioned in sec. 2(2), which in turn will guarantee the donor's altruistic motives. According to sec. 1 leg cit, a marketing of human organs has already been expressly prohibited. If

18 Examples taken from Krejci, H., 'margin numbers 69 ff. to sec. 879', in Rummel, P. (ed.), *Austrian General Civil Code. A Commentary*, 2nd ed., Vol II. Vienna, Manz 1990.

19 Cf. Kramer, H-J., *Rechtsfragen der Organtransplantation*, Munich, V Florentz, 1987, pp. 116 f.

the existence of a (presumptive) emotional bond really was the motive that led the English legislature to limit living donations to close blood relatives, it is rather curious that spouses and common-law spouses were excluded.[20]

The stipulations in the Human Organs Transplants Act 1989 are indeed very restrictive and have been the subject of severe criticism.[21] Other legal systems are more permissive and only want to guarantee that the donor have financial security should his health worsen as a result of the donation. Legal systems that take this approach usually do not specify who can be a donor or recipient. As an example, I should like to mention the law in the former German Democratic Republic,[22] which permitted living donations under the condition that no impairment of the donor's health was to be expected and that in all probability the recipient would benefit from the transplant.[23] If, contrary to expectation, the organ explantation did in fact impair the donor's health, he would be covered by social security under the law of the GDR, as would be his dependents in the case of his death.[24]

A third group of legal systems either does not touch upon the permissibility of living donations, or only does so indirectly. In these legal systems, there are scattered legal conditions that can be applied analogously to our question as to whether marketing of human organs is permissible. Austrian and German law can serve as examples for this group. On the one hand, these laws indicate that donations of certain bodily substances are absolutely forbidden, but on the other, court decisions and legal regulations recognize the living donation but do not define any clear limits for its permissibility.

In Germany and Austria, donations of ova and embryos are expressly forbidden by law.[25] In Austria, there is a law that sperm cannot be sold for profit.[26] Of course these laws do not have any real meaning within our context as the motives that led to the prohibition of donations of ova and embryos as well as of profit-oriented sperm transfer can in no way be compared with the arguments mentioned in relation to the rejection of living donation of organs and/or the marketing of organs. Donations of ova and embryos were not forbidden under German and Austrian law

20 Kennedy, I./Grubb A., *Medical Law: Text and Materials*, 2nd ed., London/Dublin/Edinburgh, Butterworth, 1994, pp. 1093 ff.

21 Kennedy, I./Grubb, A., *op. cit.*, pp. 1093 ff.

22 'Federal Regulation on the Transplantation of Human Organs of 4th July 1975', *Official Gazette* I, pp. 597 ff.

23 § 6.

24 § 11.

25 'Federal Act for the Protection of Embryos of 13th Dec. 1990', *Official Gazette* 1990 I, pp. 2746 ff., sec. 1; 'Federal Act on Procreative Medicine of 4th June 1992', *Official Gazette* no. 275/1992, sec. 3(3).

26 'Federal Act on Procreative Medicine', sec. 16; *see* Bernat, E./Vranes, E., 'The Austrian Act on Procreative Medicine: Scope, Impacts, and Inconsistencies', *Journal of Assisted Reproduction and Genetics* 10, 1993, pp. 449-452.

on the basis of concern for the health of the donor. What really was behind the prohibition were fears that can best be put under the headings of 'best interests of the child' and 'interfering with nature'.[27] Similar arguments apply to the prohibition of profit-oriented sperm donation. This is what is said in the official commentary to the Austrian bill introducing a new law on medically assisted procreation: 'The thought that the conception of a child is preceded by the purchase of sperm, and that the child could indirectly be purchased, cannot be reconciled with the dignity of the child.'[28] One can be of two minds with respect to this explanation.[29] In any case, it cannot be used to support a prohibition of profit-oriented living donations, for example, of a kidney. Other aspects must be sought here that have more substance. Interestingly, there are indications in Austrian and German law that the living donation is basically acceptable. Sec. 120(2) of the Austrian Social Security Act (ASVG) says that it is the same as an illness when a person covered by social insurance 'without financial interest donates a part of his body for transplantation into the body of another human being.' Under the circumstances described in detail in sec. 120(2) ASVG, the donor's health insurer pays for the explantation, while according to general principles[30] the recipient's health insurer pays for the implantation. German law is not explicit on this. In contrast, the Bundessozialgericht (Federal Court for Social Security Matters) ruled back in 1972 that all the expenses related to the explantation are to be assumed by the legal health insurer of the recipient.[31] The conclusion can undoubtedly be drawn from these sociolegal evaluations that living donation is generally permitted in Germany and Austria. Can it also involve a fee beyond that that is paid by the health insurer for services rendered? With an *argumentum e contrario* with respect to sec. 120(2) of the Austrian Social Security Act, this conclusion could be drawn formally. For if an insured person donates an organ with the intention of making a profit, the insurer makes no payment. Austrian social law thus is based on the fact that there could be remuneration for the living donation. Of course the social security law does not say specifically that this remuneration can also be the object of a binding contract under

27 Cf. the official commentary to the (German) Government Bill introducing the 'Act for the Protection of Embryos', *op. cit.*, reprinted in: *Records of the German Bundestag* (lower house of Parliament) XI/5460 (of 25 Oct. 1989), pp. 6 f.

28 Reprinted in: 216 of the *Appendices to the Shorthand Records of the National Council* (lower house of Parliament), 18th legislative period, p. 22 (l. col.).

29 Cf. Bernat, E., 'Das Recht der medizinisch assistierten Zeugung 1990 – eine vergleichende Bestandsaufnahme', in, Bernat, E. (ed.), *Fortpflanzungsmedizin. Wertung und Gesetzgebung. Beiträge zum Entwurf eines Fortpflanzungshilfegesetzes*, Vienna, Österreichische Staatsdruckerei, 1991, pp. 65 ff.

30 Mazal, W., *Krankheitsbegriff und Risikozurechnung. Eine Untersuchung zum Leistungsrecht der gesetzlichen Krankenversicherung*, Vienna, Braumüller, 1992, pp. 348 ff.

31 BSG, decision from 12 Dec. 1972, reprinted in: *Neue Juristische Wochenschrift* 26, 1973, p. 1432.

civil law. Current Austrian and German law rather express severe reservations on profit-oriented living donation. Even though there are no relevant court decisions as yet, some authors actually assume that profit-oriented living donations are already prohibited under current German and Austrian criminal law. They lead to a bodily injury to the donor which is performed with intent. Treatment cannot be seen here as justification for the act as it is not in fact a treatment from the point of view of the donor. The principle of volenti non fit inuiria is basically acknowledged in Austrian and German law,[32] but with bodily injuries that the injured party has agreed to, only insofar as the injury does not infringe upon bonos mores. This is assumed to be the case in Austrian and German legal scholarship by a not inconsiderable minority, insofar as the donor accepts a fee for his agreement to have an organ explanted.[33] This alone will prevent any wide-scale marketing of human organs in Austria and Germany.

B. ARGUMENTS FOR AND AGAINST A LAW REFORM

The legislature could of course assume the position that remuneration for organ donations is not an act that is to be viewed as antisocial. Which arguments could be used to support this position? First, I should like to summarize the grounds that speak for the impropriety of a profit-oriented organ donation:

(a) Living donations among relatives are generally accepted, as it is assumed that they are voluntary. The voluntary nature of paid living donations is questioned because the payment poses a temptation that could influence the capacity of the donor to make a decision of his own free will.
(b) Another main argument is that a paid donation would tend to exploit the socially underprivileged unfairly. This would have to be prevented. 'Paternalism', i.e. 'guardianship' through regulations that protect the citizen's own interests, is appropriate here. The lawmakers are paternalistic in other circumstances too; one need only consider seat-belt laws and the prohibition of hard drugs.

32 Sec. 90 Austrian Criminal Code; sec. 226a German Criminal Code.
33 For Austria *see* Brandstetter W., 'Strafrechtliche und rechtspolitische Aspekte der Verwendung von Organen Verstorbener, Lebender und Ungeborener', in: Brandstetter W/Kopetzki Ch (eds.), *Organtransplantationen. Medizinische und rechtliche Aspekte der Verwendung menschlicher Organe zu Heilzwecken*, Vienna, Facultas 1987, pp. 101 ff.; for Germany: Kohlhaas M, 'Neue Rechtsprobleme der Organtransplantation', *Neue Juristische Wochenschrift* 24, 1971, p. 1870.

These arguments can be contrasted with a number of counter arguments.[34] These are:

(a) The payment of money could be seen as an analogue to the compensation to which a person is entitled when his health has been negligently or intentionally damaged.
(b) The payment could be seen as a premium for a permissible risk.
(c) There are many countries where payment is recognized for blood and sperm donations. Why should this not also be the case for organs?
(d) If more organ donations were made, savings in the health-care sector could be realized in such cases as renal failure, where the costs for dialysis would be drastically reduced.
(e) Finally, the feasibility of a legal prohibition of profit-oriented organ donation is questioned, with reference to the analogous situation with regard to consumption of hard drugs and prostitution.
(f) As far as I am concerned, the most important argument against a prohibition of profit-oriented organ donation emphasizes that payment by no means necessarily rules out altruistic motives. What would be the difference between Father A, who donates an organ for his daughter, and Father B, who sells one of his organs so that he can afford appropriate treatment for his child, or to improve his family's miserable situation?[35]

Under ideal conditions, it seems to me that payment for organs is by no means so immoral as it is often assumed to be.

The above-mentioned, rather deontologically oriented arguments, however, tend to lose their credibility when one considers empirical works on the social effects of paid organ donations, especially in Third-World countries.[36] The paid living donation

34 These arguments are put forward mainly by American writers, *see* e.g. Brams M, 'Transplantable Human Organs: Should Their Sale be Authorized by State Statutes?', *American Journal of Law & Medicine* 3, 1977, pp. 183 ff; Bray, M. B., 'Personalizing Personality: Toward a Property Right in Human Bodies, *Texas Law Review* 69, 1990, 209 ff.; Kevorkian, J., 'A controlled Auction Market Is a Practical Solution to the Shortage of Transplantable Organs', *Medicine & Law* 11, 1992, pp. 47 ff.; Radin, M. J., 'Market – Inalienability', *Harvard Law Review* 100, 1987, pp. 1849 ff; for Germany *see* Gutmann, Th., 'Lebendspende von Organen – nur unter Verwandten?', *Zeitschrift für Rechtspolitik* 27, 1994, pp. 111 ff.

35 Example taken from Richards, J. R., 'From Him That Hath Not', in Land, W./Dossetor, J. B. (eds.), *Organ Replacement Therapy: Ethics, Justice, Commerce*, Berlin, Springer, 1991, p. 190.

36 *See* the essays of Abouna, G. M. *et al.*, 'The Negative Impact of Paid Organ Donation', in Land, W./Dossetor, J. B. (eds.), *op. cit.*, pp. 164 ff.; Reddy, K. C., 'Organ Donation for Consideration: An Indian Viewpoint', in: Land, W./Dossetor, J. B. (eds.), *op. cit.*, pp. 173 ff.; Daar, A.S., 'Rewarded Gifting and Rampant Commercialism in Perspective: Is There a Difference?' in Land, W./Dossetor, J. B. (eds.), *op. cit.*, pp. 181 ff.; Adib Rizvi, S./Anwar Naqvi, S. A., 'Fallouts of Commercialism in Organ Donation as Seen in Pakistan', in Land, W./ Dossetor, J. B. (eds.), *op. cit.*, pp. 203 ff.

there has, according to the statistics, negative effects on the donor, on the recipient and on the local transplantation centers, which gradually come to neglect organ acquisition *ex mortuo*. The effect on the donor is negative as he often is not given adequate medical treatment and often does not realize what the full effect of his decision will be. The recipients are exploited through exorbitant fees and may also receive poor treatment. Kuwaiti physicians, for example, reported in 1990 on 72 patients who had obtained organ transplants abroad.[37] A disproportionate number of these patients died, lost the transplant or were infected with diseases that could have been recognized, such as HIV. In this context, it has also been reported that relatives become less willing to donate when they realize that their sick relation could simply buy himself an organ. All in all, these observations permit the conclusion that in those countries where profit-oriented living donations could play a significant role, they do more harm than good.

If one trusts these empirical data, it would seem that profit-oriented living donations should not be tolerated by the lawmakers. This example also shows how far ideal norms for the evaluation of a biomedical scenario can diverge.[38] If deontological observations show us that profit-oriented living donations are basically not as bad as we would intuitively assume, consequentialist observations lead us to a quite opposite conclusion. The decision of the lawmaker will ultimately depend on his methodological approach to the subject, but this is a matter beyond the task of this paper.

37 Abouna, G. M. *et al.*, in Land, W./Dossetor, J. B. (eds.), *op. cit.*, p. 165.

38 For a comprehensive survey of competing ethical theories cf. Beauchamp, T. L./Childress, J. F., *Principles of Biomedical Ethics*, 4th ed., New York/Oxford: Oxford University Press, 1994, pp. 44-119; Veatch, R. M., *A Theory of Medical Ethics*, New York, NY, Basic Books Inc., 1981, pp. 141-287.

Gift Ethics and Organ Donation

Cosimo Marco Mazzoni*

As is well known, organs can be harvested in view of transplantation from either cadavers or living persons only with the consent – express or implied – of the person in question or of his nearest of kin. In both these cases we speak of an organ donation. Even many of the recent bills use the term donation.

Organ donation, or organ market. This latter prospect is purely theoretical – at least from a legislative point of view – and immediately raises fear and apprehension in any discussion on this topic. But we must bear in mind that the practice of illegal transplants is anything but theoretical: behind this practice lies a flourishing market, a growth industry. In any case, and this statement might appear banal and obvious, when a person has an asset, and there can be no doubt that an organ is an asset, this can be disposed of or alienated either free of charge or for compensation. To be able to dispose of an asset or to exert a right over an asset, in juridical terms, means to be its proprietor, i.e. to have a real right over the asset. We shall see later on in which legal category an asset which is a human organ can be placed.

The current debate on the issue of human organ transplants follows two rationales and two models that are inspired by very different ideological bases, and are almost always conflicting; but they share an equally powerful dose of dogmatism, in many cases almost becoming a sort of ideal radicalism, since the positions are so rigid and even on some occasions intolerant.

These two positions can be identified by two words: solidarity and market. The former is the 'good' position, which *per se*, in that it claims to offer solidarity, flavours the debate applying all the connotations that belong specifically to the world of ethics. The 'good' debate which is taking place in one of the central domains of bioethics – and organ transplants are undoubtedly one of the most important fields – is the sum of concepts such as donation, solidarity, liberal spirit, the gift ethic, altruism and all the other synonyms which tend to address these issues in the only way possible, if we are to guarantee an 'ethical' vision of social and individual relations.

* Professor of Law, University of Siena, Siena, Italy.

Cosimo Marco Mazzoni (ed.), A Legal Framework for Bioethics, 173-177.
©1998 *Kluwer Law International. Printed in The Netherlands.*

There is no other way, if we are to believe the radicalism of the supporters of this position, to approach transplant ethics. An ethics of individual and collective behaviour, a philosophical and juridical ethic which could advise, guide or – if necessary – impose, in our search for a rule. Which, in turn, will discipline the ways in which an act of social solidarity expressed through an organ donation for a transplant (it is irrelevant at this stage whether the organ originates from a living or a dead person) can occur, thus implementing one of the fundamental elements of bioethics.

On the opposite side of the debate is the other word mentioned earlier: market. Like the first one, this term, too, speaks for itself: it evokes synonyms such as trade, profit, appropriation, proprietary or possessive individualism, selfishness. The market thus stands in antithesis to the notion of donation. The spirit of commerce and trade as opposed to the gift ethic. And if the concept refers to organ transplants it is easy to establish a moral judgment between the *good* spirit which lies behind social solidarity and is expressed through a donation and the *evil* spirit which uses – even in this context – the tools of the market, of trade, of appropriation, of ownership.

But the market, some people maintain, is legitimized by factual considerations and by a pragmatic interpretation of ethical considerations. The rationale which leads to the concept of an 'organ market' develops out of the acknowledgment of specific priorities. The first one is the following: the main objective that all legislative policies (in those countries where it has been decided to regulate the matter legally) have set themselves is to find and allocate organs in the best possible manner, so as to ensure that the supply of organs is equal to – or at any rate, balanced with – the demand. This is the consideration on which economic analysis studies of the law in the field of organ transplants were based (Hansmann).

The issue of how these objectives can be reached – donation or market – is a matter of secondary importance, even from the point of view of bioethics. The top priority issue is how to ensure that the available organs are allocated to the highest possible number of people in need.

So, currently the discussion is entirely focussed on these two positions, and there seems to be nothing in between the two polarized visions. As we described them above, they have now become so radicalized that they are destined never to meet: *either* donation *or* market.

But there is a significant element within this debate. None of the proposed systems (or those actually applied) to find and allocate organs for transplantation is satisfactory. The market notion has never moved beyond a purely theoretical plane, where it is mentioned, in general terms, as a possible alternative to donation. It has never been included in any legislative project. On the contrary, the legislations of those countries which have regulated the matter have always solemnly refused to accept any contact with anything even remotely resembling a market, and disdainfully rejected any commercial connotation. The documents produced by Ethics Committees and the reports annexed to the bills presented to national Parliaments state that any contact with a market orientation is precluded by moral principles. The market appears to be an insult to altruism; it privileges the positions of economic advantage since it offers access only to the rich. As a result it causes and favours the supply of organs by the poorer classes.

Furthermore, the market is a factor discriminating between poor and rich countries. Only in English-speaking countries were the first steps taken towards a market-based approach, although only in theory. And perhaps an echo of that debate can be felt in some of the norms contained in the British Human Fertilization and Embryology Act (1990).

It is worthwhile to stop a while and examine the moral reasons which suggest that the market, as a concept, must be rejected in that it hinders solidarity and is antithetical to the spirit of a donation. Why does solidarity or altruism *have* to be totally without advantages for the person who performs an act of solidarity or altruism? Why *must* there *not* be any form of compensation for a person who donates? Why *must* a donation absolutely be gratuitous? Why are we scandalized, why do we smile, when we hear the term 'rewarded donors'? Western civilization has this idea of altruism and liberality. The juridical model through which liberality takes place is the donation. From the very beginning the hallmarks of that model were two characteristic elements: the spirit of liberality (the *animus donandi*) and the gratuitousness. These elements set the donation model against all other models which contemplate an act of disposing of an asset. Roman law drew a distinction between *donare* and *negotium gerere* (Archi).

Well, it is very likely that in the debate on organ donation the reference to the juridical model of the donation will be misleading. The act of donating, conceived and disciplined in the contractual forms which the law regulates with rigorous norms of very ancient origin, to a large extent is foreign to the spirit and the modalities by which a gift of organs is exercised. Two points appear to me to be fundamental here. The first is the fact that an organ donation is made *in incertam personam*, that is to an unknown recipient. One might say that the organ is donated to the collectivity which will then choose the actual recipient – the beneficiary. In this sense it is not a donation contract in the juridical sense. Secondly, this type of act of liberality requires the intermediation of third parties, acting between the donor and the recipient. These intermediaries (the medical team, the hospital or clinic, the judge), although they are not aiming at reaping a profit from the transaction, are certainly not acting out of a spirit of liberality: they are acting in the exercise of their profession.

Lastly, if an act of donation were in any way facilitated, encouraged, suggested, or made more interesting because it offered some form of advantage to the donor (for example, some medical benefit such as free medication or tax advantages, etc.) would this entirely cancel the spirit of solidarity? And if these advantages were capable of modifying considerably the percentage of organ donations, should they not be taken into consideration?

What were the practical motivations which transposed the issue of organ transplants from its original position as an act of liberality to a search for profit? One motivation which may be significant, although not everyone agrees on this, is the following: the notion of donating an organ, the gift ethic as related to the sacrifice of a part of one's own body, has not convinced the mass of public opinion. The information available does not even allow us to indicate in which countries organs are harvested and transplanted more easily and frequently than others; and even less so, does this information allow us to argue in favour of a more developed social conscience, of a different cultural background, of a different religious spirit, of a different ethic, etc.

In the United States only 15 organs per million inhabitants are actually used for transplants. The other transplantable organs are lost. In Europe, Italy comes next to last, with 8 organs per million inhabitants, whereas the country where the rate is highest – 22 – is one which is very close to us, in terms of social conscience, cultural background and religion, Spain.

How is it, then, that the donation model still appears as the only possible solution? The basic reason is that, as we stated earlier, it favours solidarity and – generally speaking – offers no privileges to anyone. Western societies stress the fundamental notion that the human body cannot be disposed of at will, it is not an asset and cannot be made the object of trade. This fundamental notion derives from the principle of the unviolability and integrity of the human body.

And it is without contradicting the concept that the human body cannot be disposed of at will that the only possible waiver to this principle develops and grows: alienation out of solidarity, with the gratuitous nature of the act being a fundamental aspect. A charitable act is the only possible exception to the rule of the sacredness of the human body. Catholic doctrine has only recently, and with a fair amount of difficulty, overcome this notion of the integrity of the body and separated it from the spiritual integrity of the human being. In recent years, in fact, the Catholic Church, although never giving a favourable opinion on cremation, has stopped condemning the practice (as it used to in the past).

So, a charitable act, performed for altruistic motives, cannot be remunerated or compensated, not even symbolically.

Now I should like to relate everything I have said so far to the topic of this discussion: new challenges to property.

To a large extent the debate on many topics in the field of bioethics is based on principles which relate to the notion of private property, the same notion that specialists in civil law know well. Whatever his cultural background (here I mean either continental or common law), the jurist will always keep as his starting point the traditional right over things, whether he is talking about a real relationship or about property right.

When we speak of human organs, or of embryos, or even of a foetus during the later stages of gestation, the jurist's basic perspective will be that of property law. My body my property. Never has a slogan had such a close identification with the technical juridical meaning of the term.

And, in fact, all resistances against the possibility, however remote, that the harvesting of human organs for therapeutic purposes should become the prerogative of the health services, in other words of the State, and therefore no longer fall under the private individual's 'right to dispose', can all basically be traced back to the proprietary aura that permeates the entire scene of bioethics. This notion makes a kidney an asset, a good, which therefore can be the object of a right, can be disposed of or alienated (and at this point it matters little whether it is donated *gratis* or not), can be bought with a contract between living persons or by succession *mortis causa*.

This is where the ultimate reason for the consensus of the nearest of kin lies, before the harvesting of an organ. I am entitled legitimately to dispose of the corpse of my deceased relative and his/her organs. Well, the rationale that lies behind almost all European legislations in matters related to organ donations is exactly this one. And even the ambiguous form of the 'presumed consent' to a donation (a presumed donation, a 'putative' donation) is based on this conceptual premise.

6. The Right to Die

The Right to Die

Ian Kennedy*

The general concern of this session of the meeting is with what some call the right to die. For purposes of analysis, I divide this into the right of patients to refuse treatment when death may be the consequence of such refusal and the right to request assistance in bringing about death. As regards the former, Anglo-American jurisprudence is now clear that a competent patient is entitled in law to refuse treatment even though death may ensue and that any doctor who thereafter attempts to treat the patient acts unlawfully.[1] (The régime of law governing the care of the incompetent warrants separate examination and will not be addressed here.)

In this paper I have chosen to concern myself with what many call euthanasia. I am not, however, at least initially, intending to rehearse all the moral arguments for and against various forms of euthanasia. You are all very familiar with them. They have long been a part of the currency of intelligent debate. They are of course also the cause of much confused thought. Out of such confusion have marched numerous armies intent on advancing their version of received truth, refusing to accept anything other than capitulation from those who oppose them. Nothing that I can say will add anything that has not been said countless times before and better.

Furthermore, I would delude myself if I thought that anything I may say will move you to change your minds.

Euthanasia and the Law

I have set for myself a more limited goal. I want to concentrate on the law, specifically the law governing the relationship between a doctor and a patient in circumstances in

* Professor of Law, Kings College, London, England, UK.

1 *See*, e.g. *Airedale National Health Service Trust* v. *Bland* [1993] 1 All ER 821 (House of Lords UK) and *Thor* v. *Superior Court* (1993) 855 P 2d 375 (California Supreme Court USA).

Cosimo Marco Mazzoni (ed.), A Legal Framework for Bioethics, 181-197.
©1998 *Kluwer Law International. Printed in The Netherlands.*

which euthanasia in one form or another may fall to be considered. Perhaps it would help if I set out what I intend euthanasia to refer to and indicate my particular concern. I take euthanasia to have acquired at least the following meanings. It refers to actively bringing about the death of a patient, whether with or without the patient's consent, and to passively allowing a patient to die, with or without consent, when it would have been possible by continued treatment to keep the patient alive. Of these forms, my concern initially is with the competent patient who asks his doctor to assist him to die.

I must concentrate on English law since that is what I know. It is my suspicion, however, that the conceptual issues raised are common to most legal systems and can, therefore, serve as the basis for discussion.

The Law is Unsatisfactory

It may be helpful to begin with my conclusion. The current state of the law, as it touches on the form of euthanasia which is my concern here, is extremely unsatisfactory. It is not fair to patients or doctors and it does not serve the public interest. It should be changed or, better put, developed. It will, however, take considerable courage and ingenuity to do so. And, it will necessarily involve having to take a view on the very analysis of the moral arguments about euthanasia which I said I intended to avoid. But it will be a different analysis. It will not proceed from some set of abstract premises. Rather, its point of departure and driving force will be the current reality of medical practice and how the law is applied to it.

Let me begin by explaining why the law is currently unsatisfactory. Dr. A and Dr. B are in all respects similar. They are caring, respected doctors with impeccable backgrounds. Dr. A's patient, Mr. X is suffering from a fatal illness which is now in its final stages. Mr. X is near to death and in great pain. He can also see the pain his suffering is causing to his family who maintain a vigil at his bedside. He asks Dr. A to put him out of his misery. Dr. A explains that he cannot do so, but he will steadily vary the cocktail of pain relieving drugs which Mr. X receives. The effect of this, Dr. A explains, will be that over a period of time, perhaps a few days the dose prescribed will be such that Mr. X will in fact die, albeit, he adds, as a consequence of the attempt to relieve pain. Two days later Mr. X dies. Meanwhile Dr. B's patient, Mrs. Z is in virtually the same situation. In response to Mrs. Z's entreaties Dr. B says that he will give her something which will bring her the relief and release she seeks. Dr. B injects Mrs. Z with potassium chloride. She dies within minutes, a rapid end to her pain and suffering.

What characterizes the two courses of conduct taken by the doctors is that the doctors' intentions were the same – to ease pain and bring about a peaceful death – their motives were the same – to be as caring as they can be for their stricken patients – their conduct was the same – the active administration of injections – and the result was the same – the death of their patients, though in Mr. X's case it took considerably longer to achieve. What further distinguishes Dr. A from Dr. B is that before Dr. A began the course of injections intended to bring about Mr. X's death, he specifically disavowed any such intention. Furthermore, he used drugs listed as pain relievers, though also recognized as causing death. Dr. B used a much more effective pain reliever but pain relief is not an indicated use for the drug. The only other thing that differentiates them is that the law regards Dr. A as a perfectly reasonable doctor while it regards Dr. B as a murderer.

'Is this not rather odd?' you may ask, 'Dr. A goes home to his family. Dr. B gets a mandatory life sentence, the penalty for murder in English law.' The legal rationale which is offered is that doctors may bring about the death of their patients in such circumstances, always provided that their first and primary intention in embarking on the course of conduct that ends in death is to relieve pain. They can know that death will result, they can want and intend that death results, but as long as they claim otherwise – that 'this is for your pain' – they are entirely within the law. If on the other hand they do something designed specifically to end the patient's life, they break the law.

Before going any further, it is important to look at this concept of intention. To the English lawyer, if not the moral philosopher, intention means either doing something for a purpose or doing something with the knowledge that as a substantial certainty a certain result will follow. This latter meaning is one which non-lawyers are not always familiar with and find difficult to accept.

Bearing in mind this second meaning, the legal rationale just offered is too easy. It will not do. Both of our doctors in fact did something designed specifically to end the patient's life. So, given that it is the only distinguishing feature, the legal rationale would have to be that the doctor in carrying out his intention must use a recognized pain killer. Only in this way can he take advantage of a legal rationale based on a so-called primary intention.

So, you may say, the law gets more odd. A doctor is or is not a murderer depending on the drug he uses and how that drug is classified, or primarily classified. But, you can reply, this is not so odd when you think about it. Giving a patient a poison is not much different in principle from shooting the patient with a gun. And, shooting patients even at their request is surely not something we are prepared to discuss. Thus, the law is right to stick to the hard and fast rule that only if the doctor treats the patient with a genuinely recognized therapeutic agent with the intention of treating him by way of pain relief can he remain within the law. All other conduct can conceptually and actually be differentiated from this and is outside the law. Furthermore, this position has the additional advantage of offering us a clear rule to follow.

Why the Law is Unsatisfactory

I repeat, however, that this is not satisfactory. Here are some of the reasons.

1. First, the law should always strive to be clear and unambiguous. Nowhere is this more so than when life and death are in the balance and a charge of murder is the consequence of breaking the rule. In the treatment of the patient whose life has become to him an intolerable burden, however, the legal rule just offered is far from clear. It relies on there being an agreed list of pharmacological agents or medical interventions which are universally accepted as having a single function. But all drugs have multiple functions and are appropriate in some circumstances and inappropriate in others. Further, it is well known that doctors will advocate a particular drug for one purpose while other doctors will decry such use as reckless or unproven. It is part of the history of medicine that drugs designed for one reason become used for another. What is to stop a doctor claiming that he intended to relieve pain albeit through unconventional means? And this alerts us to the second problem in the pursuit of clarity. Everything ultimately turns on what the doctor claims he was trying to achieve. As long as he uses the right verbal formula and records it in the patient's notes and, to be on the safe side, does not use too unusual a drug, he will stay within the law. Knowing how to play the game becomes the crucial determinant of criminal liability, rather than what objectively is done or what results. When the crime is murder, this can hardly be satisfactory.
2. The second reason follows on from this. The current state of the law endorses, indeed entrenches, hypocrisy. 'We all know what you are doing, but use the magic words, "I'm doing this to relieve your pain" and all will be well'. Alternatively, the law encourages casuistry, as those who are anxious to do right by their patients, as they see it, feel compelled to resort to subterfuge out of fear of prosecution. Fear of prosecution is of course eminently desirable when designed to deter what is accepted as wrong. But when it is neither the means nor the end which is regarded as wrong but rather the absence of attendant rhetoric or ritual, such fear becomes itself a wrong.
3. The law works against the interests of patients in a number of ways. It will be said, of course, that the crucial feature of the existing law is that it protects patients who might otherwise be abused by their doctors, and by abuse here we must include killing patients. But does it? Obviously those patients who fall into the hands of a murderous doctor appear to be protected. Mercifully there are not too many such doctors around! And, of course, when such a rarity does crop up the current law would not prevent him from carrying out his murderous intent, provided he remembered to use the 'right' drugs and make the right noises. But we can forget such doctors. They are so rare. Certainly what such a doctor might or might not do should not serve to determine the shape of the law. Instead, we should concern ourselves with the everyday conscientious doctor. How does the law fail to serve

the interests of the patient by preventing the doctor from serving him as he might wish? The answer lies in the examples considered earlier. Fearful of the law, not really understanding it, he responds to his patient's wish for a peaceful end by embarking on the process of increasing dosage until the desired objective is reached. This may, as we have seen, take some time. During this time the patient is required to continue to suffer, physically and mentally, so that the proper form may be observed. Furthermore, the patient may fall into that relatively small but no less real group of patients whose pain is beyond the reach of drugs. Such a patient must simply continue to suffer until the proper legal courtesies have been observed and the final dose can bring the intended death. It is hard to argue that the law protects the patient. In fact, the law specifically asks him to suffer so as to protect others. The irony will not be lost on you or him. If these others are anything like him, it is precisely this 'protection' which they do not want.

4. The law is also unsatisfactory in that it can harm doctors in their ability to maintain a relationship of trust and support when their patients most need it. If, out of fear of the law or uncertainty about what he may properly do, the doctor rejects his patient's entreaties, it would be no surprise if the patient felt abandoned. The patient's trust in his doctor, so critical as death approaches, is lost and suffering is compounded. The doctor, for his part, is forced to deny his training. If he is to satisfy his patient's request, he must engage in subterfuge. Alternatively, he must fail his patient by not providing the means to end the patient's pain.
5. Finally, the current law is unsatisfactory in that, so far from serving the public interest it can, in fact, undermine it. The hypocrisy it engenders brings it into disrepute. The care and support a patient receives is made to depend on how alert his doctor may be to ways of manipulating the law.

Change the Law

If the law is so unsatisfactory, something, in the oft-heard words of the irascible bystander, should be done about it. Arguably the law should be changed out of an understanding that the realities of modern medicine make the old certainties untenable. These certainties are, you will recall, that a doctor may act in such a way as to bring about death, provided his so-called primary intention, in the regime of treatment he chooses, is to relieve pain. The doctor may even stand by in certain circumstances and take no action to ward off the advent of death. But the doctor may never do any positive act with a view to bringing about the patient's death. I remind you that this is a distinction without a difference. The law permits the administration of drugs in ever-increasing doses, until death occurs. Is not this a positive act intended to bring about death, once the legal concept of intention is properly understood? Only the dose will determine whether death occurs immediately or after a suitable delay.

Legislation

There are only two ways of changing English law. Parliament has to pass legislation or the courts have to create new law or reinterpret existing law. (I leave out recourse to the European Court of Human Rights as being too complex an issue to deal with satisfactorily here. It should not, however, be discounted). What are the prospects for legislation? The simple answer is, not good. Clearly, we have to identify what Parliament could be asked to consider. In this paper I am initially concentrating on the situation in which patients ask their doctors for help to achieve relief from pain and release from a life which no longer has any value to them. So, putting aside other forms of euthanasia for the time being, can Parliament be expected to change the law so as to permit doctors to respond to such requests? In the past Parliament has resolutely refused to contemplate even the slightest change. The tenor of the times and the current composition of Parliament suggest that this opposition is likely to persist for some long time to come. One of the principal reasons for this is simply the difficulty of getting any thoughtful debate off the ground. No sooner is the issue raised than all the massed ranks of unreason form themselves into opposition. The rhetorical bogeymen are given a fresh airing. Defenders of the 'sanctity of life' represent themselves as fighting in the last ditch against those whose agenda is really one of Nazi eugenics. I use florid language because that is the language often employed. These intimidatory tactics are, of course, a denial of the normal conventions of a society which boasts the Mother of Parliaments and a commitment to free debate. But euthanasia is one of the issues which are regarded as taboo and not to be discussed. It is no surprise, therefore, that legislators responsive to such claims or simply reluctant to attract the unfavourable attention which would follow if they got involved, are far and away in the majority in Parliament. The consequence is that legislation on euthanasia, in any form, is a non-starter.

'Under-the-counter' Deals

Thus, if there is to be any change in the law, the impetus must come from elsewhere. But before exploring what may be possible, it may be helpful to notice one argument which appeals to some. It goes as follows. Admittedly, the present state of the law is most unsatisfactory. It is hypocritical and fails the patient, the doctor and the public interest. But changing the law poses so many dangers, quite apart from the more florid assertions of some, that the wisest course is to leave the law as it is while turning a blind eye to those cases in which it is breached for what we all agree are good reasons. This is what one famous commentator, Professor David Daube, once dubbed as doing 'under-the-counter deals with Death'.

The difficulty with this approach, apart from its perpetuation of the law's hypocrisy, is that it is no longer a real option. Decisions about the care of patients are not taken under-the-counter. Too many people are involved. Too much has to be recorded.

It is all far more in the open. Furthermore, of course, it assumes a critical level of agreement about the cases which justify such deals. The difficulty is that it is precisely such agreement which does not exist, particularly among those who see it as their task to ensure that no deviation from the current law goes unnoticed. And, even more important, it cannot be fair to doctors to present them with a situation in which they have to guess whether people will subsequently endorse what they have done or whether, if they guess wrong, the law will be applied in all its rigour and they will face a charge of murder.

The Courts

So, to repeat, if there is to be change, where is it to come from? The only answer is, from the courts. What I am going to suggest is that the courts can and indeed have the obligation to create more satisfactory law than that which currently prevails, given the unwillingness of Parliament to do so.

'Not for us'

We cannot examine how the courts might proceed, however, until we have disposed of an issue of principle. It will be argued by some, not least some of the judges, that on a matter as morally and socially contentious as euthanasia, it cannot be for judges to change or even develop the law. Only those elected by and responsible to the people have the authority to do so. It would be to usurp their role for the judges to presume to make new law. They exist to fill in gaps in the law and iron out anomalies. They are, according to this approach, at best interstitial legislators. This is a well-known judicial response. The cynic might observe that it never seems to restrain the judges when they feel the urge to develop the law. They go ahead and do so, relying on the alternative theory: that the law is dynamic and never stands still and it is their task constantly to be renewing it!

In truth, we all know that there is no simple dividing line which says that this is for the courts and this is for the Legislature. What is involved is a delicate calculation by the judges as to the relative authority of the courts and Parliament. A weak government or a strong judiciary will see the balance shift to the courts. Of course this is not to deny a crucial difference between them. The courts cannot, unlike Parliament, choose the issue to be decided. It is merely to suggest that when the courts are presented with an issue, whether or not they will opt for the role of legislator in the strong sense will not depend on some abstract theory of the separation of powers. Instead, it will depend on whether the judges have the stomach to take the issue on and whether they think that, if they do so, they will be able to get away with it. In short, therefore, it is and always has been for the judges to decide what is and what is not for them to decide.

After all, as Lord Denning might have put it in his heyday, if Parliament does not like what the courts decide, they can always legislate.

The Courts Have a Duty

If we can dispose of, or at least cast doubt on, the objection in principle to the reshaping of the law by the courts, we can move on to a far more important point. This is that, so far from having, as would be argued by many judges, a duty to leave the matter to Parliament, the courts instead have quite the opposite duty, as they deal with cases which come before them, namely, to reshape and develop the law relating to euthanasia. I say a duty because I do not think that as a matter of legal theory it is open to them to say that they regret the state of the law but it remains the law until such a time as Parliament chooses to do something about it.(My argument owes much to the approach adopted by Madame Justice McLachlin, albeit in a somewhat different legal context, in the landmark decision of the Canadian Supreme Court in *Rodriguez* v. *Attorney-General of British Columbia*, 1993).[2]

I ought to make my reasoning explicit. First, whenever a court reaches any decision it makes a choice. By the very nature of law, courts are never compelled by some inevitable process of logic to reach a particular view. If the process of decision-making were so automatic or predictable we would not need to go to court in the first place. Second, if courts have a choice, then to maintain the status quo is as much a decision of policy as to change it. Third, in considering whether to change it, the court must always have in mind the fundamental principles which the law is committed to uphold. In my view, in the area of medical law, the fundamental principles are those of human rights. Fourth, if a proper consideration of human rights requires that the law be changed or reshaped, then it is the duty of the court to do so.

It must be conceded immediately that there can be honest differences as to what a concern for human rights requires. Thus. a court could quite legitimately decide that no change in the law was called for. But the point of the argument being advanced is that the court may only reach this view after proper reflection on the demands of human rights. It is, to repeat myself, the court's duty to do so. And, given the unsatisfactory state of the law relating to euthanasia, it is my conviction that a court would be compelled to conclude that they should change or reshape the law.

2 *Rodriguez* v. *Attorney-General of Britísh Columbia* (1993) 82 BCLR (2d) 273.

Precedents

In case you think this is too radical or provocative a view, it may be worthwhile, as part of the process of working out what in fact the court should do, to notice a few of the better known cases in English law in which the courts have not shrunk in the past from reshaping the law, specifically medical law, even if to do so involved adjudicating on a subject of significant moral controversy and where doing so attracted criticism that the role of the Legislature was being usurped. In the case of *R* v. *Bourne*, (1939)[3] Macnaughton J. chose to carve out a defence to a charge of unlawfully procuring an abortion. In doing so he not only developed the law so as to allow Dr. Bourne to go unpunished but more importantly incorporated into the law a recognition of the need to have regard for and seek to protect the human rights of women who might find themselves in the desperate condition of the girl in the case; raped, pregnant and in danger of becoming a physical and mental wreck.

Second, in a series of cases culminating in the case of Re J (1991), the courts have established that there are circumstances in which it may be legally permissible to allow a severely handicapped baby or child to die rather than continue to treat it. It cannot be doubted that such cases raise the most profound moral questions and exercise many. They involve, after all, what many regard as a form of euthanasia, and one practised on a child who though desperately ill is not dying. Did the courts resile from deciding what was obviously such a controversial and morally charged case? Far from it. They returned to it on a number of occasions, refining the legal rule until satisfied that it was right. In doing so they acted as a court should. They recognized that here was an issue which was of the utmost importance, was not going to go away and which Parliament was most unlikely to deal with. They recognized their responsibility in such circumstances to shape and develop the law. They were not deflected by those who pointed to slippery slopes and foretold horrors to come. They shaped the law so as to give effect to the human rights of the child, recognizing that it is plausible to argue for a right to die in circumstances where continued existence is a form of torture.

The third example I cite is perhaps the most significant. It is, of course, the case of Tony Bland.[4] In that case, the courts were asked to declare that it is lawful to discontinue medical treatment of a patient, including the administration of food and fluids, if in all the circumstances the patient's condition is hopeless, (he had been in a persistent vegetative state for three years) and he is unable to derive any benefit from such interventions. This was, on one view, an epoch-making decision in that the court appeared to endorse what to some is euthanasia, (passive euthanasia – allowing

3 *R* v. *Bourne* [1939] 1 KB 687.
4 *Airedale National Health Service Trust* v. *Bland* [1993] 1 All ER 821.

someone to die or not preventing the death). On another view, it merely allowed the law to recognize and confirm the legality of what had long been medical practice.

Bland is important for our purposes. The judges had no option but to decide the question put to them. In formulating their decision, however, they could have taken refuge in the 'this is a matter for Parliament, not for us' formula. After all, the issue at stake was one of life or death for Tony Bland. The temptation to do so must have been very great. They could, alternatively, have arrived at what might be called a holding decision: that what is proposed by the doctors is unlawful under the existing law, as constituting the crime of homicide. They could even have decided that they lacked jurisdiction either because what was being asked for was their consent to the proposed withdrawal of treatment on behalf of Tony Bland, which they had no authority to give, or was a declaration as to the illegality of future conduct, which on good authority courts are unwilling to grant. They chose none of these. Instead, they chose to take the case on. They clearly saw it as their duty to develop and reshape the law. They chose to reshape it so that it was more in touch with, more sensitive to, the realities of modern medicine whereby technology and dedicated care could result in a patient who was not dead but who had no life.

Finally, and most important for our purposes, they chose to reshape the law by reference to human rights, recognizing, as in the cases of severely handicapped children, that we can validly talk of a right to be allowed to die, or at least to be free from further intervention. The language used by the courts is of crucial importance. It was that which is customarily used by the courts in cases of this kind. They referred to the best interests of the patient as the guiding principle in determining what the law allows in the case of patients unable to decide for themselves. The importance of this language lies in the fact that the best interests formula in this context, is, I suggest, another way of expressing a commitment to human rights, since it must always presumptively be the case that only by respecting a patient's human rights can you be acting in his best interests.

What these cases show us is that there is strong evidence that the English courts when faced with morally challenging and controversial problems of medical law involving questions of life and death have not shrunk from reshaping and developing the law. Conscious of the fact that the law must keep abreast with the pace of change in medicine, the courts have seen it as their duty to be the architects of change. They have not taken refuge behind some notion of the separation of powers and left matters to Parliament not least out of an awareness that, while action is called for, Parliament is unlikely to act. Indeed, medical law as a whole and not merely in cases of life and death, is largely judge-made law. It has to be said, of course, that concern for human rights has not always guided the courts: there come to mind such cases as those concerning informed consent, particularly in the case of children, the sterilization of the mentally disabled and the licensing of a Caesarean operation on an unwilling mother. But even as regards these, while it can be said that they got the law wrong, the courts clearly recognized the need to make new law and did so readily.

Law and Euthanasia Revisited

So now we come to the crunch. All that has been said so far is, in effect, by way of preamble. It has set the scene and sought to demonstrate both that the courts have a duty to reshape the law and the principles which they have applied and should continue to apply in doing so. The question now is how can the courts reshape and develop the law relating to euthanasia.

And at this point it is necessary for me to show my hand. I have so far referred to doctor-assisted suicide as being the form of euthanasia which I am particularly concerned with. I should make it plain that when I use this term I do not limit it to the situation in which the doctor assists but the last act is that of the patient. I intend to include the situation in which the last act is done by the doctor, in other words, where the doctor actively brings about the patient's death. I accept that this is provocative. In my view, however, the supposed distinction between doctor-assisted suicide, as the term is ordinarily used, and active voluntary euthanasia, whereby the doctor actively brings about the patient's death, is illusory.

On examination, the distinction collapses both factually and morally. Three examples may illustrate the difficulty in drawing any clear line on the facts:

1. The doctor agrees to set up a procedure whereby the patient may by pressing a button deliver intra-venously a fatal dose of some drug. The last act will be that of the patient. But the patient finds that he lacks the strength to press the button the whole way down and asks the doctor to help. The doctor does so. Is the last act that of the doctor or the patient? Other variations on the same theme can be imagined. The doctor guides the patient's hand to the button, or the patient's hand slips and the doctor holds the button for him.
2. The patient decides to end his life by drinking a lethal concoction. The doctor helps to hold the glass to the patient's mouth and he opens his mouth and drinks. Again, whose is the last act? And again variations can be imagined. The glass slips and the doctor puts it to the patient's lips, or the patient drinks some and then hands the glass to the doctor so that he can rest for a moment before drinking the remainder.
3. The patient asks the doctor to inject him with a fatal dose of a drug. He extends his arm to receive the injection and once the skin is punctured, presses the plunger on the hypodermic to release the drug. Again, I ask, is it possible or fruitful to seek to identify whose is the last act?

What of the supposed moral distinction between the two forms of conduct? (Of course, it must be recognized that to some all talk of even suicide, let alone euthanasia, is morally repugnant. Obviously, there is nothing in this paper for them.) Here again the distinction collapses. Our principal concern, I have suggested, should be for human rights and human dignity. If personal freedom is to have any real meaning or significance, it should not fail the patient precisely at that moment when he is most anxious to express it by seeking to take control of his destiny in the face of intolerable illness. To maintain the distinction, the argument must be that if he can bring his life to an end by his own hand, so be it. But if he cannot, he must accept his fate. This cannot be right. It is incompatible with society's commitment to respect the freedom of others that we deny him the enjoyment of that freedom simply by virtue of his physical frailty. It is a consistent theme of respect for the individual, as expressed in the language of human rights, that no one should be discriminated against simply on the basis of disability. Yet, on the facts as I have put them – the patient unable to act for himself – this is precisely the effect of forbidding the doctor to assist his patient to die. Further, I should make it clear that I would not necessarily confine the notion of disability, in the sense of the patient being unable to act for himself, to physical disability. To do so would mean that if the patient could act for himself he must be left to do so. This is far too harsh a view. It ignores the mental suffering which the patient must also endure and which may well have the result of sapping his will or ability to do anything. After all, if the patient were able to act for himself he may well not seek the assistance of his doctor, save at the level of advice as to what his options might be if he wished to end his life. And, finally, to avoid all doubt, I would emphasize that to recognize the right of a patient to ask and the freedom of his doctor to comply in no way obliges the doctor to comply. It is not part of my argument that doctors must abandon their own beliefs. This would, in the context, be too great an imposition. It is another question whether the doctor who is unable to meet his patient's request should then transfer the care of the patient to one who is prepared to do so.

So, having made explicit the true extent of my enquiry, let me now return to what I described as the crunch question: how can the courts develop the law relating to euthanasia? As a first step in answering this question, it is of critical importance to remind ourselves how far English law has already gone. At the very least this will give us some indication of the scale of the challenge faced by the courts if they are to go further. So, what does English law currently say about the various situations in which the issue of euthanasia can be said to arise?

1. The first situation is that of the patient who while entirely competent refuses further treatment and asks to be left alone. Whether the patient is dying or not makes no difference. The law is already clear. It is unlawful to treat the patient in the face of his refusal.[5] There may need to be some tidying up of the law at the edges, particularly as regards the competent minor. Otherwise the law has already been developed, and in such a way as clearly to give proper recognition to the human rights of the patient. If, as some would insist, by leaving such a patient to die the doctor commits euthanasia, then the law to that extent permits euthanasia.

5 *See Airedale National Health Servive Trust* v. *Bland* [1993] 1 All ER 821.

2. Secondly, there is the necessary logical extension of this first situation where the patient is now incompetent to express his wishes, for whatever reason, but prior to the onset of incompetence expressed a clear wish that treatment should cease in certain plainly identified circumstances so that he be allowed to die, the law is clear. His wish must be respected. Indeed, the growth of interest in Advance Directives (sometimes called Living Wills) is posited on this assumption. Admittedly, the law still requires considerable refinement, but the general principle is clear. And, it was the courts again who developed the principle.[6] Thus, if this is a form of euthanasia and some hold that it is, then the law to this extent permits euthanasia.
3. Third, there is the patient whose condition is agreed, after all appropriate tests, to be hopeless. The law again is clear. Provided the patient meets certain criteria, there is no obligation on the doctor to continue treatment which has become pointless. The law allows the doctor either to withdraw existing treatment, as in the case, for example, of the continued administration of food or drugs, or to withhold treatment as in the case, for example, of connection to a respirator.[7] Thus, if this is a form of euthanasia, and many regard it as such, the law to this extent permits euthanasia.
4. Fourth, there is the patient who is incompetent to express any wish, who has not given any prior indication of his wishes concerning treatment, and whose condition does not meet the criteria of hopelessness sketched out by the courts. Here again the law is clear. Such a patient must receive all appropriate treatment for as long as there is a real possibility that he can or may be able to benefit from it. To withhold or withdraw treatment in such a case is unlawful. A fortiori it is unlawful to do anything designed to bring about the death of the patient. Thus, if this is a form of euthanasia, and, of course, it is the form which causes most concern, the law does not to this extent permit euthanasia.

WHEN THE PATIENT ASKS FOR HELP TO DIE

5. We come, finally, to the fifth set of circumstances, the one I am particularly concerned with in this paper. The patient, while competent requests his doctor to assist him to die. To make it abundantly clear what is being considered, we will posit a patient who is suffering from intractable pain and has a fatal illness. Furthermore, we will assume either that the patient by reason of his illness is unable to do anything to bring about his own death; i.e. if he is to have his way, his doctor

6 *See* Re T (adult: refusal of treatment) [1992] 4 All ER 649.
7 *See* Re J (a minor) (wardship: medical treatment) [1991] Fam 33 and *Airedale National Health Servive Trust* v. *Bland* [1993] 1 All ER 821.

must supply the death- dealing service, or that the patient requests assistance, for example, in obtaining the means to bring about his death.

As I have made it clear, it is here that I maintain that the courts have a duty so to develop the law as to allow the doctor to meet the request of the patient without thereby committing a criminal offence. How can the courts do this? Currently, the doctor's conduct falls within the area of conduct not permitted by law, i.e. if this is a form of euthanasia, and clearly it is so regarded, the law to this extent does not permit euthanasia.

Reshaping the Law

How can the courts reshape the law so as to correct its current unsatisfactory state? How can they develop the permitted forms of euthanasia to include the circumstance in which the doctor assists his patient to die?

1. Where the last act is the doctor's

The obstacle in the current law appears formidable. It has been repeated on any number of occasions, most recently in the House of Lords in Bland, that any act done with the intention of bringing about the death of a patient is murder. But this is where we came in. The obstacle is not formidable at all. It is non-existent. It describes both the injection of the cocktail of pain-relieving drugs and the injection of potassium chloride. Either both are forbidden or both are allowed because, try as you will, you cannot get any half-way plausible analytical wedge between them.

What is required, then, is no more than a re-description of the doctor's conduct. And, significantly, I do not mean a re-description of the legal-analytical nature of the conduct. The legal analysis is common to both situations, in that there is an act, there is intention as understood in law, there is causation and there is a resulting death. What I mean, therefore, is that the doctor's conduct be so described that it may be subsumed within the range of conducts which are already permitted by law. Put shortly, the court should decide that in certain specified and carefully defined circumstances, the concept of treating a patient for dying, already well recognized by the law in the context, for example, of the severely handicapped child, should extend to the administration of that which will kill the patient. They should recognize that the law's guiding principle of seeking to ensure that the doctor acted in the patient's best interests can clearly be extended to these circumstances. After all, we are assuming that the doctor may only act on the request of the patient and who better than the patient knows what is in his best interests? And, by defining best interests in this way, the court, of course, gives effect to the underlying demands of human rights which are entailed in this concept. It will, of course, be a brave court which will take this step. Moreover, in the traditions of judge-made law, the court will be extremely anxious to establish appropriate limits and safeguards. I shall, therefore, return to the question of safeguards shortly.

2. Where the last act is the patient's
   Ironically, the legal obstacles in the way of the English courts are significantly greater here than in the case of active voluntary euthanasia. This is because by virtue of a specific statutory provision, Section 2 of the Suicide Act 1961, it is a crime to aid and abet a suicide. And, of course, the English courts do not have the power to strike down such legislation, given the absence of a written constitution.[8]

It would not be an easy task for the courts to avoid Section 2. There are, however, some arguments, of varying strength, which the courts could marshal:

a. treatment for dying is a legally accepted form of treatment, whether carried out by the doctor alone or by the patient with the doctor's assistance and as such does not constitute suicide as a matter of law
b. the word 'unlawfully' must be read into Section 2, such that the doctor will not commit the crime of aiding and abetting a suicide by assisting his patient to die, since treating for dying is a legally accepted form of treatment and, thus not unlawful.
c. even if, *prima facie*, the doctor is guilty of a crime under Section 2, he may take advantage of the defence of necessity, since only in this way can the law give proper effect to the overriding right of the patient to self-determination.
d. Section 2 is contrary to Article 8 of the European Convention on Human Rights, (a 'constitutional law' argument akin to those used in Canada and the US).

Safeguards

I referred earlier to the fact that the courts while developing the law would also have to develop safeguards. To those who regard what I propose as a proposition too far, no safeguards would be enough. But assuming that the general case is accepted so far, a court would clearly have to give its mind to a number of matters, to establish, if you will, a sort of general framework within which the doctor and patient must operate. The courts have shown themselves quite willing to do this in other controversial areas of medical law, e.g., in the case of the sterilization of the mentally disabled. I have no doubt that they could do so here.

8 Compare the *Rodriguez* case in Canada, referred to earlier, and recent developments in the United States, e.g., *Compassion in Dying* v. *Washington*, 1994, U.S. Dist., unreported: Docket No. C94-119R.

Here is not the place to set out in detail the various safeguards which may be called for. They are complex and deserve extensive analysis. Here I will merely refer briefly to what I regard as central matters.

1. the patient must be competent and appropriate mechanisms must exist to establish this
2. the decision must be voluntary and again appropriate measures must exist to establish this
3. there must be no available therapy which will alleviate the patient's circumstances (and the patient's condition must be one of intolerable suffering)
4. the patient must have received appropriate counselling
5. the patient must be suffering from a terminal illness
6. there must be an interval of time between the patient's decision and any subsequent action (save where circumstances call for immediate relief)
7. assisted suicide or active voluntary euthanasia may only be carried out by a doctor
8. the patient's death must be recorded as assisted suicide or active voluntary euthanasia in the relevant documents and reported to the appropriate authorities

(9. the court's permission should be sought through appropriate proceedings).

Obviously, these proposed safeguards will need to be kept under review by the courts. Some of them are more problematical than others. For example, I regard it as likely that the courts would stipulate that the patient must be suffering from a fatal illness. This presents its own problems of definition; it clearly covers the patient in the last stages of a malignant disease, but does it extend to the patient with motor neurone disease who has reached the point where he has had enough, even though death is not imminent? Arguably, it should extend to both. It would not, by contrast, extend to the patient crippled by arthritis and unable to derive any more pleasure from life. The law could return to such a case and others which are similar, once the initial development of the law argued for here has been assimilated.

Secondly, the courts are likely to regard it as imperative that the law should only allow doctors to act so as to assist their patients to die. Three reasons immediately present themselves. First, medical skill is required in determining the patient's condition. Secondly, medical skill is required in conducting the poignant dialogue which may culminate in the patient's request to be helped to die. Thirdly, medical skill is required in the process of treating to die. I do not advocate, nor should the law allow, the mere administration of some killing agent without regard to the process and manner of the patient's death. It is argued strongly, for example, by those in Holland who have experience that considerable care and skill must be exercised in assisting a patient to die.[9]

9 On the Dutch experience, *see* Battin, 'Voluntary Euthanasia and the Risk of Abuse: Can We Learn Anything from the Netherlands?', (1992) 20 *Law, Medicine and Health Care* 133.

Thirdly, I have made it clear that the courts will seek to establish a number of procedural safeguards. The experience in Holland is most instructive in this regard and the courts could well take advantage of the careful procedures in place there as a result of thoughtful deliberation by the representatives of the medical profession and the prosecuting authorities. Indeed, many of the safeguards which I propose mirror those adopted in Holland.

Conclusion

I will not have persuaded those who simply oppose all forms of euthanasia. I cannot dispel the fears of those who see any development of the law as the start of a slide down a slippery slope, save to remind them that there may be no slope and that, even if there is, not all slopes are slippery. I will not have persuaded those who say that no change in the law is necessary since good medical care, as practised by the hospice movement makes talk of euthanasia unnecessary. I used to hold this view myself. The difficulty is that hospice-type care is by no means available to all and in any event in some cases it does not succeed in easing the pain and burden of dying.

I hope, however, that I have succeeded in my modest ambition of persuading you of the following: that the law as it stands is unsatisfactory; that it appears to distinguish the indistinguishable; that the underlying commitment of the law to human rights demands that the patient who asks his doctor to help him to die should be treated in the same way as other dying patients whom the law allows to have a peaceful and dignified death; that the courts can readily develop the law to permit this given the developments they have crafted in the case, for example, of the severely handicapped child; and that the tools to achieve this result are available.

Euthanasia: Changes in Medicine and in Legal Regulation

Carlo Alberto Defanti*

1. Euthanasia: A Topical Issue

International debate on euthanasia has been extremely lively over the past years: I am thinking especially of a draft resolution presented to European Parliament by oncologist Léon Schwartzenberg in 1991, of the referendum consultations held in Washington State (1991) and in California (1992), both defeated by a very slim margin. But I am thinking above all of the depenalization of euthanasia approved in the Netherlands and of the very recent approval of a law in Oregon State which allows physicians to assist patients in suicide.

Euthanasia, nonetheless, remains unfortunately a difficult issue to deal with, where discussion stems not merely from differences of opinion, but from very divergent conceptions of the world. The arguments in favour or against its legitimacy are well-known, and there is nothing to suggest that the opposing parties will find an agreement on rational bases: for, with rational arguments one can demonstrate to one's opponent in a debate the fallacies in his reasoning, the contradictions within his basic thesis, but one can never eradicate the axioms on which that thesis is founded. The clash between proponents and opponents of euthanasia is especially harsh in a country like ours, where Catholic teachings, on the one hand, and a singularly clear and precise legislation, on the other, forbid both active euthanasia (Article 579 of the Penal Code: homicide of a consenting person) and physician-assisted suicide (Article 580 of the Penal Code: instigation to suicide and assistance thereto). Despite the fact that both the legal codes and the highest moral authority of this country continue to declare euthanasia unlawful (from juridical and moral standpoints, respectively), the notion is constantly gaining ground and becoming more and more accepted, both among physicians (as some recent opinion polls suggest), and in public opinion at large. It would therefore appear that – despite the fact that the debate is apparently insoluble on a rational plane – a growing number of people are changing their minds and embracing (or, at least, no longer fighting against) a pro-euthanasia stand, a position which had always been a minority one, at any rate in Judeo-Christian civilizations.

* Ospedali Riuniti Bergamo and Chairman of the Consulta di Bioetica, Milano, Italy.

Cosimo Marco Mazzoni (ed.), A Legal Framework for Bioethics, 199-210.
©1998 *Kluwer Law International. Printed in The Netherlands.*

This raises two questions.

The first is: why is it that the issue of euthanasia (and that of rational suicide, so closely linked to euthanasia), certainly not a new issue, since it was already widely debated in classical antiquity, has become so important today, as important in fact as other, totally new issues in bioethics, related to developments in science and technology?

The second concerns the reasons which can explain why so many sectors of public opinion are undergoing this new phenomenon of 'conversion' to euthanasia.

2. Changes in Medicine and in Common Sense Morality

I believe that the reasons for the change in our common-sense morality lie in the great changes modern medicine is undergoing, some of which have already taken place, while others are still in evolution. These changes involve all those issues related to death and dying. I shall try and describe some of the most significant ones, briefly.

First of all, the medical treatment of some diseases, using life-support means (initially these instruments and therapies were designed to be used in cases of acute diseases, but were later applied to chronic pathologies), today allows us to prolong – in some cases, considerably – the process of dying. This prolonged dying process can occasionally, paradoxically, lead to unexpected, negative consequences: for example, the treatment may worsen the terminal patient's suffering, in that it merely makes the whole process last longer, instead of relieving pain; or it may keep people alive in states of unconsciousness, or severely reduced consciousness, conditions which we commonly now consider degrading, or demeaning, or undignified, to use the most common expressions.

I feel it would be useful also to give some concrete examples. I am thinking first and foremost of severe brain traumas, that is, according to the definition of the Glasgow School, traumas involving loss of consciousness lasting more than 6 hours. These patients – unlike victims of milder traumas causing nothing more severe than concussion involving loss of consciousness only at the time of the trauma – reach the hospital already in a state of coma. Resuscitation treatment, in these patients, usually allows for a good recovery, or a recovery with moderate disabilities in about 40% of cases; a smaller percentage of patients (10%) experiences a slower return of consciousness, with lasting and severely invalidating neurological damage. But when the brain damage is massive, through some complex mechanisms I shall not go into here, the patient suffers a complete destruction of his cerebral matter. In these cases (about 48%) life-support therapies produce a paradoxical effect: the patient no longer shows any sign of brain activity, although he retains all major physiological activities, such as circulation, respiration (assisted), digestion, etc. This is what is normally called irreversible coma, which was first described and studied in the 1950s, and which raised one of the first and most problematic issues for the new field of bioethics. In the late 1960s the problem was solved pragmatically, thanks to the suggestion put forward by a highly authoritative U.S. institution which was eventually accepted by the entire Western world: it was agreed simply to call this state 'brain death' and to consider it to all intents and purposes exactly like death.

There is also a last possible alternative, although fortunately very rare, occurring in only about 2% of cases: severe head and brain traumas which completely destroy the cerebral cortex but leave the deeper nervous centres of the brain-stem intact: In these cases the patient loses consciousness permanently, but is still able to breathe and to vegetate autonomously. These patients are said to be in a 'persistent vegetative state' and they can survive (biologically) for several years, despite a total absence of mental life.

Although this clinical condition is relatively rare, it is extremely important from a theoretical point of view, since it proves that modern medicine can lead to a total separation between biological life (which persists) and psychological life (which does not). This is an entirely novel situation, which has profound ethical consequences: it raises the question of whether it is correct to prolong biological life when it is no longer connected to mental life.

This example clearly shows how a certain type of medical therapy (in this case, neuro-resuscitation), alongside the numerous benefits it offers, can also have very negative drawbacks for the patient and for society: not so much brain death, which is simply the total failure of the therapy, but rather this 'persistent vegetative state' and survival in conditions of severe or very severe invalidity. These cases raise the following question: to what extent can we justify undertaking or continuing resuscitation treatment when the chances of such failures are very high? Let me give you a few more examples.

A patient in hospital with an advanced malignant tumor suddenly suffers an arrythmia and has a cardiac arrest: in short, he dies. A young duty doctor intervenes immediately with a heart massage, tracheal intubation and defibrillation. The patient revives and goes on to live another few weeks in agonizing pain. Or, as occurs more commonly, a terminal cancer patient suffers a life-threatening internal haemorrhage: a blood transfusion saves his life then and there, but the evolution of his disease is the same as before. One cannot help wondering: are we doing the right thing?

One last example: lateral amyotrophic sclerosis is an incurable progressive neurological disorder which causes patients gradually to lose their ability to move, all the while retaining complete sensitivity and consciousness. In the advanced stages of this disease patients can no longer swallow or speak: during the final phases they cannot even breathe. An artificial respirator can prolong these patients' lives for years even, but this reduces them to a life entirely dependent on the machine, in a condition of total impotence, unable even to communicate. The dilemma is: is it right to do this to a patient or would not it be more ethical not to intervene and allow the patient to die?

It is not my intention to answer these questions here; some answers will become self-evident in the argument that follows. What I wanted to do was simply to prove my original premise: that is, that some life-support therapies can actually worsen the condition of the terminal patient, or can keep human beings alive in conditions that we might call 'devoid of human dignity'.

Above and beyond the indisputable (and at times, frightening) powers of modern resuscitation therapies, there are several other novelties in modern medicine.

In the majority of chronically-evolving terminal diseases, which are currently responsible for about 80% of disease-related deaths, the diagnosis and the (negative) prognosis can be made many months, even years, before the exitus. An American statistic shows that more than 50% of the population dies from a disease diagnosed at least 29 months – two and a half years – before the death occurs. And it is worth recalling that, thanks to the progress recorded in predictive medicine, it is possible today to provide a prenatal or presymptomatic diagnosis for an increasing number of hereditary diseases. To give an extreme example (a paradigm, in fact): we are now in a position to predict before an individual is born, or at the latest during the very first years of his life, that around the age of 40 he will develop Huntington's chorea, a progressive disease which will make him a complete invalid and eventually lead to his death.

Lastly, the psychological and social context of dying has changed, in that the vast majority of deaths today (80%) occur in a medical environment (hospital, clinic, hospice), far away from the family setting. This element, as well as other characteristic features of our modern ethos (our marked individualism which leads us to think of a human being as a self-enclosed monad and of death as a purely private concern; the difficulty we have in addressing death as a topic in public), are responsible for a situation which Norbert Elias has defined 'the loneliness of the dying man'.

Let me sum up what I have said so far. Modern medicine has changed the very concept of death (the core of the concept of death in this new version is now brain death). Death has lost its unpredictability and, to a certain extent, its inexorability. Lastly, death has become an increasingly medical problem. It hasn't always been like this: on the contrary, in the Hippocratic tradition the physician would leave the dying man, since death was considered in a sense outside the field of medicine.

3. Reactions to the Problems Created by the Changes Described Above

The great changes I have described raise new and difficult problems for medical science. What are the main ones?

One concerns this new concept of death (that is, the notion of brain death): we have reached a practical agreement on this concept, an agreement which has been incorporated into the legal systems of several countries. Yet, the theoretical issues this concept raises are very important and give rise to constant philosophical discussions on the topic which I won't go into here. Suffice it to say that it is quite likely that the concept of brain death will be reconsidered fairly soon: what will probably happen is that there will be an alternative between going back to the traditional notion of cardiac death and a further move 'forward' to a new concept, the notion of cortical death.

Then there is the danger of prolonging not only a person's life but also his/her suffering and pain, or of creating conditions of 'loss of human dignity'. The world of medicine is attempting to face up to this risk in several different ways. A new movement began to develop in the English-speaking world in the 1970s, the Hospice Movement. This movement developed what became known as 'palliative medicine', a new medical specialization aiming not at providing a cure for the disease, but at caring for the dying person (*sedare dolorem*). The criterion by which we judge the effectiveness of palliative medicine is not (as is the case with traditional medicine) an objective parameter based on recovery or improvement (since both recovery and improvement are impossible in the patients cared for with these methods). Rather, palliative medicine is assessed purely subjectively by the patient, which is hardly ever the case in traditional medicine. Palliative medicine is undoubtedly a huge step forward in the treatment of the dying, but several criticisms have been levelled at its basic approach: according to some recent proposals, like the one set forth by Daniel Callahan in his latest book, we need to elaborate a new philosophy of patient-care, a new medicine, which would involve training physicians (all physicians, not just specialists, as is the case in palliative medicine) to follow their patients all the way to their death, considering death explicitly as a stage in the process of illness and treatment.

At the same time, thanks to the intervention of moral philosophers, the old concept of 'extraordinary means' (borrowed from Catholic moral theology) is being revived: it is used to describe forms of treatment which it is acceptable not to employ. And in Catholic countries the new expression 'excessive therapeutic zeal' (in Italian, *accanimento terapeutico*) has been coined to describe the behaviour of doctors who resort to therapeutical means which they would do better to avoid. This brings us to the crux of the question: most scholars of ethics, whatever their orientation, agree that 'it is not always one's duty to use all means available to save human life, if the means used will cause the patient a suffering disproportionate to the quantity and quality of life they offer him'. Thus, we have a twofold statement: firstly, it is not obligatory to subject patients to the suffering caused by the so-called 'extraordinary' therapeutic means and, secondly, the distinction between ordinary and extraordinary is not intrinsic to the instruments (since something which today appears extraordinary will probably be quite ordinary tomorrow), rather it is linked to the relationship between the instrument and the expected result. Furthermore, beginning in the 1980s, we start referring to these therapies as 'disproportionate', rather than simply as extraordinary, and a fairly broad-based consensus is reached among physicians and moral philosophers of various tendencies.

At this point we can ask ourselves whether these answers are satisfactory for the questions for we have raised. More and more doctors declare that they are against all forms of 'excessive therapeutic zeal', that is the use of life-support means which serve only to prolong life in conditions of pain and suffering, without any hope. Yet, there is evidence that this practice is still very widespread.[1] In fact, among doctors old habits and notions persist; as a result it is still not sufficiently clear which treatments are to be considered 'futile' in terminal cases. Undoubtedly, the entire education process our physicians go through, as 'life-oriented' as it is, prevents them from assessing each case individually, in as natural a way as possible. A recent article by Christakis and Asch illustrates very clearly the uncertainties and irrationalities that lie behind physicians' decisions in discontinuing treatment with life-supporting means (such as antibiotics and blood transfusions). And similarly (in fact, even more dramatically), doctors have difficulty in deciding on the interruption of fundamental life-supporting therapies, such as administering food and fluids, e.g., in patients in a persistent vegetative state. The debate on this point is very heated and opinions are divided, even within the two main fields of opinion (Catholic and non) into which our country is traditionally divided. According to some, food and fluids are always 'ordinary' means, and therefore must always be administered, unless the patient is considered dead (as, for example, in cerebral death, or, according to some, in a persistent vegetative state). Whereas others maintain that food and fluids are to be viewed exactly like all other life-supporting means.

It would not be within the scope of this article to provide an analysis of this question, but I wanted to raise the issue to show that even a general consensus on the fact that 'excessive therapeutic zeal' is unjustified does not solve all our problems. On the contrary, to a certain extent the use of the term '*accanimento terapeutico*' (and bear in mind that this term is widely used in bioethical writings in neo-Latin cultures: it has no precise equivalent in English-speaking civilizations) appears to be more of a handy phrase, a trick of rhetoric, than a real step forward towards a clarification of our difficulties.

4. The Demand for Euthanasia

The most serious problems are actually caused by the failures of palliative medicine, that is those cases when the patient expresses a request for euthanasia, asking his doctor (or family and/or friends) to put an end to his life and to an intolerable pain/suffering. This is the crucial point which causes discussions and debate today, and divides consciences in Italy and in the rest of the world as well. By way of a premise, just let me say that many people maintain that modern pain therapy or, rather, palliative medicine ensures that the circumstances in which a terminally ill patient asks his doctor or someone else to put an end to his existence practically never arise, since this request

1 *See*, for example, the recent case of Federico Fellini, subjected to resuscitation therapy, including tracheostomy, when it was clear that the prognosis was negative and death was near.

usually conceals another request, which is a plea for help and for pain abatement. But, in actual fact, however caring and effective palliative care may be (and we are still very far from having a satisfactory palliative medicine available for all), it is easy to predict that it will nonetheless have a percentage of failures. And requests for euthanasia will certainly not be a rarity. The element that still needs to be examined is to what extent this type of request is rationally conceived and formulated, and not simply the expression of a curable depressive state. Once this distinction has been satisfactorily drawn, there is no denying that there is still a percentage – albeit small – of rational requests for euthanasia, to which we must provide an answer. And I feel it necessary to specify here – as is clear from the context – that I am speaking of euthanasia as a deliberate interruption of the life of a terminally ill patient, following his/her explicit request, in order to spare him/her pain or conditions of total loss of dignity. As is well-known, we normally distinguish between two types of euthanasia (according to the modality employed): passive euthanasia, that is the interruption of life-support treatments (e.g. antibiotics, transfusions, mechanical ventilation, artificial administration of food and fluids) and active euthanasia, meaning a direct intervention aimed at putting an end to life (e.g. an injection of a lethal substance). Many moral philosophers attach a huge moral importance to this distinction, and state that the first type (passive euthanasia) is to be considered legitimate, whereas the second (active euthanasia) is not: it is legitimate to allow someone to die, while it is never legitimate to kill (an innocent person, that is). The Italian legislation would appear to share this position: it openly declares active euthanasia unlawful in Article 579 of the Penal Code, whereas it never refers explicitly to passive euthanasia. In recent years, however, the principle of informed consent in the case of the administration of medical therapies (and, consequently, the refusal of such therapies) has become a principle that is accepted and applied by lawyers and judges alike. One need only think of the sentence passed recently in Florence. Now, if informed refusal of treatment is legitimate, then the interruption of that same treatment must also be legitimate (the discontinuation of all treatment, that is), if the patient has explicitly formulated this request: in other words, passive euthanasia is legitimate.

5. An Argument in Favour of Active Euthanasia

It is my firm belief that active euthanasia is ethically justifiable and that Italian law is plagued by an internal contradiction. My opinion is based in part on an argument put forward by J. Rachels. Schematically, my argument can be summed up as follows:

Premise A. All other things being equal, it is the duty of us physicians, as such, to cure diseases and fight against death. In the face of a life-threatening disease, our decision not to use a life-support therapy or to discontinue its use after we have begun treatment, cannot be considered a simple omission, an action of not-doing, but rather an active and deliberate decision. This becomes even more evident when we interrupt a treatment, when we 'pull the plug', but applies just as much to a decision not to begin treatment at all. The deeper personal intentions of the physician are irrelevant here: he knows that by his actions he is speeding up or facilitating death. If the doctor decides not to sustain life, for example not to resuscitate a patient entrusted to his cares (despite the fact that the means needed to do this are available), even if the decision not to intervene is in the patient's interest, he is at the very least a contributory cause of the patient's death and bears responsibility for the event.

Premise B. In circumstances of a terminal illness with unalleviable pain it is commonly considered legitimate (generally speaking, and even more so if the patient specifically requests it) not to begin or to discontinue life-support therapies, since they are deemed to be 'extraordinary' or 'disproportionate' compared to the benefit the patient can be expected to gain from them (by definition: no benefit or even a worsening of the situation). As a result of these considerations, physicians tend not to do anything to fight the death process (and in these cases one speaks of 'natural' death). Catholic morality goes even further by accepting as legitimate an active intervention to alleviate pain with analgesics (mostly opioids) which, as a side effect, cause a depression of consciousness and breathing activity thus accelerating the death process itself. According to this position, the determining factor is that the physician's intention is to alleviate pain and not to speed up the dying process. The reference here is to the classic doctrine of the double effect, which I do not intend to criticize here.

If it is legitimate under certain circumstances to not begin or to interrupt life support practices, it would appear equally legitimate to interrupt life actively, by administering a lethal injection, for example, if it is done in the patient's interest and following his specific request. It is actually easy to demonstrate that an active intervention, which interrupts the patient's (unbearable) life in an instantaneous and painless manner, is certainly a greater benefit for the patient than a passive 'waiting for events to unfold' would be. The ethical distinction drawn by many people between killing and allowing someone to die may appear reasonable for people outside the medical field, but it is much more difficult to accept for those who live at close quarters with the terminally ill: the experience of long drawn-out terminal stages, with patients not 'managing' to die, would easily convince anyone of the truth of what I have argued above. It is not the outer form of the action (active or passive) which we physicians believe is what counts morally, but rather the motivations the action is based on: if the patient requests it, then active euthanasia is morally justifiable, but there can be no justification whatsoever for cases of omission due to negligence, professional incapacity or actual perverse intentions.

This argument in no way purports to deny that there may be (and, indeed, there is) a psychological difference between acting and omitting to act, as there is between not even beginning a treatment and interrupting it once it has begun. The greatest dilemmas the physician is faced with when accepting the idea of an action leading to euthanasia rather than merely omitting to do something, or when deciding to interrupt a treatment as compared to never even beginning it, are very real and difficult even for those who

– like myself – support active euthanasia. But, in my opinion, these are quandaries of an emotional nature which reflect the 'life-preserving' tradition of our profession, the idea (never explicitly theorized) implicit in our basic medical training that the fundamental purpose of our actions is always to save a life at all costs. It would thus appear that the real issue is whether the prime goal of medicine is to save lives, or rather to promote well-being and eliminate pain and suffering. I believe that this commandment (to save lives at all costs), although generally speaking valid as a '*prima facie*' principle to be followed, must be set aside and subordinated to considerations relating to the patient's well-being and respect for his autonomy. The so-called principle of the 'sacredness' of life, which in the past played a very positive and important role, today, in the context of all the latest medical developments, appears wholly inadequate to provide us with foolproof guidelines, unless we re-interpret it: what really counts morally is not a purely biological life, but rather the personal life of the patient, what Rachels calls his biographical life.

6. Arguments Against Euthanasia

Very briefly I would also like to mention some of the arguments most commonly put forward by opponents of euthanasia. There are two kinds of arguments:

(a) Euthanasia is never legitimate since it violates the fifth commandment, 'Thou shalt not kill'. To put it more clearly: 'It is never legitimate to kill an innocent human being'. That one can describe euthanasia in these terms (the killing of an innocent human being) is basically true, but what is open to question is whether killing is always unlawful, when it is done following the rational request of the patient and in his interest. Those who are on principle against euthanasia – the intentional killing of a patient, in compliance with his request and in his interest – can be justified only with reference to an absolute principle of the 'sacredness of life' (seen as a gift that we may not dispose of at will, a gift of God) and not on the basis of moral considerations connected to the patient's interest.

(b) Euthanasia is not legitimate because of the severe social consequences it might engender; but on this point we are beginning to have empirical data available, as in the case of the experience in Holland, where a widespread use of euthanasia does not appear to have jeopardized in any way the patient-physician relationship, nor does it appear to have had the terrible social consequences the opponents of euthanasia had predicted (in their opinion, euthanasia threatens the very foundations of the medical profession, corrupting professional ethics and integrity, inducing very subtle coercion mechanisms on weak elderly persons; in other words it is truly the 'slippery slope' leading to a devaluation of the lives of the weak, the elderly and the handicapped).

The supporters of euthanasia, on the other hand, argue that it brings with it a whole series of positive consequences: it promotes self-determination (the patient is entrusted with the responsibility for his own death and his own life); it allows physicians to keep pain under control; it does not threaten – but rather strengthens – the patient's trust in his doctor (since the latter accepts the task of caring for his patient till the end). According to the proponents of euthanasia, today's medicine calls for a new vision of the issues of life and death: death, like birth, is part of life and needs medical treatment, exactly as we treat birth medically, if necessary even aggressively (think, for example, of labour room treatment and of procedures such as episiotomy).

7. Euthanasia in the Debate on Bioethics in our Country

Is it possible (and, if so, how?) to apply the theoretical proposals illustrated above in the Italian situation?

We must start from the consideration that there is a deep division on this issue. Alongside the official positions, as expressed in the Italian laws (which, incidentally, date back to the 1930s) and in Church tenets, both of which are decidedly against euthanasia, a different standpoint is emerging: it is only to a minor extent declared openly and, although it is still not well structured, it is gradually gaining ground. In 1991, during the discussion on the Schwartzenberg Resolution, the Italian National Committee for Bioethics addressed the issue, although indirectly. The Committee expressed a critical opinion on the vagueness of the wording and on the fact that the Resolution appeared to suggest that it was the duty of every physician to choose to perform euthanasia. But it did not actually discuss the legitimacy of euthanasia itself, thus avoiding the risk of not being able to make a unanimous statement: this tends to be the usual pattern of behaviour in this institution, which has so far only ever produced documents of a very general and elusive nature.

There have been very few official positions expressed on euthanasia in this country. Among them, I would like to mention the statement made by the Bioethics Council, which I belong to, in January 1993. In this pronouncement the Council recognizes the existence, in secular society, of a pluralism of values and stresses the need to protect this pluralism appealing to a higher value, tolerance. Alongside the traditional notion of the sacredness of life there is another vision of the world which is gradually gaining ground: this conception is based on the ethics of the quality of life. And all those who accept this ethical conception of the world must be granted the 'right to die with dignity' and the right to 'help others to die with dignity'. In its document the Council makes no proposals as to how one might apply this principle in the legal system, since it recognizes the need for an in-depth discussion of these issues beforehand.

8. Some Proposals for the Future

HOW WILL THIS DEBATE DEVELOP?

I believe that a significant step forward could be the formulation of a bill on advance directives, following the model of what has taken place in the United States. Just a few words on this matter, since I am not a legal expert. Advance directives are directives expressed in writing by the patient, and concern the medical treatments which he accepts or refuses for the future. There are two kinds of advance directives. The first is the living will, that is a document drawn up by the person when he is in full possession of all his faculties in which he states what treatments and therapies he would like to be administered to him should he become incapacitated (generally speaking, these living wills state that the patient refuses to be kept alive with life-support means once he is no longer in a state of consciousness). The second is the durable power of attorney, a legal tool by means of which the person appoints an attorney who will be responsible for taking the more difficult decisions, in collaboration with the physicians, should the patient himself no longer be in a position to do so. In the living will the patient expresses his own will and his choices, whereas by granting a durable power of attorney he delegates to another person the authority to decide. This power of attorney is usually granted to a person who has an in-depth knowledge of the patient, his history and his preferences, and can take any decision by 'putting himself in the patient's place' as it were.

I don't know how and if these legal tools, which have been in use in the United States for many years already, could be integrated into the Italian legal system which is so different. Nor do I think that advance directives would solve all the difficulties that arise in the terminal stages of an illness, when a patient has lost his decision-making ability. Yet, the introduction of these instruments might offer a concrete signal of a different relationship between patient, disease and physician which is already gaining ground in society: a relationship which is no longer one of passivity, of being subjected to the benevolent action of a doctor, but rather a more active involvement in the decisions affecting disease and treatments, an indispensable prerequisite for the complex and difficult issues related to euthanasia.

As far as the long term perspectives are concerned, I find it interesting to mention the proposal made recently by a group of American physicians, jurists and philosophers in the *New England Journal of Medicine*. The basic point of this proposal is the approval of a law allowing doctors to assist patients (both as doctor-assisted suicide and as active euthanasia) following the patient's request, in the framework of a broad spectrum of medical activities covering all forms of care to be given to terminal patients. This proposal calls for the appointment of consultants in matters of palliative care, doctors with practical experience in this field and with an adequate theoretical training: these consultants would be called in by the physician when difficult problems related to pain alleviation arise and in all cases when a patient requests euthanasia. Thus, all such cases would be overseen by two physicians, one of whom would be an officially recognized expert in the field. As well as solving the (basically rather rare) cases of a request for euthanasia, these consultants could also considerably improve the conditions of terminal patients who have not requested euthanasia. At the same time, regional committees for palliative medicine would be set up, including health workers and others who would be responsible for the training of health care providers and for educating public opinion on palliative medicine, for drawing up basic health care guidelines and monitoring tools for palliative medical care and/or euthanasia.

This proposal is extremely well articulated; one particularly positive feature of this proposal is that it does not isolate the problem of euthanasia – a fairly rare occurrence – but deals with the much broader field of palliative medicine. We know, unfortunately, that even in countries like Italy where euthanasia is illegal and everyone pays great lip service to palliative care, in fact human and technical resources available for palliative medicine are very scarce. A serious and continuous commitment to palliative medicine is in any case the first answer our society must offer in response to the terminal patient's cry for help.

The Right to Die and The Penal Code: The Arguments of a Problematic Relationship

Fausto Giunta*

In the Italian legal system there are no specific regulations governing mercy killing (euthanasia), namely regulations that explicitly consider the phenomenon, taking into account the circumstances and grounds specifically related to euthanasia. Hence, in its so-called active form, which is the form that the term refers to in its strictest sense, euthanasia is governed by general regulations, that is to say, by laws that ignore the distinctive features of the phenomenon being examined and that are conceived to provide protection against appreciably different criminal acts. Now, since the protection of life is ensured by an articulated constellation of categories of murder, it is on the basis of the latter that the cases which usually fall under the heading of euthanasia must necessarily be viewed in criminal proceedings.

The result is frequently a paradoxical situation: for instance, a murder *pietatis causa* committed without the consent of the patient may on the one hand be attenuated by the fact that Art. 62 n. 1 of the Penal Code attaches importance to special moral and social reasons, while on the other it will very likely be burdened by premeditation as an aggravating circumstance (Articles 576, para. 1 and 577, para. 1, n. 3 Penal Code). And so the lapse of time between the decision to act and the accomplishment of the action (necessary for a decision that is in any case a difficult one) may be the element according to which the Italian legal system will classify this act amongst the instances punished with life imprisonment. The judgment would be the same if the person were to use poisonous substances as death-inducing means which, although not particularly rapid or painless, are at least bloodless; the same applies to an ascendant or descendent of the patient even if he/she were to provide only moral support to the action (Articles 576 and 577, para. 1, n. 1 and n. 2, Penal Code).

Nor can it be accepted that euthanasia is not to be penally classified as murder – as suggested some time ago – on the grounds that putting an end to the agony of a person doomed to death for an incurable disease is not murder. It is an unquestionable

* Professor of Law, University of Ferrara, Ferrara, Italy.

Cosimo Marco Mazzoni (ed.), A Legal Framework for Bioethics, 211-233.
©1998 *Kluwer Law International. Printed in The Netherlands.*

teaching even in the Italian doctrine that murder means that the victim has been deprived of his/her life, regardless of the victim's living potential, as demonstrated by the fact that killing an individual sentenced to death even only an instant before the prescribed time of his execution is indisputably considered murder.

The inadequacy and the severity of the current legislative approach to euthanasia are only partially compensated by the fact that the homicide of a consenting individual (Art. 579, Penal Code) is less severe than homicide (but is punished nevertheless with a penalty of up to fifteen years imprisonment).

It is worth recalling that the introduction by the Rocco Code of the idea of the homicide of a consenting individual was a major and significant innovation with respect to the Italian legislative tradition, since this issue was unknown to the Zanardelli Code of 1889 and to the codes in force prior to the unification of Italy. And even though, as said earlier, the indictment does not openly take into account the case of euthanasia, the raison d'être of the present Art. 579 (Penal Code) is not wholly unrelated to the debate on euthanasia undertaken by penal doctrine last century. The debate originated from authoritative stances squarely in favour of euthanasia and of the possibility of enjoying life as an asset, but above all as a consequence of some of the rulings contained in the Zanardelli Code. Indeed, the excessive strictness of the legislation in force at the time (namely grouping all cases of malicious murder into a single undifferentiated class) had forced legal experts to resort to distorted interpretations of the facts, in order to avoid indictment for murder, and worse, premeditated murder, in the case where there was consent by the passive individual. It is clear then, in this context, that the introduction into the new Code of a concept of attenuated murder – subject to the requirement that the victim must have given valid consent – aimed at restoring the full effectiveness of a protection of life and, in another respect, at denying at least in principle any legitimation of euthanasia *pietatis causa*. It is by no chance that it was on the basis of this new concept that the most extreme attempts were made at interpreting human life as a community asset, almost turning it into the 'property' of the State.

The attitude against regulating euthanasia adopted by the Rocco Code emerges also from an important observation. Namely, with respect to murder in general the only specializing element in the attenuated case provided for in Art. 579 is the objective fact that the victim gives his/her consent, whereas there are no doubts as to altruistic motivations being an inseparable part of merciful euthanasia; motivations whose importance is deliberately downgraded to the level of being mere circumstantial elements.

This point deserves closer attention because the requirement of consent raises a series of applicational problems which makes it more difficult *de iure condito* to have the cases of euthanasia classified within the scope of Art. 579, instead of general murder. Indeed Art. 579 sets forth that 'consent given by mentally ill patients or by persons with psychic deficiency, due to other infirmities' is not valid. The most delicate interpretational issue is related above all to the 'conditions of psychic deficiency' as can be easily understood. It is widely believed that the expression 'psychic deficiency' serves to indicate any condition, even the non-morbid and clinically non-defined forms of lowering of intellectual performance, any undermining of the skills of criticism, any weakening of will-power and of the affective function that make the individual easily suggestible and depress his ability to defend himself from the power of psychological coercion or suggestion. It is evident that there derives another and virtually insurmountable obstacle to the eligibility of applying Art. 579 to euthanasia. Indeed, even when the disease does not cause a condition of mental infirmity in the passive individual, it is difficult not to find that there is a condition of psychic deficiency in a terminal patient who agrees to terminate his life in the grip of intolerable pain, which cannot help but influencing his psychological equilibrium, especially in the case of person who is probably also under the effect of strong narcotics or painkillers.

A presentation of the body of regulations currently governing the issue of mercy euthanasia would be incomplete if one were to overlook the theoretical and practical implications deriving from the fact that incitement to suicide (as well as aiding and abetting suicide) is considered a crime in itself and is punishable with up to twelve years' imprisonment (Art. 580 Penal Code). This is an indictment which is unknown to other European legislations and which strengthens the ideological prevention against euthanasia present in the Italian legislative tradition enhancing it with a cultural background which is worth mentioning.

The fact of regarding as a crime any contribution given to someone's suicide, a concept which was present even in the Codes of the last century, has made it possible to reconcile the failure to punish suicide (obviously attempted suicide) with the principle that life cannot be disposed of at will. It can be stated that the penal unlawfulness of inciting and helping someone to commit suicide is the traditional conceptual backbone of the collectivistic view of life and of personal integrity which was later confirmed and further strengthened by the introduction of the concept of homicide of a consenting individual. The terms of this approach can be summarized as follows: the fact that law is 'substantially' against suicide can be inferred from that it is a crime to be an accomplice in someone's suicide, because if inciting and helping someone to commit suicide is unlawful, then a *fortiori* the resulting incited and facilitated action is to be considered just as unlawful. On the other hand, even though nobody denies the anomaly of this discipline, failure to penally repress the attempts to commit suicide is justified at times by the fact that the penalty to be assigned to someone who seeks to inflict injury upon himself would be ineffective.

At a closer look, this formal reasoning is little more than a tautology, aimed at transforming a moral belief into a juridical principle. Indeed, as is recognized even by those who maintain that suicide is unlawful, Art. 580 envisages an autonomous crime so that 'only for ease of discussion' can one say that this provision punishes an activity of complicity in the crime. Even if in the *mens legislatoris* the 'substantial' unlawfulness of suicide was a cultural and ethical premise from which the regulation derived, it does not contain any provision. And since it is from the provision that one would infer that a certain fact is against the law, once one excludes the possibility of inferring the 'formal' unlawfulness of suicide from Art. 580, there remains to be seen only whether there are other positive regulations which allow us to conclude that suicide is not contrary to the legal system. Indeed, in the Italian legal tradition there have been several legal provisions suggesting the unlawfulness (even if not penal) of suicide. For instance the Sardinian Code of 1839 (Art. 585), which envisaged security provisions for persons having attempted suicide, stated that the will of a suicide was null and prohibited funeral honours.

But no matter how hard one tries, in the existing body of legislation there is no regulation to be found that, like the one recalled above, punishes suicide (albeit only under the Civil Code).

Having made such remarks, the existence of Art. 580 in the Italian legal system has an immediate impact on practice. Indeed he who helps a patient to commit suicide *manu propria* will answer for that crime if the suicide is committed or if a severe or very severe personal lesion derives from any such attempt. Unlike what happens in the other legislations which do not penally punish the help one person gives to someone else's suicide, the provisions contained in Art. 580 raise a series of additional problems, first and foremost (as far as penal accountability is concerned) whether the last causative act leading to death is accomplished by the patient or by a third party, namely the doctor or a family member. In this latter case the crime would be homicide of a consenting person, if it is the patient who produces his own death, and the accountability of the third party may consist in having knowingly given the patient the means or having explained the functioning of the means that produced his death.

The existing legislation makes no mention of cases of so-called consenting passive euthanasia, i.e., when the doctor, with the consent of the terminal patient, stops administering the treatment that is keeping the patient alive. The debate focuses on the lawfulness of similar actions, which some experts accept while others find entirely unlawful.

Resorting to a variety of arguments, the more conservative positions underscore the principle that life cannot be disposed of and that suicide is anti-juridical by nature, inferring implications which do not derive from the contents of the laws: the main one is that a terminal patient cannot lawfully refuse a treatment that is keeping him alive since it would be tantamount to asking for death, something which is not permitted by our legal system. Another argument states that, by violating the juridical duty of providing care (a duty to which the physician is bound), discontinuing treatment is a criminal omission.

But this approach to the issue is unacceptable on both accounts. As to the first argument, it must be pointed out that the Italian system not only does not prohibit, but it actually recognizes the freedom to die, which can be exercised in any of a number of ways, e.g. by refusing food, or treatment. Though starting from the opposite premise, according to which suicide is *contra jus*, even the majority of legal experts come to the conclusion that a person cannot be forced to live, by invoking the provision of Art. 32, para. 2, of the Constitution, where it is stated that medical treatment for a patient is a right and not a duty, even in cases when refusing treatment can lead to death. This is a right guaranteed by the Constitution, and derives from the principle enshrined in the Constitution that it is unlawful to administer compulsory medical treatment. Therefore this is the argument on which the lawfulness of consenting passive euthanasia is based. It is inferred from the following argument: since the therapy is in the interest of the patient, he/she can decide to refuse it (*voluntas aegroti suprema lex*), allowing the disease to follow its course ... as far as the law is concerned, death will thus become a natural event. But this also means that – for the prevailing doctrine – this is not a case of the right to die, but of the narrower right to refuse treatment, guaranteed by Art. 32, para. 2 of the Constitution.

We can also reject the second argument put forward by those experts advocating a more conservative interpretation, namely that it is a physician's duty to treat his/her patients. Indeed, once it is accepted that the patient does not have the duty to keep on living at all costs, the physician's duty is to respect his/her patient's wishes. This derives, once again, from Art. 32, para. 2 of the Constitution which, by ruling that compulsory medical treatment is an exceptional event and that the cases in which it is to be enforced are to be specifically set out in the law, clearly considers that medical treatment falls within the individual's rights and personal freedoms. From this standpoint – and except for the case of an unconscious patient that will be dealt with further on – the conscious consent of the patient is important not only as a condition for the lawfulness of a medical action, but also as a precondition and limit of the scope of a physician's duty. Consequently when the patient exercises his full right to die, his request to do so puts an end to the physician's juridical duty to dispense care and to ensure the patient's health. And since in this case we are not confronted with homicide by omission, but with a limit to the physician's duty to dispense care aimed at avoiding an undesired excessive therapeutic zeal (*accanimento terapeutico*), according to some authoritative juridical experts one should not even use the expression 'passive euthanasia' in this connection.

Now, even though there is some significant agreement on these conclusions, so much so that there is only a minority of experts who on principle question the lawfulness of passive euthanasia, one cannot deny the difficulties encountered by ordinary law in identifying the boundaries within which passive euthanasia is lawful. Indeed, whereas the failure to regulate active euthanasia is intentional and the fact of considering it among the crimes identified by Articles 579 and 580 of the Penal Code is neither a shortcoming nor an oversight, but a precise choice, the same cannot be said for passive euthanasia, whose importance grows as new advanced technological devices are introduced into the field of resuscitation, first and foremost the means that prolong biological life. Since it derives from general principles, the lawfulness of passive euthanasia is *de iure condito* like an interpretational postscript, perhaps less unintentional, but nonetheless worthy of being carefully examined.

Focussing our attention only on the main aspects of the question, the lawfulness of passive euthanasia is particularly of concern in two assumptions.

Firstly, consider a case in which the therapy that the terminal patient refuses does not consist of drugs but rather of a machine or support mechanism that is being used to keep the patient alive. From a purely practical point of view the act of switching off an artificial life-support machine is an active conduct, therefore we must clarify whether at the juridical level this action is tantamount to not administering a treatment which the patient refuses. The question is very delicate, because if the answer is 'no' it would be inevitable to consider the turning off of the machine as active euthanasia (and we can consider legitimate only those cases in which the patient's wish to die can be respected by the physician by his *non facere*).

Now, since consensual passive euthanasia has acquired legitimacy, juridical experts now agree on not considering the discontinuation of artificial life-support mechanisms as an accessory to the homicide of a consenting patient and hence an abetting of suicide brought about by an action performed by the patient, whereas the physician merely provides the means or gives the instructions as to how to stop the machine. But, in fact, the reasons underpinning this solution are not always fully convincing. Indeed to begin with, equating the two conducts is rather questionable from the juridical standpoint, even though one may share the idea. Indeed the very reasons for equating the two conducts are not clear. And the fact that the burden of providing arguments to bear out the assumption of the equivalence of the two conducts lies with those who maintain that the two conducts are equivalent, intuitively depends on their unquestionable naturalistic difference, as well as on the teaching according to which, where there are doubts, the behaviour of the agent is always to be considered active.

German juridical experts have dealt with this issue very thoroughly, also because of the attention that is being paid to the controversial discrimination between action and omission seen against the broader framework of the theory of crime. As to the active or omissive nature of technically discontinuing treatment, it has been pointed out that the interpretation depends on the social meaning of such discontinuation, according to which an action of this kind should be likened to the interruption of resuscitation measures begun with a heart massage. But in such a problematic field it is difficult to claim the univocal nature of 'social meaning' to skirt round the variables of people's points of view; the risk is that of getting stuck in a vicious circle of arguments or of presenting as social awareness the viewpoint of those who are expressing a judgment. Therefore it is preferable to justify the equivalence between discontinuation of therapy and the turning off of a machine by interpreting the latter conduct as an action-based omission (*Unterlassung durch Tun*), which – as such – is not of penal relevance. Some Italian juridical experts support this assumption.

However, as acknowledged by its very supporters, the assumption of action-based omission is not all that obvious in Germany, and even in the field of positive law in Italy there are some limitations that deserve being discussed further. As is self-evident, the expression 'action-based omission' presents itself as being the conceptual opposite of the better known category of 'committing a deed by omission'. Both these concepts express an antinaturalistic idea of a penally relevant action. What is different, however, is how they are considered by the regulations on conduct: in one case the fact of not preventing an event that one has the duty to prevent is equated to causing it; in the other case, the discontinuation of mechanical therapy that one has the duty of not prolonging is equated to the discontinuation of treatment. However, whereas in the former case the equivalence between omission and action is possible in view of the clearly expressed provision of Art. 40, para. 2, Penal Code, one can ask, what is the regulatory basis according to which one can consider the switching off of the machine as the equivalent of treatment discontinuation? And one cannot beg the question by stating that there is no juridical duty demanding that the physician should prolong the life of terminally ill patients through mechanical devices and against the patients' wishes. As Articles 579 and 580 of the Penal Code are based on 'cause', the absence of any regulation imposing that automatic treatment be continued is not sufficient to allow us to state that disconnecting the machine is legitimate. What is required is a regulation that establishes that it is a duty to discontinue such treatment.

In the Italian system this regulation is precisely Art. 22, para. 2 of the Constitution: whereas in the case of discontinuing therapy one is just barely within the boundaries of a typical case of omission, in the assumption of switching off a machine, the individual will be exonerated from criminal liability because he is merely fulfilling his duty (Art. 51, Penal Code), i.e., discontinuing a treatment in accordance with the wishes of the patient. In both cases, and beyond the theoretical categories involved, the lawfulness of the conduct derives from Art. 32, para. 2, Constitution, which sets forth that a physician is not to administer a treatment against the wishes of the patient, thus making it compulsory also to discontinue a treatment when this is expressly requested.

The second assumption of passive euthanasia, whose boundaries of lawfulness are being discussed *de iure condito*, concerns so-called pain therapy, which is at times definitely considered as being penally unlawful, whereas in other occasions, in too absolute a manner, it is deemed to be the only case of legitimate passive euthanasia. We are referring here to cases in which, with the consent of the terminally ill patient, a physician administers drugs that relieve the patient's pain but which are predicted to have side effects that will speed up the patient's death. Treatment against pain is clearly legitimate, in fact it is a duty, and this exonerates the physician from criminal liability in pursuance of Art. 51 of the Penal Code. It is widely accepted, besides being expressly laid down in the law, that the task of a physician is not only to restore health but also to relieve the pain and suffering caused by disease. As a result, being in its own right a part of medical and surgical treatment, painkilling therapy is interpreted as a dutiful assistance given to the patient in the dying process, and not as a way of helping the patient to die, which is prohibited in accordance with Art. 579.

However, even though this line of reasoning can be shared in its basic approach, it may present some shortcomings in that it does not clarify the boundaries within which pain therapy exonerates from criminal liability, or those beyond which, even if there is only a doubt (which would be inevitable) that it may shorten the patient's life, it would inevitably fall under Articles 579 and 580, with or without the assumption of malice. In order to provide a discretionary criterion, some German theorists refer to the multifaceted clause of legitimate risk which, instead of solving the issue, simply reproposes it in an apparently different form. Indeed, it is necessary to ask oneself: up to what extent can the risk to life inherent in pain therapy be allowed? The answer to this question cannot ensue from the clause of allowed risk.

It is therefore preferable (and perhaps inevitable) to have the lawfulness of pain therapy depend on how proportionate the means used are. This is a judgment mode applied typically to other cases of exoneration from criminal liability. What then needs to be determined is the term of reference for establishing the dimensions or proportions: namely according to what standard should such means be gauged. And it is unfeasible to seek the answer by calculating the probability of death ensuing, since this would introduce an arbitrary element in evaluating the duty of dispensing treatment. Indeed, if the treatment of pain is amongst the duties of the physician on a par (where possible) with the duty to cure, it supplements an absolute duty which, just like the duty to cure, finds its sole limitation in the medical knowledge available at a given point in time and in the available technology at that point in time. This remark serves also to rule out the possibility that the 'proportions' of the treatment be related to the direct or indirect death-related effect, admitting that pain therapy is lawful only when it is not a direct cause of death, but causes in its own right two distinct effects: on the one hand it shortens pain and on the other it shortens life. Once again it is the absoluteness of the juridical 'duty to relieve pain' which does not allow space for evaluations (and complex ones at that) of the main and secondary causal effects of pain therapy.

In spite of all the uncertainties due to the silence of the law on this issue, what can be done is to establish the relationship between measurement of the reduction of life, brought about by available therapeutic means, and the degree of tolerance (to what extent the pain is unrelievable), thus striking a delicate balance between the amount of life being sacrificed and the quality of life which is restored.

Limitations to the duty to treat and the corresponding right to die have been examined thus far by referring exclusively to terminally ill patients capable of expressing their refusal of further medical treatment. What we must now examine are the boundaries of the duty to treat a terminal patient who is unconscious and who is thus unable to ask to be allowed to die, nor can he accept a proposal along these lines offered by a third party.

In order to approach this issue correctly, we must recall that a partial clarification has been afforded by Law 578 of 29 December 1993 which, embodying the outcome of international discussions on this issue, identifies death for all juridical purposes with the irreversible cessation of all brain functions (Art. 1), so that the concept of death is to be considered as a regulatory element of penal matters. With the much called for legislative establishment of a unitary concept of death, all the uncertainties ensuing from the previous regulatory structure have been overcome, uncertainties which, on the basis of Law 644 of 2 December 1975 (Articles 3 and 4), applied the concept of brain death only for regulating cases of organ harvesting for therapeutic transplantations. Having established therefore that the ascertainment of brain death marks the boundary of therapeutic activity, what logically ensues is the duty to switch off any automatic devices being used to keep the patient alive.

A contrariis, until brain death sets in, the duty to assist the patient must be fulfilled to the fullest of its potential, even where the prognosis is unquestionably fatal. Indeed, even where the protection of life is not subordinated to the vitality of the passive individual, there are no doubts that the life-protecting role of the physician includes his duty to keep the patient alive. As a consequence, *vis-à-vis* the terminally ill patient who is in a state of unconsciousness, the duties of the physician are exactly the same as those that the physician has towards a patient who has agreed to treatment, even if the juridical foundation underlying the duty to treat is different. Indeed, in the case of a consenting patient, the physician's duty to treat him derives from the subordination of the intrinsically solidaristic nature of medical activity and of the protection of health (Art. 32, para. 1, Constitution) to the wishes of the individual patient (Art. 32, para. 2, Constitution). Different is the case of an unconscious or incapacitated patient where the duty to dispense treatment is exclusively based on solidaristic considerations, and not subject to the wishes of the patient, but 'heterolimited' by the provision of Art. 32, para. 1, Constitution, which, by stating that the protection of health is a fundamental right of the individual, requires that the activity of the physician be carried out in the exclusive interest of the patient.

As a consequence, the regulation governing the treatment of an unconscious terminal patient – summarized in the *brocard in dubio pro vita* – turns out to be the application of the same principle underlying the duty to dispense treatment to any unconscious individual. Just as when there is some likelihood that the health of an unconscious patient be restored the physician is compelled to treat him, even when therapy entails suffering or lesions (within reasonable limits, of course) to the patient's physical integrity, in much the same way, it is the physician's duty to intervene even in the case of an unconscious terminal patient when the treatment will significantly slow down the evolution of the disease, provided that this objective is proportional to the degree of sacrifice entailed by the therapy.

The issue becomes complicated when the therapy to be delivered to the unconscious terminally ill patient will neither slow down the disease nor enable the patient to recover consciousness so as to be able to decide whether to exercise his right to life or to death. In this connection there have been discussions on the lawfulness of discontinuing treatment even before all brain functions stop.

Those who believe that it is legitimate, refer in their arguments either to the criterion of the patient's best interest or to his right to die with dignity. And a distinction has also been made between the use of ordinary therapeutic means and recourse to extraordinary therapeutic means, pointing out that there is a duty to use only the former and not the latter in the case of an unconscious terminal patient.

A closer examination of the issue, however, shows that these arguments are not sufficient to establish that it is unquestionably lawful to discontinue treatment, also because in Italy such arguments do not enjoy adequate support in terms of positive law. In fact the former argument takes for granted, in principle and in the absence of an explicit source, that others can decide what is in the 'best interest' of the patient. But as is self-evident, this is in contrast with the principle that nobody can dispose of another individual's life; not even the physician, who in such cases would inevitably be assigned the burden of the choice. It is not by chance that the 'best interest' of the patient relates this issue to the domain of human rights; an aspect which confirms that per se the 'best interest' clause does not solve the problem. As to the right to die with dignity, it needs to be demonstrated that it can take the form of discontinuing treatment and, above all, that it overrules the duty to dispense treatment; the affirmative solution moves from the idea of the right to die with dignity that may not always coincide with the patient's idea of dying with dignity. And the duty of using only ordinary therapeutic means, lastly, besides raising the difficult problem of making a distinction between ordinary and extraordinary means, does not explain in terms of penal law why it is not a duty to resort to all means available in the attempt to prolong life.

Indeed, for a correct approach to the issue a distinction needs to be made between two different situations.

One is the case of a person who falls into a coma. As is pointed out by medical science, even in the case of a deep coma, one cannot rule out the possibility of the individual regaining consciousness, even if only for a short time. And it is in view of this possibility that the duty that the physician has to dispense treatment is not modified in the slightest: thus, discontinuing treatment would constitute a grave criminal omission. In order to reach this conclusion, it is not necessary to presume that the patient has given his consent; apart from the fact that presumed consent would be questionable in itself, where exoneration from criminal liability for an offence against the individual is concerned, it has already been said that *vis-à-vis* an unconscious patient the juridical foundation of medical activity and the duty to dispense medical care derives from the provision laid down in Art. 32, para. 1, Constitution.

Quite different is the case of a patient who is in a permanent vegetative state, in a condition that is of irreversible unconsciousness, even if the patient is not necessarily in terminal conditions.

By way of introduction it is worthwhile recalling that the physician's duty to treat is not repealed only because the therapy will not lead to the patient being cured. Indeed, from a more general point of view, it can be stated that the task of medical science is to provide treatment, not necessarily to cure, since the fatal outcome of therapy may depend on the limitations of medical science. In any case irreversible unconsciousness is a very special condition; even though the individual in vegetative conditions is alive from the juridical and biological standpoint, his so-called biographic life has ceased forever. Of course this does not mean that his purely biological life is not protected by Penal Law and that the dignity of this life is to be considered lower than the life of a conscious individual; and indeed, any aggression against purely biological life is condemned by the law exactly as an aggression against the life of a conscious individual would be. The issue of a possible differentiation in protection may arise, instead, in relation to omissive conduct, given its peculiar nature. With regard to the liability for omissive behaviour, the duty to act is not unconditionally important, but is subordinate to the suitability of the dutiful action *vis-à-vis* the protection of life. It should not come as a surprise then that the obligation to prevent an event may express a degree of evitability of the offence which is less than that corresponding to the obligation of not producing damage (through an active conduct). Now going back to the case of an individual in a permanent vegetative condition, whereas there are no doubts that the asset of biological life is fully protected against active conducts that may produce damage, with respect to omissive conduct it can be deemed to be protected to the extent to which the biological life exists autonomously. Being autonomous, indeed, biological life is an asset with regard to which one may question whether treatment is suitable or not. Conversely, *vis-à-vis* a non-autonomous biological life, the duty to intervene no longer has the instrumental function typical of medical treatment, but enters the field of excessive therapeutic zeal (*accanimento terapeutico*). There ensues that in the case of individuals in permanent vegetative conditions it is lawful to discontinue a pharmacological treatment which together with a mechanical support is keeping the patient alive. Indeed, since the machine is no longer at the service of biological life, but the purely biological life has become a product of the machine, protecting this type of biological life through the imposition of further therapeutic activities means protecting the functioning of the machine *per se*. Only in this condition therefore can the persistence of therapy envisage the case that some international juridical experts indicate as disthanasia: a newly coined word that has a negative connotation and that refers to the arbitrary prolonging of the natural course of death. What goes on being penally unlawful instead is disconnecting the artificial life support since, as pointed out earlier, this is a positive action.

In the wake of the discussion which has been developing on the international scene, Italian juridical experts have also raised the issue of the value to be attributed to the so-called living will, also called biological will. This expression is used to refer to a statement made by an individual in full possession of his mental faculties, in which he indicates which therapies he would wish to receive and which he would refuse in the event of unconsciousness and – what is most relevant to this discussion – if he/she were to find him/herself in the position of terminal illness.

If there is agreement on the assumption, *de iure condito*, of the right to die, there will be no grounds for the objections raised by some legal theorists who question the legitimacy of a living will because – they maintain – it is unlawful to refuse treatment. But there is another argument against the living will which is undoubtedly more convincing and more widely shared: the refusal of therapy contained in the living will refers to a situation which may occur in some future and – what is more important – abstract time, and so at the time when it would have to produce its effects, the statement will be out-of-date. There ensues that the living will does not ensure that there is true correspondence between the will it expresses and what its author would have decided, if he were in a position to do so, in a concrete situation. The result, according to this position, is the total loss of efficacy of an instrument which has been developed ultimately as a last attempt to bind physicians to respecting the wishes of the patient and avoid excessive therapeutic zeal.

A more attentive study, however, reveals that the position illustrated above is not wholly convincing. Having said that, in the absence of an appropriate body of regulations governing the various aspects of the issue, one must go on solving the problem on the basis of general systematic considerations, it does not appear logical that a living will should be invalidated because it represents a superseded wish and is thus an ineffective tool, since there are other well-known instances in which it is considered valid by the legal system, even in the case of provisions that are not related to assets or property (for example, the recognition of illegitimate offspring, ex Art. 254 Civil Code). On the other hand, we cannot invalidate a living will simply by making a comparison with the active consent given by the person in question, or by using the argument that up-to-date consent is commonly considered a tacit requirement for exoneration from criminal liability. Let us leave aside for the moment the observation that with a living will the drafter does not consent to his injury, but simply exercises his right to not be treated, thus making the implementation of his wish to die penally legitimate in that it is atypical and not because it is justified. Rather, at this point, it is worth stressing that when one speaks of up-to-date consent, one is referring to the fact that it must be given before the injury, and not necessarily only at the time of injury. And it is on the basis of this consideration that it can be stated that, being a characteristic of decision-making, up-to-dateness is a logical and not a purely chronological-temporal requirement. Along such lines of reasoning one could reach the absurd situation of acknowledging as juridically valid only those manifestations of will occurring concomitantly with the lesion, undermining in an unreasonable manner also the mechanisms of consent exonerating from criminal liability, which would no longer justify amongst other things most surgical procedures since in those cases consent is expressed by the patient before surgery begins; this is taken for granted when the patient undergoes total anaesthesia. Thus, if for the law a will which is out-of-date is not the same thing as a will expressed 'beforehand', the latter may be considered up-to-date provided that the desired event matches the circumstances as they evolve. In compliance with the general principles according to which all statements intended to be applied in the future are considered valid, the above-mentioned match between predicted and actual events renders null and void the time lag between the drawing up of the will and the future situation in which the conditions contained in it will be applied. It can be stated that when a statement of will is conditioned to the occurrence of future events, the requirement of this will being up-to-date is prolonged, in that the will is up-to-date from the time when it is first expressed to the occurrence of the future condition unless the will is cancelled.

Having said this, in order to avoid the paradoxical conclusion of having some hypothetical or unexpressed will prevail always and in any case over the last manifestly expressed will, it appears to be more correct to accept the validity of the living will, albeit subject to some conditions, in the absence of which one would go back to operating according to the assumption *in dubio pro vita*, which governs the treatment of unconscious patients. First of all, in order for the will to exercise one's right to die to benefit from the effectiveness that the living will can ensure, it is necessary that the statement refers clearly to the future circumstances in question, which must be defined very accurately. The statement has more chances of being perceived as being accurate if it refers not to individual diseases, but to the therapies and to the effects of the disease (degree of disability or level of suffering) with regard to which the individual refuses treatment. In the case of Jehovah's Witnesses, who carry with them a written and clearly expressed refusal to accept blood transfusions, which is to be respected should they be in danger of life or unable to express their will, a widely accepted opinion (and practice) is that such a living will is binding (and exonerates from criminal liability). Secondly, a living will is valid only if it has not been cancelled, even tacitly, that is to say where such a change of heart can be reasonably inferred from a conduct which is inconsistent with the will to die expressed previously. In order to evaluate the drafter's persistence in his will to die, the proposals of living wills that have been put forward, and the patterns that are used abroad, are characterized by a predetermination of the time span of their validity; the shorter the time, the easier it is to dispel possible doubts as to the will continuing to be an accurate representation of the wishes of the individual.

The final part of these notes – as should be quite clear by now – addresses the legal regulation of euthanasia in the future. Indeed, while the opinion according to which mercy euthanasia is an area which should be governed only by practice and which should be ignored by the law is not widely shared today, there are many who advocate the idea that the penal reorganization of this area should develop *de iure condendo*. Unlike the approach adopted by other legal systems, in ours this task can be carried out only by the legislator who must be very careful, exhaustive and clear; he must avoid the ambiguity (and, one might say, the hypocrisy) of the present legislation which makes the treatment of mercy euthanasia uncertain, and at times unjustly severe, without providing clear regulations. Indeed, it is all too evident that, for their absolute importance, neither the protection of life nor the effective exercise of the rights of each individual in the face of death can tolerate legislative silence, especially when this silence causes uncertainties in applying the law ... or worse, when it becomes a means for the system to shirk its responsibilities in a field where each choice has to be made with a profound sense of responsibility. Moreover, as far as such choices are concerned, as seen earlier, the viewpoint of the criminal law expert has no specific and special competence. This is another reason why it is worthwhile to focus immediately on some technical aspects of the possible reform of this field, which can prove useful for further reflection; it deserves a more in-depth scientific debate, before being examined from the legislative point of view. In particular two aspects will be touched upon: one concerns the type and limits of the restrictions that the principles of the Constitution can exercise on the discipline of euthanasia, the other concerns the ways in which reform may occur and the impact it may have.

If we consider the first of the two above-mentioned issues, it must be pointed out that it is possible to infer – from the Italian Constitution – the existence of a real right to die with dignity as a specific aspect of the more general right to human dignity, even if it is not expressly stated. We refer here to the regulations that – by guaranteeing, with absolute priority, the fundamental assets of the person – identify as the pivot of the entire legal system the so-called personalistic principle. In contrast to the opposite utilitarian concept based on the assets of an individual, the personalistic principle considers man as an end in himself, making it unlawful for any individual to be sacrificed in any way for the good of the community. In particular Art. 2 sets forth that human rights are inviolable even by the State, and Art. 3, para. 2 assigns to the State the duty of being instrumental in ensuring the full development of the human person. Secondly, the personalistic principle finds specific, but just as important, confirmations in the consecration of the human person's rights and freedoms (e.g. amongst others, Articles 13-19 and 21, which attach absolute importance to such rights and freedoms). Other important articles in this respect are Art. 32, para. 2 for the aforementioned reasons and Articles 41, para. 2, and 27, para. 3, which provide for the protection of human dignity. Finally, the personalistic principle is inferred from the provisions which, in close connection with the content of Art. 3, para. 2, impose upon the State specific and positive tasks in view of the full development of the human person in such matters as labour (Articles 4, 35 and 37), culture and scientific research (Art. 9), assistance in court proceedings (Art. 24), the family (Art. 29), health (Art. 32), education (Art. 34), social services (Art. 38) and economic activities (Art. 41, para. 1.).

But, hermeneutics does not allow us to draw from such regulations all the possible meanings of the right to die with dignity, so much so that in legal theory there is widespread agreement only on some of its contents. It is thus acknowledged that the rights of the person as a whole are valid also before death, including, as discussed earlier, the right to refuse a treatment that may offer hope for survival or more simply that delays death. The indications in the Constitution on the right to human dignity are of no help in clarifying whether the right to die with dignity may be the foundation on which to base the legitimacy of mercy euthanasia taken in its broadest meaning, that is including active euthanasia also in its form without the patient's consent. A similar solution could indeed be based only on the position – frequently expressed by legal theorists who uphold the legitimacy of euthanasia – according to which the value of life (and, therefore, its protection as an asset) is subordinated to the quality of life. Besides not being contained in our Constitution, this stance would be difficult to interpret given the different meanings attached to 'quality of life', a parameter which is very difficult to define, as has been seen. While the subjective connotation of this concept reveals its vagueness and stresses what a risk we run of it being misused, its objective meaning evokes a more general interpretation which is only marginally less vague and only succeeds in protecting collective sensitivity from the suffering of a dying person, by stressing the notion of a standard of dignity.

Similar objections are levelled against attempts to base the constitutional legitimacy of euthanasia on the notion of the patient's best interest. Apart from the fact that this notion is not expressed in any clause in the Constitution, it does, however, refer back to the theme of human rights, and is subject to the same fluctuations between general meaning and the various subjective connotations attributed to inalienable human rights.

A more plausible argument is offered by the attempt to find Constitutional foundations to the prohibition of excessive therapeutic zeal (i.e. prolonging the purely biological life of an individual, made possible today thanks to the progress achieved in the medical field), using the clause prohibiting cruel treatment as stated in Art. 27, para. 3 of the Constitution. Indeed, this solution which has been used in other countries (for instance in Spain where the Spanish Constitution contains a general statement prohibiting cruel treatment) could be supported by an *a fortiori* reasoning: considering that an individual sentenced to a punishment (in particular, imprisonment) maintains all the rights that he is entitled to as a human being, provided they are not in contrast with the sanction inflicted upon him, we can infer that prohibiting cruel treatment may have a much broader scope, irrespective of whether such treatment is or is not part of a penal sanction.

However, this approach to the issue is not fully satisfactory either. First of all because one cannot overlook the fact that, unlike the other fundamental Charters, in the Italian Constitution the prohibition of cruel treatment is stated in a context that (Art. 27, para. 3, devoted to the description of penalties), though not ruling out an interpretation in terms of general principle, considers a case which is undoubtedly different from excessive therapeutic zeal. Secondly, it goes without saying that, when the idea of cruel and inhuman treatment does not refer to a punishment, its contours become quite blurry. In particular we would have to demonstrate that prolonging life and the 'sacred' protection of its biological dimension are tantamount to cruel treatment. Thirdly, it must be pointed out that the Constitutional foundation of prohibiting excessive therapeutic zeal derives from the more fitting and decisive provision of Art. 32 of the Constitution, i.e., the regulation that describes and restricts the duties of medical treatment. Indeed, by stating that it is a duty to provide medical care when it is requested, and when the patient is unable to express valid consent, Art. 32 of the Constitution, on the one hand allows all those therapies carried out in the best interest of the patient (including pain therapy therefore), while on the other it offers a guarantee, a form of security for the physician, by envisaging a duty to act which is not unconditional but restricted to therapeutic needs. And even though the duty to administer a therapy exists even where there are no prospects for a cure, there are sound grounds to doubt that the mere prolonging of non-autonomous biological life can come under this concept of therapy.

In short: the principle of human dignity does not allow euthanasia to be a choice undertaken by a person other than the patient, even if it is done for the sake of the patient's dignity or in his best interest. As a consequence the patient's dignity in dying and the best interest of the terminal patient are to be protected as aspects of the more general freedom of the patient's right to self-determination: against the patient's wishes, or without his free and conscious consent, no intervention can be made which shortens his life. All this, however, is not the same as stating that, in terms of Constitutional principles, the assets of a human person are to be considered as private assets, with regard to which any protection measure is to be subordinated to the wishes of their owner. Indeed, whether (and to what extent) each person can dispose of himself is a query that does not seem to allow a single and final response. There are multiple responses which differ appreciably from one another depending on the type of collective interest according to which the right to free and conscious self-determination is examined. It has been frequently pointed out that no indications are given in the Italian Constitution as to the limitations to the right to dispose of one's body, and in any case the indications on this issue that can be inferred from the clauses of the Constitution are not entirely without contradictions.

This issue deserves some attention. Indeed, it goes without saying that it is not possible to strike a perfect balance between the collective interest and the personalistic principle simply by referring to the elements contained in the Constitution, as they can be applied by the ordinary legislator, in particular with reference to the Penal Code.

This is a rather concrete risk if we bear in mind the widespread tendency, mentioned earlier, to infer from a biased interpretation of Articles 579 and 580, Penal Code that suicide is unlawful and that life is an asset the individual cannot dispose of at will. These conclusions are influenced by preliminary conditions that are independent (at times avowedly so) of the regulatory system. Suffice it to mention the assumption of the structural unlawfulness of suicide, according to which even in the absence of a relevant provision suicide is deemed to be *contra ius*, because it is felt to be in contrast with the function of law and in particular with its preconditions of coexistence and of intersubjectivity. According to this approach suicide is perceived as a social as well as an existential defection; in the past it was used consistently (albeit paradoxically) to bring together under the common banner of unlawfulness both suicide and emigration, and to extend the notion of not being allowed to dispose of one's own body to the concept of not being allowed to dispose of one's physical integrity either.

But we can infer from the pre-eminence of the personalistic principle that limitations (no matter how many and whatever their nature) to the right to die – including the right to committing suicide – are exceptions to the principle of the incoercibility of living implicit in any unbiased reading of the ordinary legislation. Indeed, the duty to live is potentially in contrast with the pre-eminence of personal freedoms confirmed by the Constitution. The same observation can be made in relation to physical integrity. Thus, the Constitutional legitimacy of any limitation to the right to die and the boundaries of protection (even penal), if any, 'against oneself', will depend on the significance of the specific solidaristic value which opposes the lawfulness of voluntary death and the freedom to dispose of one's body at will, including sacrificing its integrity.

In other words: for a correct approach to the issue it is not sufficient to invoke the needs of the collectivity which, even after the drafting of the Republican Constitution, were called upon to justify the compression of the rights that the human being can exercise over his life and integrity, in the name of the generic interest of the conservation of society. In order to be legitimate, any choice which delimits a human being's rights over his own life and his own body must demonstrate the reasons why collective needs are to be given priority. In order to deny its Constitutional legitimacy, it is not enough to say that the *contra se* action is without social value: in other words, that it reflects an individualistic idea of man and of his property. The significant and undeniable differences that exist, both ethically and philosophically, between the individualistic and personalistic ideas tend to disappear in the legal system of a lay and secularized State. In this context the individualistic view loses its conceptual autonomy according to which any self-aggression not aimed at fulfilling a need of the individual is viewed as a sort of misuse of the rights over one's body. Indeed, given its lay nature, the State cannot prohibit a *contra se* conduct for its cultural and ethical values; no matter how unacceptable, these values belong to the inner jurisdiction of the person and are his/her absolute prerogative. As a result, self-aggression is either prohibited on the grounds of precise and predominant solidaristic needs, or it must be considered legitimate, albeit an expression of the reprehensible extravagance of a single individual.

Given its scope and complexity this theme would deserve to be thoroughly explored. But here it is sufficient to point out that, in principle, in order to avoid that individual instances of the prohibition of self-aggression be merely the expression of authoritarianism or of paternalistim, the solidaristic need may prevail over the *ius in se ipsum* where exercising it would produce social damage; namely a cost that would have to be incurred by individuals other than the agent.

Moreover, the recent interpretations of juridical experts show that the Italian legislation seems to be developing in line with this approach. Indeed such actions as:

(a) donating a kidney for transplantation (Law 458 of 26 June 1967);

(b) transexualism, that is to say surgical transformation of a person's sexual identity and ensuing recognition of the new identity in compliance with Law 164 of 14 April 1982, which could even be considered an adjustment to the psycho-behavioural sex of the individual and hence viewed as an advantage for him/her;

(c) voluntary sterilization, which denies those who undergo the procedure one of the most intense projections of human personality, namely generating offspring ... are undoubtedly legitimate because they do not entail damage to others even though they do impair the physical integrity of the individual. Conversely, consistent with

> the general principle of offensiveness, the punishment by Criminal Law of fraudulent self-mutilation (Art. 642 Penal Code) does not go against the above-mentioned Constitutional principles because such conduct offends the asset-related interests of the other members of the community.

There is no doubt that the issue of evaluating the damage that an act *contra se* produces to others is extremely delicate, even from this standpoint. Especially when the offence is addressed to the community considered as an impersonal whole. Indeed, if it is not correctly understood, the need to protect the other members of the community could make of any violation of solidarity rights an act which produces social damage. In particular, there are some problematical cases with regard to which one might wonder whether, by reasoning along these lines, the risk is that of reaching interpretational solutions that lead to viewing the individual as property of the State to the detriment of the freedom of self-determination.

Let us consider for instance the voluptuary consumption of drugs: an approach to the issue that intends to be consistent with the above-mentioned premises must be based on the principle according to which the free and fully aware choice of the consumer of drugs should not be subject to judgment, not even when such consumption causes a condition of drug addiction. And the same should apply to alcoholism and smoking. The Constitutional aspect of the right to become ill rules out any limitation to such freedom. Nor can one discriminate between action-based self-aggression behaviour and the offence to health deriving from exercising the right to refuse treatment, attributing the dignity of an inalienable right only to the latter. Once there is agreement on approaching the whole issue from the standpoint of the self-determination of the individual, whether the way such wishes are put into practice is through action or through omission is of secondary importance.

But if the issue is examined from another standpoint, it is difficult to deny that drug addiction has a negative impact on the whole of society. In this forum we shall not be discussing the crime-generating effects of drug addiction which, according to legal theory, would in themselves justify the penal punishment of the consumption of drugs, in full conformity with the Constitutional principle of offensiveness and on the basis of the rediscovered legitimacy of the crimes of abstract danger, where supraindividual assets are to be protected. The aspect that is of interest for this discussion is that the voluptuary consumption of drugs entails a considerable social damage consisting in the cost (also economic) of treating drug addiction. It is true that this cost can be avoided by abandoning the drug addict to his fate, that is to say by applying the (inhumane and cynical, but undoubtedly consistent) principle according to which each free choice must be accountable for the consequences it generates. However, when acts *contra se* are involved which produce damage to the individual's health, one cannot have recourse to the criterion of *imputet sibi* because of the duty of solidarity consecrated amongst others in Art. 32, para. 1 of the Constitution, which sets forth that the State has the duty to ensure health as a right of its citizens, and that it is to provide treatment free of charge for the most underprivileged. In short: given its general nature and being conditioned only to the consent of the individual involved, the duty that the State has of providing for the care and health of the individual applies also to drug addicts (and the same goes for alcoholics and heavy smokers) whether they expressly ask for such treatment or whether they are unable to do so.

Having said this it would be truly unreasonable to deem that in such cases the duty of solidarity should not be mutual, hence imposing on the individual (even under threat of a penalty) limitations to the freedom of disposing of himself, to prevent the occurrence of the preconditions whereby the State is obliged to offer solidarity to the individual. The same applies with regard to the obligation that motorcyclists and car drivers have to wear helmets and seat belts respectively. This obligation and the penalty envisaged where this duty is ignored are justified only in the name of the need to contain the social cost of the duty of solidarity in case of injury to the individual.

Now, as is even too obvious, once the Constitutional legitimacy of the possibility of prohibiting the acts *contra se* which entail social damage is acknowledged, there is nothing to suggest that the decision to stigmatize these acts, even penally, ultimately depends on political and legislative evaluations, based on the one hand on the principle of proportionality between conduct and penalty, and on the other, on a comparison between cost and benefit of their criminal punishment. So, going back to the case of drug addiction, the Constitution does not prevent the legislator from setting up a legislative policy driven by the idea that drug addiction is the product of modern society, instead of being an individual choice and from approaching the prevention of the problem entirely from the standpoint of rehabilitation, hence excluding any punitive or deterrent sanction. After all, with regard to the less severe phenomena of alcoholism and smoking, while the Constitutional principles do not exclude the legitimacy of their being stigmatized, it is the principle of proportion even before the principle of subsidiarity that demands that the penalty be kept within the administrative area or at the most within the sphere of civil liability compensation.

In drawing some conclusions on the Constitutional legitimacy of consent-based euthanasia, the foregoing remarks suggest that, if the self-aggression undermining the individual's integrity can be prohibited to the extent to which it causes damage to the other members of society, the same does not apply to the case of self-aggression aimed at terminating life, since it is rather difficult to identify any social damage to oppose to the right of the individual who chooses to bring about his/her death. After all, going back to the comparison between emigration and suicide, in order to use it in favour of the assumption that suicide is not subject to any penalty, Beccaria points out: 'He who commits suicide produces less damage to society than he who leaves the country forever, because the former leaves behind all his assets, whereas the latter takes with him a part of his belongings'.

Moving on, in conclusion, to a profile of the possible sectors and levels to be reformed, the possibilities for reform in Italy are extensive and varied, provided that there is agreement on the fact that the Constitutional principles not only do not prevent but rather prompt a legal configuration which may even be appreciably different from the one in force at the moment.

A. A first step could be to explicitly declare the legitimacy of passive euthanasia, with the individual's consent, in those cases where there may still be doubts; namely in the cases in which the survival of the patient depends on a machine that is already operating. This is a possible reform that should receive considerable support, also because the briefness of the current legislation could be interpreted by physicians (in these days of medicalization and hospitalization of death) as delegating the power to decide even against the wishes of the patient. Now, this need for legislative clarification could be satisfactorily met by issuing an *ad hoc* provision – obviously extra-penal – requiring that the physician discontinues therapeutic treatment in cases when the patient has made a clear and conscious request. By integrating the exoneration from criminal liability for fulfilling his duty, this regulation would eliminate any possible and residual interpretational doubts and would have the advantage of ensuring the effectiveness of the right to allow oneself die. Once a similar line of conduct is accepted as dutiful at the legislative level, the lawfulness of the same conduct on the part of an individual other than the physician, for instance a relative of the patient, should be less problematical. A similar solution could be suggested to clarify the lawfulness of pain therapy, even in cases where it may shorten the life of the patient. As pointed out earlier, however, the sensitivity of this issue lies in particular in the difficult balance between the duty to relieve pain and the effect of shortening the patient's life: an aspect which cannot be solved by resorting to an abstract assessment parameter. It would seem preferable to base the exoneration from criminal liability on a requirement, namely that of proportion, which is expressly established in other cases of exoneration from criminal liability. This means, of course, that the judge will have to make the necessary evaluations in the light of the progress of medical science.

As to active euthanasia of a consenting patient, it is difficult to conceive of any intervention, however slight, that moves away from the idea of it being absolutely unlawful unless we first revise the legal category of murder of a consenting individual. Indeed, as seen earlier, the provision of Art. 579, para. 3, n. 2, which envisages that the consent given by a mentally ill person or by an individual in conditions of psychic deficiency is not valid, makes it difficult to apply this regulation in practice. Without prejudice to the need of a provision aimed at ensuring the capacity of an individual who consents to his killing, instead of using terms such as mental illness and psychic deficiency it would be preferable to refer to a condition that might have some bearing on the action in question, i.e., bringing about the death of a consenting individual. It could be sufficient to refer to an absence of psychic disorders in the patient, to rule out that the wish that has been expressed does not correspond to his innermost will. Apart from this and for the very purpose of preparing a specific discipline governing euthanasia, adequate importance should be attached to the situation of he who acts with the purely altruistic aim of preventing the terminal patient from suffering a painful death. From this point of view, a fitting decision was the creation of a separate indictment from the charge of homicide in cases of the killing of a consenting individual: this charge now carries a less severe punishment and is characterized by the fact that the agent pursues a purely altruistic goal and that the passive individual is a patient who is terminally ill and is suffering unrelievable pain.

And finally these conditions should be taken into account to introduce, for the case of active euthanasia without the consent of the patient, a precise extenuating circumstance for wilful murder having special efficacy (namely having the capacity of decreasing the decreed penalty by over one third) that cannot be offset by other aggravating circumstances and incompatible with the aggravating circumstances of premeditation and blood ties. Indeed, even though this form of euthanasia will inevitably continue to remain in the area of criminal unlawfulness, this does not mean that the way in which it is regulated at present should not be appropriately modified. This solution is at any rate preferable to the recourse to pardon, as is the current practice, a measure commonly felt to be inadequate, not least because it avoids addressing the real terms of the problem.

B. The phenomenon of active euthanasia of a consenting individual would require a different and more effective type of intervention. There are two basic situations: the case of an individual who enables the patient to terminate his/her life *manu propria*, and the case of an individual who carries out the action on behalf of the patient.

With reference to the former case which, as seen earlier, is regulated by Art. 580 of the Penal Code, it must be pointed out to begin with that the importance the Constitution assigns to the 'right to die' does not in any way diminish the validity of the provision in Art. 580 which punishes incitement to commit suicide. Indeed, the concept of exercising one's right to die presupposes that the suicide makes up his mind of his own free will; this provision states that it is unlawful to suggest to another individual that he/she should commit suicide or to reinforce the idea of suicide that another individual has autonomously conceived. A different approach is adopted in the case of someone who helps an individual to commit suicide: namely the situation of a person who, without taking part in the action (which would otherwise be regulated by Art. 579), simply facilitates the actual suicide in any way (by providing the means or any information that is necessary). At a closer examination it is not easy to justify the penal unlawfulness of such conduct, which, as already said, is not punished in several other legal systems. Two sorts of juridical interpretations of this provision have been put forward: the first, and least convincing, suggests that the person intending to commit suicide should be left alone, since without any form of assistance he may desist from his suicidal intentions. The second, although more plausible, is nevertheless questionable: to help an act of suicide is simply immoral and therefore must be considered unlawful. This latter interpretation reflects a paternalistic concept of the relationship between the State and the individual and – as such – is in contrast with the modern-day secularization of criminal law.

Indeed, to confirm this impression we can point out that in the Italian legislation the aiding and abetting of conducts or actions, which in themselves are not considered criminal unlawful, is nonetheless a penal offence, and a behaviour commonly deemed to be immoral; suffice it to mention aiding and abetting of prostitution (Art. 3 of Law 75, 20 February 1958) and of the consumption of drugs (Art. 79 of Law 309, 9 October 1990) which is nevertheless a civil offence. These connections, however, have not escaped the attention of authoritative juridical experts, who justify considering this behaviour as a criminal offence by pointing out that the conduct which is being aided and abetted is one that is merely tolerated, and as such disapproved of, although not unlawful. But even approaching the argument from this end, it is difficult to uphold its validity. Unless one wishes to base one's disapproval of suicide on the notion that facilitating suicide is penally unlawful (and this would clearly show up the vicious circle), the freedom to commit suicide set out in the Constitution is inconsistent with the punishment of the conduct of anyone materially taking part in such action. In short: since aiding and abetting suicide is not an offence against a juridical asset, its depenalization would represent an adjustment of penal regulations to the principles in the Constitution, and this would exert an unquestionably positive impact on those cases of euthanasia – that today are considered penal offences under Art. 580 of the Penal Code – in which the physician provides a patient (in answer to his request) with the means and the instructions needed to accomplish his free and fully aware decision to commit suicide.

And finally, as far as the problematical issue of active euthanasia of a consenting individual is concerned, let us consider the possibility of total depenalization, which can be argued on the basis of the same arguments that can be invoked in favour of the assumption that suicide consists in exercising a right of freedom of choice. Since it has now become generally accepted that the killing of a consenting person is substantially 'a suicide committed by someone else', there are no reasons in principle why this act should be listed among the cases that are criminally punishable, once aiding and abetting suicide has been depenalized.

On the other hand it is also true that by upholding the right to die, we strengthens the idea of viewing euthanasia in a social perspective: in other words, without in any way diminishing the very personal nature of the decision, the right to die is seen as a right towards the achievement of which the State has a duty to contribute. The case provided for by Art. 579 of the Penal Code creates an evident discrimination between a terminally ill patient who is physically capable of killing himself and can put an end to his suffering *manu propria*, and the terminally ill patient who is unable to do so (a person affected by an irreversible paralysis of his/her limbs, for example) and needs to be helped by the physician. Indeed, at least in these cases, and without infringing the right of conscientious objection by the medical staff involved in the decisions concerning a terminal patient, the idea of depenalizing active euthanasia of a consenting individual seems to overcome the objections raised: that is to say the concern that, by accepting the lawfulness of active euthanasia of a consenting individual, we may be weakening our prohibition of murder. The absolutely special nature of the phenomenon of euthanasia makes it possible to reasonably suppose that its depenalization in cases of consenting individuals will not bring about a depreciation of the value of life. The risk of this choice lies in the possibility that the depenalization of euthanasia may become an alibi for social negligence which – especially in the cases in which keeping a patient alive costs a great deal, in terms of both human and technical resources – could induce the terminally ill patient to opt for an early departure, so as not to create problems for his/her family. A concern which can be fully shared. And it is true that in no other sector as in this one the real value of life is not protected by criminal law but rather by an adequate social policy.

Self-determination and Living Wills

Pietro Rescigno*

So we have come to the end of this conference, and we are here, a small group of friends who can talk things over as though at a private meeting. I should like to thank Cosimo Mazzoni for having organized the conference which has certainly achieved what it set out to do (unfortunately, I was not able to be present at all sessions, but this final day and the echo of the previous sessions allow me to state this with certainty). It offered a frank and stimulating exchange of ideas, covering a wide range of issues and presenting suggestions and solutions. I have often thought about the specific topic addressed in today's sessions, but the discussion I witnessed here goes to prove that it is always necessary, in all topics, to keep updating one's knowledge and thoughts. In a discussion on 'Law and Material Life' (the title we gave to a conference organized at the Accademia dei Lincei in 1982) I was asked to speak about the end of human life: my limited knowledge in this field and all the developments which have occurred in the meantime, made me feel very much behind the times today. I am grateful for your help in filling in some of the gaps.

Some time after that first conference, a seminar was organized in Rome by the periodical 'Nuova Scienza' and I was invited to give a paper: the occasion was a bill presented by a Member of Parliament who was especially interested in topics linked to personal freedom (his bill proposed a legal regulation at least for the form known as passive euthanasia). And, more recently, the topic has been addressed, as Professor Defanti pointed out, by the National Committee on Bioethics; but this Committee – which I have been a member of since it was formed – in an admirable but restrictive attempt at reaching unanimity or at least the broadest possible consensus of opinion, ended up by pronouncing itself only on the most essential aspects of the problem, shunning away from taking any clear position (the same applies to the Schwarzenberg document). One statement of a very general nature made by the Committee was that it is necessary (and juridically it must be made possible) for doctors to listen to and accept the request for euthanasia made by a patient. But we must always bear in mind the possibility that a doctor may have conscientious objections to euthanasia and these

* Professor of Law, Università La Sapienza, Roma, Italy.

Cosimo Marco Mazzoni (ed.), A Legal Framework for Bioethics, 235-238.
©1998 Kluwer Law International. Printed in The Netherlands.

must be accepted, despite the fact that the initial premise of the argument is that the request is legitimate and can legitimately be met.

Certainly the 'right to die' as a notion arises out of a changed context: an event in the past considered unavoidable and inexorable, can today be for the most part – if not totally – predictable.

This leads us to a sort of 'management' of death and self-determination is not the only factor that will influence or play a role in the overall picture of a possible management of the end of life. In the past, too, if you think of the ways society allowed men to live, and thereby favoured their decline and death, the phenomenon was to a large extent 'regulated' by society and by laws. Today we are faced with much more dramatic issues: one need only think of the technical means that are now available – and by means of which a human life at a purely vegetational stage can be prolonged – to realize that a threshold must be decided upon, either through common practice or by law, to discipline the use of these methods of artificial prolonging of life. Think also of the issue (analyzed primarily by specialists in the economic analysis of law) of the distribution of life-saving therapies, of support therapies, which are not available for all and therefore require the legislator or the public administrator in a hospital or a larger community to choose which individual shall benefit from the limited resources available.

The decision as to which individual shall be allowed to continue living is part of this concept of death 'management', and even the profile of self-determination, normally used to explain the 'right to die' also falls within the general sphere of a 'managed' death, although it is linked to a juridical value such as autonomy and free will of the person. In this case it is tied to a personal decision and this is why it is less disconcerting to move from nature (in a limited context in which only nature appeared to exert an influence on man's destiny) to the decision to be taken concerning one's own life or that of other persons.

Whether a legal regulation is possible or desirable: this was one of the questions asked at this conference. And the need for legal intervention is an issue debated in all fields of bioethics, which cover human life from the beginning to the end and view death as an event and a procedure. In fact, one might even consider a legal regulation that does not go through legislative activity: a corpus of laws can be laid out, legally binding to varying degrees, through the codes of conduct of the professional corporations. From this point of view, medicine appears to be more advanced (although not without problems) than science and traditional practices, still rooted in the notion that duty and function (i.e., the physician's freedom of action) lie in an intervention aimed at improving or conserving the patient's health status.

From this viewpoint, all topics dealt with here this morning, from organ transplants to methods for artificially prolonging life, were considered outside the sphere of the subject: classical medicine thought its duties were over when the death-event began, since it viewed its presence as useless in front of an unavoidable fact of nature. Here, too, we sought solutions that might satisfy the jurist even outside the field of legislative rules, from the field of past experience, taking into account a range of behaviour patterns and attitudes which all merge into the positive elements of legislation and case law (and the latter is the most accurate reflection of customary behaviour, since it adapts the rules to the peculiar features of each case).

It is a matter of marking the boundaries of the right to self-determination as it relates to death: interrupting extraordinary technical means prolonging life and the legitimacy of interrupting them and what is known as '*accanimento terapeutico*' finds most experts in agreement, although the positions vary more as we approach the topic of active euthanasia. In stressing the legitimacy of suspending measures prolonging life one tends to mention as examples cases involving famous people, where the desire to keep them alive beyond reasonable limits was due essentially to their fame and their importance, and this was the reason why their life was prolonged. Although for some people in the public eye there were political motivations for a disproportionate application of life-prolonging means, in the case of ordinary people the discussion can be much more interesting.

The refusal to be treated medically is accepted as a legitimate decision by an ever-growing number of people, especially if motivated by an ideology which refuses medical therapies. This promotes a notion of self-determination. And the evolution in our legal codes in which suicide was considered a crime (and there are still traces of this notion) is paralleled by a more positive outlook on self-determination, granting greater legitimacy to an individual who chooses to conclude his/her existence.

If the system has progressed in recognizing more and more the legitimacy of self-determination and the decisions a person can make concerning his/her own life, the topic of euthanasia takes us one step further. It has already been pointed out that the distinctions suggested to lay down the acceptable limits are often based on language conventions, when they are not reduced to mere plays on words used to mark the boundary between practices which public opinion and jurisprudence judge permissively (and which we link to the notion of a purely passive euthanasia) and practices which might end up in what is sometimes called 'mercy killing'.

The discussion is left up to each person's sensitivity; the English-speaking jurist constantly repeats that he has no intention of persuading anyone and concludes by saying that he hopes he has not exerted undue pressure in trying to convince his audience. Perhaps, as jurists preoccupied primarily with private law, we should have devoted greater attention to an institution which can more effectively be legally regulated and which introduces a mechanism that could guarantee the legitimacy of suspending or not beginning life-prolonging therapies, thus exonerating the physician from this type of decision. I am referring here to 'living wills'. There was a bill presented in Italy which attempted to apply this type of will to Italy as well. Even those people who are not wholly in favour of a legal regulation of the matter, or who believe that it is advisable to resort to the codes laid down by the professional corporations, might think that a legislative intervention in this direction is technically possible and desirable. Mention was also made of possible abuses or misuses and of what remedies should be found for them: the term abuse is here used in a very unusual manner, since in principle it is applied to a person who has a prerogative but uses it for reasons contrasting with those for which it had been granted him to begin with.

Index

A

B

C

Cosimo Marco Mazzoni (ed.), A Legal Framework for Bioethics, 239-245.
©1998 *Kluwer Law International. Printed in The Netherlands.*

D

E

Nijhoff Law Specials

1. D. Campbell: *Abortion Law and Public Policy.* 1984 ISBN 90-247-3107-0
2. J. Pictet: *Development and Principles of International Humanitarian Law.* 1985 ISBN 90-247-3199-2
3. J. van Houtte: *Sociology of Law and Legal Anthropology in Dutch-speaking Countries.* 1985 ISBN 90-247-3175-5
4. C. D. De Fouloy: *Glossary of NAFTA Terms.* 1994 ISBN 0-7923-2719-5
5. H. L. Zielinski: *Health and Humanitarian Concerns. Principles and Ethics.* 1994 ISBN 0-7923-2963-5
6. K. S. Foster and D. C. Alexander: *Prospects of a US-Chile Free Trade Agreement.* 1994 ISBN 0-7923-2885-X
7. F. J. M. Feldbrugge (ed.): *Russian Federation Legislative Survey. June 1990 December 1992.* 1995 ISBN 0-7923-3243-1
8. R. Platzöder (ed.):.*The 1994 United Nations Convention on the Law of the Sea.* Basic Documents with an Introduction.1995 ISBN 0-7923-3271-7
9. D. Warner (ed.): *New Dimensions of Peacekeeping.* 1995 ISBN 0-7923-3301-2
10. M. van Leeuwen (ed.): *The Future of the International Nuclear Non-Proliferation Regime.* 1995 ISBN 0-7923-3433-7
11. E.-U. Petersmann: *International and European Trade and Environmental Law After the Uruguay Round.* 1995 ISBN 90-411 -0857-2
12. V. Gowlland-Debbas: *The Problem of Refugees in the Light of Contemporary International Law Issues.* 1996 ISBN 90-411-0085-7
13. A. Kaczorowska: *International Trade Conventions and Their Effectiveness.* Present and Future.1995 ISBN 0-7923-3362-4
14. T. F. Acuña: *The United Nations Mission in El Salvador.* A Humanitarian Law Perspective. 1995 ISBN 90-411-0123-3
15. H. Wiggering and A. Sandhövel (eds.): *European Environmental Advisory Councils.* 1996 ISBN 90-411 -0873-4
16. E. A. Ankumah: *The African Commission on Human and Peoples' Rights.* Practice and Procedures. 1996 ISBN 90-411 -0130-6
17. B. de Rossanet: *Peacemaking and Peacekeeping in Yugoslavia.* 1996 ISBN 90-411 -0192-6
18. A. Webster and K. Packer (eds.): *Innovation and the Intellectual Property System.* 1996 ISBN 90-411 -0907-2

19. H. Bocken and D. Ryckbost (eds.): *Codification of Environmental Law.* Draft Decree on Environmental Policy.1996 ISBN 90-411 -0911 -0

20. K. Lescure and F. Trintignac: *International Justice for Former Yugoslavia.* The Working of the International Criminal Tribunal of the Hague.1996 ISBN 90-411-0201-9

21. G. de Nooy (ed.): *The Hole of European Naval Forces after the Cold War.* 1996 ISBN 90-411 -0227-2

22. M. Bertrand and D. Warner (eds.): *A New Charter for a Worldwide Organisation?* 1997 ISBN 90-411 -0286-8

23. E.-U. Petersmann: *The GATT/ WTO Dispute Settlement System.* International Law, International Organizations and Dispute Settlement.1996 ISBN 90-411-0933-1

24. G. de Nooy (ed.): *Cooperative Security, the OSCE, and its Code of Conduct.* 1996 ISBN 90-411 -0316-3

25. M. Bertrand: *The United Nations.* Past, Present and Future.1997 ISBN 90-411 -0337-6

26. D. Dijkzeul: *The Management of Multilateral Organizations.* 1997 ISBN 90-411-0356-2

27. G. de Nooy (ed.): *The Role of European Ground and Air Forces after the Cold War.* 1997 ISBN 90-411 -0397-X

28. M. Hilaire: *International Law and the United States Military Intervention in the Western Hemisphere.* 1997 ISBN 90-411-0399-6

29. D. Warner (ed.): *Human Rights and Humanitarian Law.* The Guest for Universality.1997 ISBN 90-411 -0407-0

30. J. C. Hathaway (ed.): *Reconceiving International Refugee Law.* 1997 ISBN 90-411 -0418-6

31. G. de Nooy (ed.):.The *Clausewitzian Dictum and the Future of Western Military Strategy.* 1997 ISBN 90-411 -0455-0

32. Canadian Council on International Law and The Markland Group (ed.): *Treaty Compliance: Some Concerns and Remedies.* 1997 ISBN 90-411 -0732-0

33. B. de Rossanet: *War and Peace in the Former Yugoslavia.* 1998 ISBN 90-411-0499-2

34. C. M. Mazzoni (ed.): *A Legal Framework for Bioethics.* 1998 ISBN 90-411-0523-9

640018

DEPAUL UNIVERSITY LIBRARY
3 0511 00647 1775